The Territorial Dimension of Judaism

W. D. Davies

The Territorial Dimension of Judaism

With a Symposium and Further Reflections

Fortress Press   Minneapolis

THE TERRITORIAL DIMENSION OF JUDAISM

First Fortress Press edition 1991. Originally published by the University of California Press in 1982.

Cover design: Ned Skubic
Author photograph: John C. Manapace

Library of Congress Cataloging-in-Publication Data
Davies, William David, 1911–
    The territorial dimension of Judaism : with a symposium and further reflections
/ W. D. Davies. — 1st Fortress Press ed.
        p.   cm.
    Originally published: Berkeley : University of California Press,
1982.
    Includes bibliographical references and indexes.
    ISBN 0-8006-2553-6 (alk. paper)
    1. Palestine in the Bible.   2. Palestine in Judaism.   I. Title.
BS1199.P26D38   1991
296.3—dc20   91-29502
                                                                      CIP

The paper used in this publication meets the minimum requirements of American National Standard for Information Sciences—Permanence of Paper for Printed Library Materials, ANSI Z329.48-1984.   ∞™

Manufactured in the U.S.A.   AF 1-2553

95   94   93   92   91   1   2   3   4   5   6   7   8   9   10

In memory of

Abraham Heschel
James W. Parkes
Marcel Simon
Ephraim E. Urbach

and for

Louis Finkelstein
John Gwyn Griffiths
Edmund Jacob
Marc Tannenbaum

habêrîm hacâmim rôshîm

Contents

List of Abbreviations

Abbreviations of books from the Old Testament (Tanak) and from the New Testament will be familiar to readers and hence are not listed.

APOT: R. H. Charles (ed.), *The Apocrypha and Pseudepigrapha of the Old Testament.* See also Glossary, p. 143.

BT: The Babylonian Talmud.

DJD I: D. Barthélemy, O.P., et al., *Qumran Cave I: Discoveries in the Judaean Desert,* I

GL: W. D. Davies, *The Gospel and the Land: Early Christianity and Jewish Territorial Doctrine*

JEDPH: The materials that went into the making of the Pentateuch (the first five books of the Tanak).

J: The source or tradition from the south, using the name *Yahweh* (Jehovah) for God, dating from the eleventh to the early eighth century B.C.E.

E: A source or tradition coming from the north, also dating from the eleventh to the early eighth century B.C.E., using the term *Elohim* for God. Probably fused with J into one complex after 722 B.C.E.

D: Deuteronomy, dating in its earliest form from the seventh century B.C.E.

P: The Priestly Code of the postexilic or Persian period, dealing with cultic laws and the history of the cult

H: The Holiness Code (Lev. 17–26), dated 600–570 B.C.E., emphasizing holiness, The Land as polluted by sin, sacrifices, the duties of priests, and the calendar. Emerged between *D* and *P,* to which it seems related

LXX: *The Septuagint,* the Greek version of the Hebrew Old Testament

NEB: *The New English Bible*

RSV: *The Revised Standard Version of the Bible*

Apocrypha and Pseudepigrapha (see Charles, *Apocrypha and Pseude-*
pigrapha of the Old Testament)

Asmp. M.: The Assumption of Moses

2 Bar.: 2 (or Syriac) Baruch. Greek or Hebrew, from
Palestine, ca. 90 C.E.

Ecclus.: Ecclesiasticus, or The Wisdom of Jesus ben
[the son of] Sirach. Hebrew, from Palestine
(Jerusalem?). Ben Sirach wrote the Hebrew
text ca. 180 B.C.E. His grandson translated it
into Greek ca. 130 B.C.E.

I En.: 1 Enoch or Ethiopic Enoch. Hebrew and/or
Aramaic, from Jerusalem (?), of composite date
(ca. 150 B.C.E.–early first century C.E.)

4 Ezra: Also known as 2 Esdras. Greek version is a
translation from Hebrew or Aramaic. Palestinian, ca. 90–100 C.E.

Jub.: Jubilees or Little Genesis. Hebrew, from Palestine, second century B.C.E. Essene?

1 Macc.: 1 Maccabees. The present Greek text is a translation from Hebrew. Probably written ca. 100
B.C.E.

2 Macc.: Not a continuation of 1 Maccabees. In its present form, presumably produced in Alexandria
ca. 50 B.C.E. Based on the lost history of Jason
of Cyrene

Ps. Sol.: Psalms of Solomon. Hebrew, from Palestine,
ca. 50 B.C.E.

Sib. Or.: Sibylline Oracles. Greek, from Alexandria.
Bk. 3 ca. 150 B.C.E.; bk. 4, ca. 80 C.E.; bk. 5,
ca. 100–150 C.E.

Test.Ab.: Testament of Abraham. Hebrew (but the
Greek does not read like a translation), early
first century C.E.

Test.Job: Testament of Job. Greek, perhaps from Alexandria, first century B.C.E. or first century
C. E.

Test.Levi: Testament of Levi. In its present form, a Christian composition of the second century C.E.,
but based on a Jewish Palestinian text from the
second century B.C.E.

Tob: Tobit. Hebrew or Aramaic, ca. 200 B.C.E.
Egypt or Western Syria has been suggested as
the provenance: Babylon and Palestine have
not been ruled out (text does have Persian influences)

Wisd. Sol.: Wisdom of Solomon. Greek, reflecting the style of the Septuagint from Alexandria, second or first century, B.C.E.

Texts from the Dead Sea Scrolls

11QPsª: Manuscript from cave 11, Qumran, containing forty-one canonical psalms and several apocryphal psalms

CDC: The Damascus Rule. Preserved in two medieval manuscripts. Fragments have also been found at Qumran

1QS: The Manual of Discipline from cave I, Qumran

1Qp Hab and 1QpH: The commentary on Habakkuk from cave I *(pēšer Habakkuk)*

1QIsaª: A scroll of Isaiah from cave I, Qumran, exemplar *a*

1QM: The sectarian War of the Children of Light against the Children of Darkness *(milḥāmāh)*

4Q Flor.: 4 Q Florilegium. Published by J. Allegro in the *Journal of Biblical Literature* in 1956 and 1958

For introduction and English translation of the Dead Sea Scrolls, see G. Vermes, *The Dead Sea Scrolls in English.* The Temple Scroll referred to herein has not been translated into English: for an introduction to it see J. Milgrom, "The Temple Scroll"; German translation: J. Maier, *Die Tempelrolle vom Toten Meer;* French translation: A. Caquot, "Le Rouleau du Temple de Qoumran."

Preface to the Fortress Press Edition

The warm reception of readers and reviewers to this small volume has prompted its republication. It was first published in 1982 under the direct impact of the Six Day War of 1967 and now in 1991 because of the mounting need to understand its theme in the light of events in the Middle East culminating in the Gulf War and its aftermath. I am very grateful to Mr. W. J. McClung, sponsoring editor of the University of California Press, Berkeley, and to Dr. Marshall Johnson, editorial director of Fortress Press for making its reappearance possible; the latter has generously shared his thoughts with me on The Land.

Parts of this volume were communicated to seminars at the Center for International Security and Arms Control, Stanford University, and at the Graduate Theological Union, Berkeley, California. I recall with real pleasure and appreciation the courtesy of Professor John Lewis, Director of the Center, and of Dr. Lewis Mudge, Dean of San Francisco Theological Seminary.

W. D. D.
Duke University

Preface

In 1967, just before the Six Days' War between Israel and Egypt, a letter from Dr. E. E. Urbach urged support for the cause of Israel. It was informed by assumptions that, despite my immersion for years in the study of Judaism, I had never fully faced, and it compelled a deep examination of what is—I soon realized—the Cinderella of both Christian and Jewish scholarship: the theme of territory in Judaism. The result was *The Gospel and The Land: Early Christianity and Jewish Territorial Doctrine,* published by the University of California Press in 1974. But the subject continued to burn in my bones like a fire, and this short book carries on the consideration of the territorial theme, this time exclusively in Judaism, against the larger context of Jewish history since the first and second centuries C.E. There is here no attempt to deal with the specifically Christian response to the theme.

What happens when the understanding of The Promised Land in Judaism conflicts with the claims of the traditions and occupancy of its other peoples is also not discussed here. From different points of view, my friends and mentors Professor David Daube and Dr. J. S. Whale, who, were it necessary, would have made it impossible for me to underestimate the tragedy of the conflict between Israelis and Palestinians, have urged me to deal with it. From their criticisms I have greatly profited. However, apart from the question of competence, to engage that issue would demand another volume. Here I have concentrated on what in my judgment must be the beginning for an understanding of this conflict: the sympathetic attempt to comprehend the Jewish tradition. This is the justification for my brief study, which is designed primarily, first, to introduce the subject for discussion among a wide public, and secondly, since the territorial theme touches upon matters beyond the competence of any one student, to stimulate specialists to consider this much-neglected subject now forcing itself upon the world's attention.

My warmest gratitude goes to Professors D. N. Freedman and Jacob Neusner and to my colleagues Martin Golding and Edward Tiryakian; to Mr. Dale C. Allison, my assistant, for much valuable stimulus, and Mr. Richard Countie, for help in the final stages; to my secretary, Mrs. Sarah Freedman, for her interested help; especially to the Librarian of Duke Divinity School, Professor Donn M. Farris, who seems always to go beyond the call of duty, and to his staff, particularly Ms. Harriet Leonard and Ms. Linda K. Gard; and to Mr.

Richard Judd and Mr. George Mandel of the Oxford Centre for Post-graduate Hebrew Studies. I wish to acknowledge the help and concern of Mr. William J. McClung, Executive Editor in Berkeley, and the extraordinary efficiency of Ms. Marilyn Schwartz and Mr. Peter Dreyer, editor and reader for the Press. My debt to my wife, in this as in all my endeavors, cannot adequately be expressed and I do not attempt it.

W. D. D.

Introduction

This volume attempts to answer the question whether there is an essential territorial dimension to Judaism. Put concretely, it assesses the nature and place within Judaism of the doctrine which in various ways asserts that there is a special relationship among the God of Israel, the People of Israel, and The Land of Israel. Is that relationship primary or secondary, dispensable or indispensable? Is the territorial doctrine of Judaism accidental and peripheral or essential, an aspect of Judaism without which Judaism would cease to be itself?

At first encounter the question would seem to be open to strict historical investigation and an unequivocal answer. However difficult, the sources for understanding Judaism are abundant: the practice of Jews as it bears upon Eretz Israel[1] is open to scrutiny. But in the course of Jewish history especially in this century, internal and external factors affecting Judaism have clouded as well as clarified the issue and compel caution. The complexities, paradoxes, and obscurities of the territorial theme cannot be sufficiently emphasized.

Besides the inherent difficulty of the sources and the factors at which we have hinted, there is another reason the question of The Land remains one of the most neglected aspects of Judaism: the contemporary approach of Gentile (largely Christian) scholarship and also, by way of reaction to this, of much Jewish scholarship, to the Jewish tradition. Christian origins have usually been approached in two ways. One approach, bearing the authority of a long history and renewed with vigor in this century, has emphasized the radical newness of the Gospel as a supernatural phenomenon breaking into this world with startling discontinuity in a manner that defies rational analysis. The other approach, more characteristic of the nineteenth and early twentieth centuries, has sought to understand the emergence of the Christian faith as a phenomenon within history which, partly at least, can be

---

1. Two Hebrew terms are translatable as "land," and in some cases have a similar meaning, but they are not identical: 'adâmâh primarily designates the land as habitable, without political or national connotations; 'eretz can, and very often does, have such a connotation. It is with Eretz Israel (henceforth The Land), with that connotation, that we are concerned here. The Land was never defined with geographic precision. See W. D. Davies, *The Gospel and The Land* (henceforth GL), p. 16, n. 3, and p. 73; also N. Avigad and Y. Yadin, eds., *The Genesis Apocryphon,* col. 21, lines 15–18, pp. 45–46.

interpreted in relation to contemporary religions. This second approach has forked in two directions, one leading to the Graeco-Roman world and one to the Jewish: and the Christian faith has correspondingly been illumined in terms either of Hellenistic syncretism or of the Judaism of the first century. Only in recent decades have scholars recognized that the Hellenistic and Judaic cultures and religions of the period reveal deep interpenetration.

Even when Christian origins are understood in the Hellenistic and Jewish setting, Christian scholars have usually determined how that setting is used and what aspects of it are significant for the illumination of the Christian faith. This is especially true of the way Judaism has been examined as a background to Christianity. Long before the emergence of modern scholarship, the pagan faiths of the Graeco-Roman world that vied with Christianity for the allegiance of men in the first century had died. But because Judaism has persisted as a living faith to the present, a peculiarly contemporaneous relevance and urgency have always characterized the discussion of the relationship between it and Christianity. One might expect that Judaism would have helped formulate the terms of the discussion between the two faiths. In fact, because of the overwhelming dominance of Christianity, the discussion has been governed almost entirely by concerns Christians have deemed important. Despite their emphasis on the Word made flesh (that is, "material"), doctrines in which Christians have been particularly interested—theological and metaphysical abstractions such as God, Creation, Time, Man, Sin, Revelation, Prophecy, Reward, and Punishment—have been emphasized in attempts to understand how the Gospel emerged from and impinged upon Judaism. The Jewish faith came to be understood largely in terms of Christian categories, seldom in terms native, or peculiar, to itself. And once Judaism came to be interpreted as a body of ideas or doctrines, the assumption followed that its ideas, to be true, must be valid for all persons at all times and places. Local or geographic, particularistic elements in Judaism could be disregarded as insignificant—or, at best, secondary.

This explains why the question of The Land in primitive Christianity has been neglected. Even rabbinic theology, borrowing its philosophical tools and methods from, and stimulated by, Christian theology, concentrated on themes dictated by the need to defend itself against specifically Christian challenges, and neglected such awkward, particular doctrines as that of The Land. Rabbinic thinkers, understanding Judaism in terms of, or in reaction to, Christianity, did not appreciate what significance a particular place, Palestine, could have in their faith: and Christian scholars, naturally governed by their own doctrinal interests, easily neglected the *realia* of Judaism and especially its traditional concentration on The Land. So it is that neither *the Interpreter's Dictionary of the Bible,* published in 1962, nor two recent

French biblical dictionaries contain articles on The Land. *The Peake Commentary* (1962) has two references to the theme in its index: *The Jerome Biblical Commentary* (1968) virtually ignores it; and the *Wörterbuch* of Kittel-Friedrich (1933) allots just under four pages to it. Although there are innumerable references to The Land in the document of their concern, until very recently the neglect of this theme has been as marked among scholars of the Tanak (the term used by Jews for what Protestant Christians call the Old Testament) as among those of the New Testament.

But, despite its comparative neglect until recently, even in formal rabbinic theology, the emphasis on The Land in Judaism is one of the most persistent and passionately held doctrines with which the early Church had to come to terms. The doctrine is traceable throughout the Tanak, the Apocrypha and Pseudepigrapha, the Qumran Scrolls, and the rabbinic and Hellenistic Jewish sources.

1

A Marked Theological Tradition

The Tanak and other sources of Judaism reveal certain ideas concerning The Land that reflect, or are parallel to, primitive Semitic, other Near Eastern, and, indeed, widespread conceptions about the significance of their land to a particular people. Israel is represented as the centre of the earth. Mircea Eliade has connected this notion with that of sacred and profane space, which is common in human societies. Sacred space is that space which has manifested an irruption of the divine, and which alone, therefore, is real or possesses being. The religious man desires to live as near to this sacred space as possible and comes to regard it, the place of his abode, his own land, as the centre of the world. To this belongs cosmos, order: outside it is chaos, where demons and alien spirits rule.

The belief that The Land of Israel is the centre of the earth occurs in Ezek. 38:12. In the end of days, when many people out of the nations will have been gathered upon the mountains of Israel to dwell in security, Gog, of the land of Magog, is to advance against them. The people of Israel are described as those

> who dwell at the centre of the earth.

This notion also emerges in Ezek. 5:5: "Thus says the Lord God: This is Jerusalem; I have set her in the centre of the nations, with countries round about her." Here the emphasis is demographic—that is, on the visibility of the conduct of Jerusalem to all the nations of the world because of her centrality. The idea persisted, as in the Ethiopic Enoch 26:1, where Enoch's visit to Jerusalem is described as his going to "the middle of earth." In Jub. 8:12, Noah assigns to Shem as his lot, "the centre of the earth." We learn what this is explicitly in Jub. 8:19, where Mount Zion is described as "the centre of the navel [omphalos] of the earth." The context of these verses is geographic, the division of the earth among the sons of Noah. But the centrality of Jerusalem is connected also with other holy places—the Garden of Eden as the Holy of Holies, and Mount Sinai as the centre of the desert, a combination that became important in later Christian speculation (Jub. 8:19). Josephus, *Jewish Wars*, III, 3.5, refers to Jerusalem as lying at the very centre of Judaea, "for which reason the town has sometimes,

1

not inaptly, been called 'the navel of the country.' " The Sibylline Oracles V, 248–50, refer to "the godlike heavenly race of the blessed Jews, who dwell around the city of God at the centre of the earth."

Israel, then, is the centre of the earth; Jerusalem the centre of Israel; Mt. Zion the centre of Jerusalem; and, further, according to *BT* Sanhedrin 37a, the meeting place of the Sanhedrin lies within Mt. Zion and, again, within the Temple on its summit. The passage from *BT* Sanhedrin 37a reads:

The Gemara on Mishnah Sanhedrin 4:3,4 is as follows:
Whence is this derived?—R. Aha b. Hananiah [third century Amora] said: Scripture states, "Thy navel is like a round goblet" ['*aggân ha-Sahar*] wherein no mingled wine is wanting [Cant. vii, 3]. "Thy navel"—that is the Sanhedrin. Why was it called *"navel"*? Because it sat at the navel-point [i.e., the centre] of the world [compare *Tanḥuma, Wa Yikra,* xviii, 23].

And, finally, at the very centre of all the earth, stands the '*eben shetiyyah,* the foundation stone, which in the Second Temple occupied the place of the Holy Ark.

Such ideas had much influence on later Christian speculation, but for our specific purposes they are not of primary significance. They are widespread outside the Tanak in many cultures. In no way do they belong to the peculiarity of the biblical understanding of The Land. They belong mostly to the same category as the arrangement of the maps of the world that I knew as a boy. In these, the earth was not only largely colored British red, but invariably had its centre in the British Isles, and, on closer inspection, in England, and, on still closer inspection, in London, until finally one detected Greenwich, by which the world set its clocks, but on which not even the sun itself would ever set. Nor are such ideas peculiarly British in the modern world. Readers of the very first page of Charles de Gaulle's *Memoirs of Hope* (translated 1971), will recall his understanding of his beloved France as "this human amalgam, on this territory, at the heart of this world." The very word *China* means centre of the universe.

Another notion of The Land, also not belonging to the peculiarity of the Tanak and Judaism, but important in its own right, is that of The Land of Israel as the place where Yahweh abundantly gave material gifts of all kinds to his people: it is this emphasis that makes so many passages in the Tanak useful in Harvest Thanksgiving services. We encounter here that element in Israel's thought on The Land which it probably owed primarily to Canaanite culture, but which it may have met before it settled in Canaan. Because primitive man was primarily concerned with the satisfaction of immediate physical needs, any area that offered such satisfaction became marked. On grounds of its fertility, usually because of the presence of a stream or spring or some other source of water, a certain spot would gain the reputation of being unique. Or, again, a peculiar conformation of rocks might create the belief that a place was in some way different. For whatever reason, a place would become associated with an irruption of the divine and come to be regarded as a gateway to a god. But because primitive man was a nomadic tribesman or huntsman, he could not conceive of the god as limited to one spot. The god surely moved within the area of man's seasonal migrations in search of water and grassland. And so the entire area which the god was considered to frequent became identified as his land, even though the first spot where he had manifested himself continued to be regarded as his home. Against such a picture, the patriarchal period has often been understood in terms of animism and the like, but few would now argue that the patriarch's religion is thus explicable.

The continued settlement in Canaan and the encounter with a static culture dominated by Baalim made the relationship (or the idea of such a relationship) between a god, as the giver of good gifts, and his land open to acute question. For the Canaanites, the god who guaranteed the fertility of the soil and the abundance of the harvest was Baal, "the husband" or "lord" of the land. The sanctuaries of the Baalim were usually situated in secluded, isolated spots near a source of water. The temptation for Israel to adopt them—sanctuaries and Baalim—was almost irresistible. During the battle waged by Israel against the Baalim in the interests of Yahweh, the functions of the Baalim were transferred to Yahweh, and it has been held that the reiterated emphases on the blessings of The Land came into Yahwehism through Canaanite Baalism. G. von Rad thinks that even the phrase "the land flowing with milk and honey" is from this source, as are

the descriptions of an almost paradisal blessing on human progeny, on the offspring of the cattle, on basket and kneeding-trough, the fruit of the fields, rain for the earth, peace, deliverance from wild animals and so on; these descriptions would surely seem to have been composed under the influence of Canaanite nature-religion (Lev. 26:3–12; Num. 13:23, 28; 14:7 f.; 24:3 f; Deut. 28:2–7).[1]

We may be allowed to question the exclusive ascription of such motifs to the influence of Canaanite religion without rejecting von Rad's main emphasis.

The question of the relationship of Yahweh to The Land of Israel cannot be isolated from the relationship of Yahweh to the whole universe. In the Tanak the notion of creation as a totality is late: the term

---

1. G. von Rad, *The Problem of the Hexateuch and Other Essays,* p. 89.

bârâ', to create, is not used of Yahweh before the Exile.[2] But certainly in the later strata of the Tanak Yahweh was always the creator, so it became wholly natural to regard him as the source of the gifts of the natural order entirely apart from his special relationship to Israel; the Canaanite heritage in this respect could easily be assimilated without any sense of incongruity.

These two peripheral aspects of The Land in the Tanak and Judaism—its centrality and abundance—do not, however, constitute its peculiarity. Before we pass on to that peculiarity, we might add a purely geographical factor which greatly affected Israel's understanding of its land: the difference between The Land of Israel, which received rain as proof of Yahweh's constant concern, and the land of Egypt, which was at the mercy of the fluctuations of the Nile. Israel was under Yahweh's immediate supervision in a way Egypt was not: the soil of Israel received water by the direct will and decision of Yahweh (Deut. 11:10–12). But few peoples have failed to discover some geographic sign of grace. The peculiarity about which we speak lies elsewhere, in the concepts of the Promised Land and of The Land as the peculiar property *(s^egûllâh)* of Yahweh.

THE LAND IN BIBLICAL SOURCES

The Hexateuch

First, The Land is a promised land. To disentangle the various currents that have gone into the concept of the promise of The Land is exceedingly difficult. Let us begin with those texts where the promise emerges in the oldest strata of the Pentateuch, which, it is generally agreed, occur in Gen. 15 [*EJ*]. In Gen. 15:1–6 we read as follows:

After these things the word of the Lord came to Abram in a vision, "Fear not, Abram, I am your shield; your reward shall be very great." But Abram said, "O Lord God, what wilt thou give me, for I continue childless, and the heir of my house is Eliezer of Damascus?" And Abram said, "Behold, thou hast given me no offspring; and a slave born in my house will be my heir." And behold, the word of the Lord came to him, "This man shall not be your heir." And he brought him outside and said, "Look toward heaven, and number the stars, if you are able to number them." Then he said to him, "So shall

2. On *bârâ'* see W. H. Bennett, *The Post-Exilic Prophets*, pp. 30 f. It might be objected that the exclusively postexilic appearance of *bârâ'* is not significant, because its equivalent, the verb *'sah,* occurs earlier. Nevertheless, the increasingly transcendent character of Yahweh after the Exile can hardly be gainsaid, as also the importance of the doctrine of creation in Judaism (see J. Bonsirven, *Le Judaïsme Palestinien,* I, 162 f.).

your descendants be." And he believed the Lord: and he reckoned it to him as righteousness.

Here Abraham is promised an heir. There is no explicit reference to land, but there is an implication in 15:4 that the land which Abraham possessed at that time was to be handed on to his son. Later in the same chapter, in 15:17 ff. [*EJ*] we read:

When the sun had gone down and it was dark, behold, a smoking fire pot and a flaming torch passed between these pieces. On that day the Lord made a covenant with Abram, saying, "To your descendants I give this land ['*eretz*], from the river of Egypt to the great river, the river Euphrates, the land of the Kenites, the Kenizzites, the Kadmonites, the Hittites, the Perizzites, the Rephaim, the Amorites, the Canaanites, the Girgashites and the Jebusites."

The promise is referred to again in Gen. 12:1–3 [*J*] in the following terms:

Now the Lord said to Abram, "Go from your country ['*eretz*] and your kindred and your father's house to the land that I will show you. And I will make of you a great nation, and I will bless you, and make your name great, so that you will be a blessing. I will bless those who bless you, and him who curses you I will curse; and by you all the families of the earth shall bless themselves.

What is common to all these passages is that a land is promised to Abraham's descendants: the land they are to possess is to be theirs by divine authority. In other respects, the passages differ: in Gen. 15:17–21 the land defined is possibly, by implication, less extensive than that contemplated in Gen. 12:1–3, where Abraham's descendants are to become a great nation and to impinge upon all the families of the earth.

These passages have been variously assessed. According to some, they are creations of a late period, the Exile, when Israel felt that its possession of The Land was in jeopardy. She accordingly sought to bolster her claims by recourse to a supposedly ancient divine promise to Abraham. The promise is not grounded in early tradition, but is a late literary and theological construction, in this view, which has gained few adherents.

It has been urged that the promise is exceedingly ancient, going back to pre-Israelite and even pre-Canaanite times, when the god of Abraham, the god of a nomadic clan, promised to his devotees the two great needs of nomads—a land and numerous progeny. Later, when the descendants of this clan were incorporated into Israel, their god, the god of Abraham, later known as the God of the Fathers, was identified with Yahweh who had brought Israel out of Egypt. In this interpretation, the promise was given by the god of Abraham before

Israel had entered Canaan: it envisaged not the gift of the whole Land of Palestine, but simply the strict inheritance of Abraham.

Recently, in the third place, the view has been forcefully presented that Abraham had already entered Canaan when the promise came to him. Of necessity, the god who gave the promise was not the god of a nomadic group, who had no land of his own to give, but the god of a settled community who owned the land which he gave in promise. The god concerned was, in fact, the *El* deity of Mamre at Hebron where Abraham dwelt. His name was possibly *El Shaddai:* the land he promised was the territory around Hebron referred to in Gen. 15:19 as the land of the Kenites, Kenizzites, and Kadmonites, etc. It is essential, in this view, to recognize that the patriarchs were not merely nomads but leaders of settlements in the agricultural land of Canaan. The emergence of the promise of The Land is to be understood as the legitimization of the settlement of the patriarchs in Canaan.

For the understanding of our task in this volume, what is important is not the rediscovery of the origins of the promise to Abraham, but the recognition that that promise was so reinterpreted from age to age that it became a living power in the life of the people of Israel. Not the mode of its origin matters, but its operation as a formative, dynamic, seminal force in the history of Israel. The legend of the promise entered so deeply into the experience of the Jews that it acquired its own reality. What Jews believe to have happened in the Middle East has been no less formative in world history than that which is known to have occurred.

The reinterpretation to which we have referred concerned two things: the identity of the author of the promise and the content of the promise. As for the author of the promise, historically, if we follow Exod. 6:3, the god who gave the promise could not have been called Yahweh, because Yahweh was unknown by name to the patriarchs. Perhaps most scholars would agree that it is the Yahwist, that is, the formulator of what is known as the *J* tradition in the Pentateuch, who identified the original deity who had given the promise to Abraham with Yahweh. In this way it could be claimed that the god who gave the promise to Abraham also led Israel out of Egypt and became the God of Israel.

The history of the content of the promise is far more complicated. If we follow Clements,[3] it was governed by the political vicissitudes of the people of Judah and Israel and largely formulated by the Yahwist.

---

3. R. E. Clements, *Abraham and David,* pp. 47 ff. It is of the utmost significance that the borders of The Land were never precisely defined in the ancient sources, and that, like the early secular Zionists, even religious Jews have never in this century attempted to follow the broad biblical boundaries mechanically (see chapter 2, n. 27).

In the original promise to Abraham, the content of the promise consists of progeny, blessing, and a land. In three passages, a new relationship to God is also promised. It is the promise of land alone that concerns us. The promise of the possession of the hereditary land of the clan or tribe, whether around Hebron or not, implied in Gen. 15:1 ff, was expanded to include the land from Egypt to the Euphrates (Gen. 15:18). Further, Israel is to become a great nation, numerous as the stars of heaven in number (Gen. 15:5). Thus the promise is made to foretell the rise of the Davidic empire and subserve the interests of that empire. According to Clements, the covenant of Yahweh with David at his installation at Hebron (2 Kings 5:1 ff.) both reflects the Abrahamic covenant and influenced its interpretation and transmission. The Yahwist saw a connection between Abraham and David: for him the Abrahamic covenant found its fulfillment in the extension of the Davidic kingdom; the promise to Abraham was of the rise and triumph of that kingdom. The local dimension of the land in the promise originally made to Abraham was transcended. This means that the Abrahamic covenant became subsumed under the covenant with David, which helps explain why there are so few references to Abraham and his covenant in the preexilic prophets and in the preexilic cultus.

As long as the Davidic dynasty prevailed, the appeal to the promise to Abraham, now absorbed into the Davidic covenant, could be neglected. But in times of dire crises, as in the eighth century, when the threat of Assyria was real, and the self-identity of the people was shaken, the Abrahamic covenant again gained recognition and importance. In Deuteronomy, although the covenant at Horeb is given preeminence, appeal is also made to the promise to Abraham, in reassurance that behind Israel's existence and its tenure of the land of Canaan lay the divine purpose. The Abrahamic covenant is now referred to as having been made with all the three patriarchs and is understood as exclusively concerned with the land of Canaan. The land promised to Abraham has been promised to Israel as a whole, and the promise has found its fulfillment, both in the covenant at Horeb and in the conquest under Joshua.

Deuteronomy, then, fused together the promise of The Land made to the early patriarchs and the tradition of the giving of the Law at Sinai. The relationship of the commandments to The Land is regarded in Deuteronomy as twofold. On the one hand, the commandments are regulatory; that is, they are intended to provide guidance for the government of The Land, for the conduct of the cultus, and for the arrangements demanded by the settlement. On the other hand, the commandments are conditional; that is, only if they are observed can The Land received because of the promise to the Fathers be possessed. According to Deuteronomy, under the terms of the covenant entered into at Sinai, Israel, if it disobeys the commandments, can be expelled from The Land: in this sense, the occupancy of The Land has a "legal" basis. Yes: but Deuteronomy finds reassurance for Israel in the promise to Abraham. That promise was irrevocable: it can therefore, provide a rationale for forgiveness, even though the commandments have been broken. In this way, the promise to Abraham gives grounds for ultimate hope. In Deuteronomy the covenant of "grace" with Abraham can be read as a guarantee and safeguard against failure to observe the covenant of "the Law"—even as a "gospel" for Israel. Particularly revealing of this are the words of Moses to the people in Deut. 9:24-29.

When later we come to P, the priestly document, the strict historical origins and limits of the promise to Abraham are still further modified. The priestly document seeks to provide Israel with a renewed theological basis for its existence. Taking up J and E, P makes the divine promise to Abraham the bedrock on which all Israel's subsequent history rests. P's understanding of that covenant is seen in Gen. 17:1-14 [P]:

When Abram was ninety-nine years old the Lord appeared to Abram, and said to him, "I am God Almighty; walk before me, and be blameless. And I will make my covenant between me and you, and will multiply you exceedingly." Then Abram fell on his face; and God said to him, "Behold, my covenant is with you, and you shall be the father of a multitude of nations. I will make you exceedingly fruitful; and I will make nations of you, and kings shall come forth from you. And I will establish my covenant between me and you and your descendants after you throughout their generations for an everlasting covenant, to be God to you and to your descendants after you. And I will give to you, and to your descendants after you, the land ['eretz] of your sojournings, all the land ['eretz] of Canaan, for an everlasting possession; and I will be their God."

And God said to Abraham, "As for you, you shall keep my covenant, you and your descendants after you throughout their generations. This is my covenant, which you shall keep, between me and your descendants after you: Every male among you shall be circumcised. You shall be circumcised in the flesh of your foreskins, and it shall be a sign of the covenant between me and you. He that is eight days old among you shall be circumcised; every male throughout your generations, whether born in your house, or bought with your money from any foreigner who is not of your offspring, both he that is born in your house and he that is bought with your money, shall be circumcised. So shall my covenant be in your flesh an everlasting covenant. Any uncircumcised male who is not circumcised in the flesh of his foreskin shall be cut off from his people; he has broken my covenant."

Here Abraham is to be the father of a multitude of nations; all the land of Canaan is to be an everlasting possession; the god of the

Abrahamic covenant (*El Shaddai* was probably his name historically) is to be the god of Abraham's descendants; and circumcision is to be the mark of god's people. The content of the covenant has thus been changed: its promissory character has been heightened; its inviolability has been affirmed—it is everlasting. *P* exhibits what is already found in Deuteronomy—an appeal to divine grace, the promise, as a bulwark against failure to observe the commandments of the Sinai covenant, which *P*, like Deuteronomy, connects with the Abrahamic covenant. The appeal to the Abrahamic covenant means that Israel's election, and with it the possession of The Land, can never, for *P*, become conditional on obedience to the Law; that election, resting upon the Abrahamic covenant, cannot be annulled by human disobedience. Israel, it follows, cannot be destroyed, and The Land *will* be hers.

According to von Rad, the whole of the Hexateuch in all its vast complexity was governed by the theme of the fulfillment of the promise to Abraham in the settlement in Canaan. "The chief purpose of this work," he wrote, "was to present in all its biblical and theological significance this one leading conception, in relation to which all the other conceptions of the Hexateuch assume an ancillary role.[4] Like Clements, von Rad holds that it was the work of the Yahwist to fuse the whole complex of the patriarchal sagas together: for him, the entry into Palestine under Joshua is the fulfillment of the promise. Later modifications of this basic pattern of *J* and *E*, in von Rad's view, were trivial.

Of all the promises made to the patriarchs, it was that of The Land that was most prominent and decisive. It is the linking together of the promise to the patriarchs *with* the fulfillment of it in the settlement that gives to the Hexateuch its distinctive theological character. For the Hexateuch, The Land is a promised land, and that inviolably. The significance of the promise as a fact in the Hexateuch is immeasurable, for a very simple reason. However much the Prophets and the Writings gained in significance, in later ages the Pentateuch remained the bedrock of revelation for Jews, so that the references to the promise of The Land embedded in it must be accorded great weight in any assessment of Judaism.[5]

4. Von Rad, *Problem of the Hexateuch,* pp. 85 ff.
5. In *Torah and Canon,* J. A. Sanders has concentrated on the distinction between the Hexateuch and the Pentateuch. He asks the simple question why the Pentateuch, not the Hexateuch, came to constitute the heart of the Torah for Judaism. The "story," the memory of which alone kept "Israel" alive, in *J* and *E* (composed or collected between the eleventh and eighth centuries B.C.E.) included the conquest of the land, and stretched on to include the monarchy of David. Sanders has pointed out in an unpublished paper that the conquest of Canaan in the book of Joshua "culminated in the very place where

We now turn to the second of the concepts that lend peculiarity to the understanding of The Land in the Tanak. G. von Rad lays great emphasis on Lev. 25:23: "The land *(hâ-'âretz)* shall not be sold in perpetuity, for the land *(hâ-'âretz)* is mine; for you are strangers and sojourners with me."[6] This verse introduces a concept which von Rad refuses to connect with Canaanite ideas of the relationship between the Baalim and The Land. In the rest of the Hexateuch, The Land is nowhere declared to have belonged to Yahweh, but rather to the nations whom Israel dispossessed. In the Hexateuch, The Land is invariably referred to as "the land of Canaan." Not until 1 Sam. 13:19 does the phrase "the land of Israel" appear. Joshua 23 makes it clear that Yahweh himself only gained possession of The Land through conquest. The conquest gave him The Land for the sake of Israel (23:3), according to his promise (23:5). But, despite her success in war, which she owed to Yahweh (23:9 f.), Israel does not own The

---

Abraham first settled, at Shechem: the promise of the land, which was made to Abraham at Shechem, was symbolically fulfilled at Shechem." Would it not have been natural for Judaism to elevate the Hexateuch to a normative position? Apparently so. Yet it was Deuteronomy, a document from the seventh century which leaves Moses looking to the Promised Land but not entering it, that formed the climax of the Torah of Judaism. Why? Sanders answers that the crisis of the sixth century B.C.E., in which The Land, the city, and the Temple were lost and ceased to sustain "Israel," compelled the Deuteronomist, and later *P* (sixth-fifth centuries B.C.E.), to look back to the period before the conquest, the Mosaic age, as that which supplied an authoritative norm, and to which both *D* and *P* ascribed the laws which were to give life. While this deserves serious examination, we would simply ask whether Sanders has not too rigidly separated *torah* as "law" from *torah* as "story," and whether, although Judaism did elevate the Pentateuch, it did not isolate it.

The story of the "conquest" in the book of Joshua still remains part of the Tanak. (Cf., especially, D. N. Freedman's review of *GL*, and B. S. Childs, *Introduction to the Old Testament as Scripture,* pp. 56–57.) If Sanders should be able to establish his case, it would be difficult to account for the persistence of the territorial doctrine with which we are here concerned. His work suggests at least that there was much flexibility in the attitude to The Land, and we shall see that this flexibility continued. That the question of the history of the tradition and its formulation is far from being settled appears from the important and stimulating work of J. van Seters, *Abraham in History and Tradition,* and T. L. Thompson, *The Historicity of the Patriarchal Narratives;* see also J. Huesman, "Archaeology and Early Israel." There is a brilliant statement of the assurance provided for the fulfillment of the promise, despite its being conditioned by obedience, in D. N. Freedman, "Divine Commitment and Human Obligation."

6. Von Rad, *Problem of the Hexateuch,* ad rem.

Land. Disobedience to the commandments of Yahweh, through intermarriage with the inhabitants of The Land, will inexorably incur withdrawal of Yahweh's support and the loss of The Land (23:13-16).

There is evidence that Israel had a bad conscience about the act of expropriation, which we call the conquest or the settlement, and sought to justify its conduct. In Josh. 24:13, Israel is reminded that she did not develop The Land herself. In Josh. 24:8, The Land is called unequivocally the land of the Amorites. Similarly, in Judg. 11:19 ff., the consciousness that Israel had dispossessed a people of its land is clear: it had avoided doing so in the case of the Moabites and Edomites (Judg. 11:17–18). According to 2 Sam. 7:23, the conquest of Canaan was made possible only through "great and terrible things" wrought by God in driving out a nation and its gods. In Num. 33:50 ff., the sole justification for the occupation is that Yahweh has seen fit to give Israel The Land; the initial price of occupation is high in destruction (33:52); and then the demands of safety take their human toll (33:55). Compare with this Josh. 23:13. In Deut. 9:4 ff., a reason for Yahweh's gift of The Land is offered: it is "because of the wickedness of these nations that the Lord is driving them out before you": the conquest is, thereby, justified. The same justification appears in Deut. 18:9–14, and it is implicit in Deut. 29:2 ff. Can we also detect a need for justification in Ps. 44:3? It is Yahweh, not the sword, who gave Israel The Land: here it is as if the conquest were divorced from Israel's own volition. In Ps. 105:44 f., the taking of another people's toil in the conquest is justified, without elaboration, in terms of observance of the Law (is it implied here that only in The Land can the Law be observed?). As late as the turn of the first century B.C.E., the "bad conscience" over, or the need for a justification of, the conquest remains (1 Macc. 15:33). But with the recognition in such passages that The Land really belonged to the Canaanites, there coexists also the very ancient notion that The Land belongs to Yahweh (the God of the Fathers—*El*; probably equated with the chief god of Canaan, also *El*) and is his to dispose of, so that he can promise it to Abraham.

This notion, that The Land belongs to Yahweh himself, persisted throughout the Tanak, and beyond. It expressed itself in the conviction that the soil of Israel was not tribal property, but was given by Yahweh for cultivation by lot: the individual received his parcel of land by lot, and so, too, did the tribe. The whole Land was divided according to lot (Num. 26:55). Judgment rendered by lot was thought to be that of Yahweh himself. Thus, when Yahweh commanded that The Land be divided according to lot, it was he himself who decided upon its division: because The Land was Yahweh's alone, he alone could decide its allocation (Ezek. 47:13 f.).

Cultic statements about the harvest are to be understood in the light of Yahweh's ownership of The Land. This explains the demand for

the offering of firstlings; of the first son in Exod. 22:28; the tithe given
to the Levites in Lev. 18:24; the tithe of all the yield of the seed in
Deut. 14:22; and of all the produce in Deut. 26:9–15. In the Hebraic
mind, the first of a particular series was the archetypal form, and as
such represented the entire species. Thus, the offering of the firstfruits
symbolized the offering of the entire crop or harvest. Since Yahweh
was the owner of The Land, the firstfruits offering was only a rendering
to him of his proper portion. For as The Land belonged to Yahweh
so, rightfully, did all the produce. The same concept governed the
custom of gleaning.

Yahweh's possession of The Land is further acknowledged in the
commandment that The Land should keep a sabbath to the Lord (Lev.
25:2, 4). The sabbath of The Land has been variously explained, but
Lev. 25:2 reads: ". . . the land shall keep a sabbath to the Lord." It is
not the people who are commanded to allow The Land to rest: rather
The Land itself, personified, seems to be addressed. The Land, too,
owes worship to Yahweh, to signify that special relationship which it
enjoys with him. The Land's rest recalls the seventh-day rest of the
Lord himself after the creation.

Yahweh's possession of The Land was expressed in terms of "holiness," a conception which in its origin had little, if anything, to do
with morality, but rather denoted a relationship of separation for, or
consecration to, a god. Since The Land was Yahweh's possession, it
enjoyed a certain degree of closeness to him; for Yahweh dwelt in the
midst of Israel (Num. 25:34). Because Yahweh was near to it, his own
holiness radiated throughout its boundaries. Note that the term "holy
land," which suggests that The Land itself was inherently "holy,"
seldom occurs in the Tanak; that is, the holiness of The Land is
entirely derivative.

Nevertheless, the potency of the concept of the holiness of The
Land, though only derived from its relationship to Yahweh, emerges
particularly in passages which forcibly and vividly personify The Land.
Consider especially Lev. 20:22–26 *(H: P)*. Here The Land is conceived
of as itself ejecting Israelites when they are unfaithful to the commandments. One might conclude from this that it was the transgression of the specifically Israelite Law, the Torah that provoked The
Land and caused it to react violently. But in Lev. 18:24–30, The Land
had been defiled by its pre-Israelite inhabitants, who did not know
the Torah of Moses, but had broken the demands that The Land itself
imposed. It was not the military prowess of the Israelites, nor even
Yahweh's fighting for them, which had caused the expulsion of the
earlier inhabitants of The Land. When it became defiled by their abom-
inations, The Land itself thrust them out. The implication is that it
was already holy in Canaanite days, because Yahweh owned it and
dwelt in the midst of it. This is the import of Num. 25:34: "You shall

not defile the land in which you live, in the midst of which I dwell, for I the Lord dwell in the midst of the people of Israel."

The relationship of The Land to Yahweh also governed the relationship of the Law to The Land. If the Israelites were to live in Yahweh's Land, in his very presence, they had to approximate to his holiness by following his Law: the verse "You shall be holy; for I the Lord your God am holy" (Lev. 19:1) implies that Israel is to obey Yahweh's Law. And, in much of the Tanak, obedience to the Law becomes the condition of occupying The Land, as we have already seen. We shall return to this theme later. Suffice it here to refer to Isa. 1:19 and Deut. 4:40. Here it is important to recognize that Yahweh had imposed on The Land—indeed upon nature—a sacred order or pattern or law, the violation of which produced a dissolution, a return to chaotic disorder and formlessness. This can best be illustrated from those laws which, when disobeyed, are specifically stated to pollute or defile The Land of Israel. We note prohibitions:

1. Against harlotry (Lev. 19:29)
2. Against shedding blood (Num. 29–34; Deut. 21:6–9; Ps. 106:38 f.)
3. Against allowing a corpse to remain hanging on a tree (Deut. 21:22–23)
4. Against remarriage with a former divorced and remarried wife (Deut. 24:1–4; compare Jer. 3:1)

To examine the background of these prohibitions in full is not possible here. Fundamental is the concept of totality within the Israelite community. Everything within that community had its proper place: everything in the natural order was divided according to function or kind. For example, there could be no violation of species, no crossing of the boundaries set between differing groups. This explains the prohibitions expressed in Lev. 19:19; 22:5, 9, 10, 11. There is a Yahweh-given order to the cosmos; a division is made between the sacred and the profane (Lev. 22:5 ff.).

And it can safely be asserted that each of the prohibitions singled out here is directed against the violation of that order and the mixing of the sacred and profane which leads to the disintegration and profanation of the whole cosmos. Thus prostitution violated the concept of totality. The prostitute withdrew from the community as an integrated whole: by dissolving the boundaries between kinds, she violated the sacred divisions established by Yahweh. Again, blood was especially holy to Semites: blood was life: it was the possession of Yahweh as his portion of a sacrificial feast, and as such was sacred. To shed blood was to handle what was sacred as though it were profane. So, too, because dead bodies were one of the major sources of uncleanness, to allow a corpse to lie in The Land, and especially to hang it on a tree overnight was to subject The Land, which in virtue of its relation to Yahweh was holy, to uncleanness. From the corpse, uncleanness spread like a contagion throughout the surrounding area: the totality of nature was thereby affected. And, finally, the prohibition against remarrying one's divorced wife who had remarried was governed by the recognition that such a woman was in a similar case to the prostitute: she had known two different men. To return to her first husband was to mix diverse kinds and ipso facto to join together one who was clean (the first husband) with the one who had, by her second marriage, become unclean. Again, such a violation of the natural order involved the whole cosmos, and was particularly manifested in The Land itself.

But it is merely for the sake of clarity that we have concentrated on the above four prohibitions. What is true of them holds true of every violation of Yahweh's commandments. Yahweh dwells in Israel. Through the "contagion" of his holiness, The Land becomes clean. Violation of Yahweh's Law is a profanation of the order which he has implanted in the cosmos. And when, through the violation of that Law, Israelites have profaned themselves, they can no longer remain in the holy-clean Land; either The Land itself ejects them, as in some passages, or The Land suffers under the wrath which they have brought upon it, in which case, as Isa. 24:4–5 puts the matter:

The earth mourns and withers, the world languishes and withers; the heavens languish together with the earth. The earth lies polluted under its inhabitants: for they have transgressed the laws, violated the statutes, broken the everlasting covenant.

In the above pages, we have distinguished two peculiar emphases in the understanding of The Land in the Tanak. The first is an historical one, centered on the promise to Abraham and appearing chiefly in the narrative portions of the Hexateuch, in *J* and *E*. The second is a cultic one, concentrating on the conception of The Land as Yahweh's own possession and appearing chiefly in the legislative portions of the Hexateuch, *D* and *P*. Although derived from different sources, these two emphases became merged in the cultic life of Israel and in its transmission of various traditional documents, so that, as the Tanak now stands, they have to be carefully disentangled. Proper assessment of the role they played throughout the history of Israel is difficult, and will be postponed for the present.

The Prophets: Doom and Restoration

The second source to which we turn is the prophetic literature. One thing seems clear: concern with The Land and hope for The Land emerges at many places in the Tanak outside the Hexateuch. While the promise was regarded as fulfilled in the settlement, that settlement was not regarded as a complete fulfillment. Deuteronomy makes it clear that there is still a future to look forward to: The Land has to achieve rest and peace. This points to what von Rad calls one of the most interesting problems of Tanak theology. He expresses it thus: "Promises which have been fulfilled in history are not thereby exhausted of their content, but remain as promises on a different level, although they are to some extent metamorphosed in the process. The promise of the land was proclaimed ever anew, even after its fulfillment, as a future benefit of God's redemptive activity."[7] Promise and fulfillment inform much of the Tanak, and the tradition, however changed, continued to embody the hope of life in The Land.

Thus it is arguable that it was as inconceivable to the prophets as to the people as a whole that Israel should finally be deprived of her Land. At this point, we encounter a notorious problem of proportion in the interpretation of the prophets. It has been easy and, indeed, almost customary, to assert that the prophetic sources suggest something along the following lines: the prophets insisted on Yahweh's freedom to choose and to reject Israel from the beginning, but they recognized that Israel as a whole had been unfaithful to her covenant with him, and maintained that Yahweh could exist without his people—that, indeed, it might become his will to destroy them. The prophets pronounced doom on people and Land: it is this predominant message of doom that rings like a knell in their works. And it has been pointed out that one, at least, of the greatest of the prophets seems to have been able to feel only a loose commitment to The Land, deep as was his love for it. The advice of Jeremiah in a letter to the exiles in Babylon reveals this (Jer. 29:1, 4–9). In the popular mind, return from Babylon was an absolute necessity; for Jeremiah it was no urgent matter, although he was hopeful that someday it would occur: for the moment, to return to The Land would be to follow false prophecy.

But it is not only in 29:1, 4–9 that Jeremiah takes a positive view of the Exile. Jeremiah 29:16–20 and 38:2 make clear that those who were not deported, but remained in The Land and in the city of Jerusalem, would know the sword and famine and pestilence. The words of Jer. 38:2 are unequivocal: "Thus saith the Lord, He who stays in this city shall die by the sword, by famine and by pestilence; but he who goes out to the Chaldeans shall live; he shall have his life as a prize of war, and live." Equally striking is the vision of the good and bad figs in Jer. 24:1–30. The good figs are the exiles (Jer. 24:5). The evil figs are those who remain in The Land (Jer. 24:8–9). For Jeremiah, the Exile is the fulfillment of the purpose of God: the exiles are blessed in their disaster. The same theology reemerges in Ezek.

7. Ibid., pp. 92 f.

17 in the parable of the eagle and the cedar. As in Jeremiah, the Exile proves a blessing.

But no other prophet so unequivocally asserts the possibility of the good life apart from The Land and we may well question whether the attitude of Jeremiah and Ezekiel was as unclouded as we have suggested. As the prophetic books now stand, alongside prophecies of doom against The Land because of Israel's sin, there are promises of restoration. This is particularly conspicuous in Amos (9:14–15). Compare also the incidence of prophecies of restoration in Hos. 1:10; Isa. 2:1–5; 9:1–9 (both possibly Isaianic); 9:10–16; 24–27; 26:15–20; 29:16–21; 32:15–20 r. 3:18–19; 11:4–5; and Ezek. 4:15. Many such messages of restoration in the prophetic sources, as they now stand, are doubtless due to emendation aimed at the domestication of the prophets. Like the generality in Israel, stung by prophetic denunciation and foreboding, pious scribes could not reconcile themselves to the severity of the prophets, and provided addenda to soften their implacable stance. To such scribes, the prophets' messages of doom could not possibly have been their last word. The question, however, is whether *all* the prophecies of restoration to The Land are to be so understood.

If we exclude Amos and Isaiah, all the prophets of doom reveal a persistent yearning for the ingathering of the dispersed of Israel into one national entity in their own Land. At first sight, there is nothing in Amos to suggest the recognition of a peculiar relationship between Israel and her Land. Amos 7:17 is instinct with awareness of the significance of The Land, however, and there may be a glimmer of hope for people in The Land expressed in 5:14, notwithstanding that the closing words of Amos 9:11–15, speaking of a coming salvation, cannot with certainty be derived from the prophet. It is significant that Israel's punishment for her sins takes the two forms, among others, of a redistribution of The Land and exile from it (7:17; compare 5:26). Future restoration of the people and its Land can only be very tentatively found, if at all, in Amos.

It is otherwise when we turn to Hosea. The words of hope in Hos. 1:10–11 can only very doubtfully be ascribed to the prophet, but those of 2:14–25 may be taken as his. Here Yahweh is to entice his unfaithful Israel (2:2–15) back to himself in the wilderness. But notice: it is not in the wilderness that Israel is to enjoy new fertility, but as she reenters the promised Land, through the Valley of Achor, where Achan sinned (Josh. 7:24 ff.). This has now become a door of hope. Unlike the Rechabites, whom we shall mention later, the prophet does not wish a return to the desert: such a return as is envisaged in 2:2–14 is merely a prelude to a new entry into the land. And that land is Yahweh's Land. That the land of Canaan is The Land of the Lord appears in 9:3. The attitude towards The Land in Hosea is a positive one: despite its apostasy, Israel is to dwell in The Land.

The role of The Land in Isaiah is less easy to assess. But one thing is clear: that the reward of sin is thought of in terms of The Land indicates its significance (see Isa. 24). There is no doubt that The Land is the Land of Emmanuel (Isa. 8:8; cf. 14:25). The seminal passage is 1:5–9 (compare Isa. 5:13, where exile is the punishment for sin, 7:23–4; and 9:19). Beyond the destruction of The Land, Isaiah looks forward to a renewal of Zion and the perpetuation of a remnant of the people. True, unlike Hosea, he makes no reference to an exile and a return, but he does look forward to a new king and his kingdom (Isa. 9:7). Here The Land is not explicitly mentioned, but the kingdom of the new David implies the restored Land—restored in justice and righteousness, not in its old sinful form.

When we turn to Jeremiah, the evidence leads to the same attitude. Born in Anathoth, which is situated in the territory of Benjamin, it was perhaps natural that Jeremiah should have been concerned not merely with his own kingdom of Judah but also with the fate of the northern kingdom exiled in 722 B.C.E., because Benjamin (although politically it was possessed by both north and south at different times) ethnologically belonged to Israel. At any rate, his prophecies reveal an absorbing interest and a constant love for the Rachel tribes; it is his heart's desire that the northern Israel as well as Judah should ultimately return from exile. Here we must emphasize his purchase of a portion of his family inheritance: this is symbolic of his belief in the ultimate salvation of all his people and their establishment upon their own soil (Jer. 32:6–25). If we take Jer. 31:2–6, 18–26 as authentic and accept the literal interpretation of them that Skinner favours, they reveal the same longing. This means that for Jeremiah the nation was still the sphere, if not the unit, of religion. As Skinner puts it: "The main point is that in some sense a restoration of the Israelite nationality was the form in which Jeremiah conceived the Kingdom of God." It is essential to note in the vision of the figs in Jer. 24 that the "good figs," the exiles, will be brought again to The Land (Jer. 24:6) (compare Jer. 12:14b–15; 16:15; 24:6; 29:14; 30:3; 31:9, 12, 14, 23–25, 33–34).

In Ezekiel we find the idea that Yahweh is a jealous god who can brook no rivals. He therefore inflicts punishment on Israel because of her apostasy, but the restoration of Israel is assured, because Yahweh's name must be upheld among the nations; the failure of his people would bring dishonor upon himself. The ingathering of all scattered Israelites in The Land is a constant theme of Ezekiel; the reassembled nation will be purified in heart and spirit; there will be one flock under the shepherd Yahweh (Ezek. 17; compare Ezek. 20:42; 36:9–12; 39:26). The end of Ezek. 47:15–48:35 describes the redistribution of The Land among the tribes of Israel.

The same motif runs through Deutero-Isaiah. True, Israel is to be a missionary to the Gentiles, but its first task, before turning to them, is to seek the return of the lost sheep of the house of Israel (Is. 49:5 f.). There is a core of particularism in the most universal of the prophets.

That the hope for the future in the prophets' messages is not to be neglected is confirmed by recent studies. It is preserved even when the promise seems obliterated in the announcement of doom. The "Day" of Yahweh, which spelt judgment, would also witness the outpouring of his mercy. This hope comes to explicit expression in much-noticed concepts: that of the remnant in Isaiah, that of the new covenant in Jeremiah, and that of the spirit revivifying the dry bones in Ezekiel. These concepts have been treated so often that we need merely pinpoint the pertinent aspects. The remnant which is envisaged, not only by Isaiah but also by Amos, assures not only survival but continuity with the old community, and it exists not for its own sake, but for the sake of the whole community: within the perspective of Israel itself, it is *always* a saving remnant. Likewise, although the new covenant of Jeremiah suggests a radically new beginning, it is with Israel, albeit a changed people, that this new covenant is to be ratified; just as it is the people of Israel which is to be reconstituted when, in Ezekiel's vision, the spirit revivifies the dry bones. It may be objected that neither the remnant nor the new covenant nor the spirit specifically refer to The Land. But this may be questioned in the case of Isa. 7:3, where clearly the remnant *(She'ar yâshûb)* is involved in the very physical existence of the nation. In any case, in view of the passages we have cited in this connection, the prophets did include The Land in their hopes for the future. Despite the difficulty of their precise delimitation, if we bear in mind the passages promising restoration in the prophets, together with references to the remnant, the new covenant, and the spirit, it is difficult not to recognize with Sifre[8] that the prophets first addressed hard words of judgment to Israel, but in the end spoke words of consolation.

Finkelstein, in a controversial work[9], has connected the prophets with the legal tradition that came *after* them, that is, with the development of the rabbinic tradition (just as Alt, Buber, von Rad, Zimmerli, and others have connected the prophets with the Law in Israel *before* their day). If his interpretation is accepted the concern of the prophets with, and their anticipation of, the future life of their people in The Land becomes exceedingly probable, however dark the doom

8. Cited without exact reference in *New Light from the Prophets,* p. 14, by L. Finkelstein, who translates: "And 'all' the Prophets learned from him [Moses], at first addressing harsh words to Israel, but in the end turning about and speaking words of consolation." Finkelstein notes, as examples, Hosea, Joel, Amos, Micah, and Jeremiah.

9. Ibid.

they proclaimed. In Finkelstein's hands, the prophets become, to use Rudolf Otto's phrase, architects of the future, as well as heralds of destruction: they reveal the essential irrationality of the eschatological mind, which can hold doom and a promising future in living tension.[10]

THE LAND IN EXTRABIBLICAL SOURCES

The Apocrypha and Pseudepigrapha

After the last of the canonical prophets, hope for The Land is taken over into later eschatological thinking in Israel. The problem of how far Apocalyptic is an outgrowth of prophecy or is a new emergence primarily instigated by the influence of Iranian and other factors on the life of Israel need not directly concern us. What does need recognition is that eschatological thinking was not alien to the main currents in Judaism. The antithesis drawn between Pharisaism as the heir of the Law and Apocalyptic as the heir of prophecy—so that, with the increasing significance of Pharisaism, Apocalyptic became correspondingly peripheral in Judaism—has had to be abandoned. This means that concepts that appear in the apocalyptic sources need not be regarded as insignificant fringe elements in Judaism. In these sources, The Land is given the kind of attention that is accorded to it in the Tanak and in the rabbinical sources, although notably less frequently.

The incidence of specific references to The Land in the Apocrypha, the Pseudepigrapha, and the Qumran scrolls, especially in comparison with the Hexateuch, is meagre. But the awareness of The Land—its holiness, its possible pollution by sin, and consequent need for purification—is unmistakably clear. The connection of Israel with The Land is an assumption. The term "holy land" appears (Wisd. Sol. 13:3, 4, 7; 2 Bar. 65:9, 10; 71:1; Sib. Or. 3:266 f.), and "goodly land" (Tob. 14:4, 5; Jub. 13:2, 6; 1 En. 89:40), and "the land which is in thy sight the most precious of all lands" (Wisd. Sol. 13:3, 4, 7). In 1 En. 89:40, the phrase "pleasant and glorious land" occurs, and in the Letter of Aristeas, line 107, The Land is "extensive and beautiful." The notion of The Land of promise occurs in Jub. 12:22; 13:3; 22:27; Ecclus. 46:8; Asmp. M. 1:8 f.; 2:1. The connection between Israel's conduct and The Land is marked. In Jub. 6:12–13, failure to observe the demands of Yahweh is incompatible with occupation of The Land. Again, in Jub. 15:28, the reward of those who observe circumcision is that "they will *not* be rooted out of the land." The cultic recital of Yahweh's acts in history was the vehicle for the transmission and perpetuation of the understanding of the relationship between people and land, as of other motifs. Even the rationalization of the conquest as a punishment for

10. R. Otto, *The Kingdom of God and the Son of Man,* pp. 59 ff.

the sins of the pre-Israelite inhabitants reappears in the Wisdom of Solomon (cf 2:7). The insistence on the mercifulness of Yahweh, even in the conquest, however, breaks through in 12:3–11.

The understanding of The Land found in the Tanak, then, reappears in the Apocrypha and Pseudepigrapha, showing the growth in intensity of the idea that Yahweh must vindicate his choice of his people by restoring them to their land according to their tribes as a united people. Perhaps the most well-known expression of this idea is found in Psalms of Solomon (first century B.C.E.). Speaking of the son of David, whom the Lord shall raise up, the author writes:

> And he shall gather together a holy people. . . .
> And he shall divide them according to their
> tribes upon the land
> And neither sojourner nor alien shall
> sojourn with them any more.

In 4 Ezra 13:48 (first century C.E.) we read of the last days that: "The survivors of thy people, even those found within thy holy border (shall be saved)." The same thought occurs in 2 Bar. 9:2 (first century C.E.). In the end, Yahweh will protect only the people who live in Israel: that land will be surrounded by his holy presence:

For at that time I will protect only those who are found in those self-same days in this land.

In 2 Bar. 1:1 the author asserts that The Land itself will act on behalf of Israel:

And the holy land shall have mercy on its own and it shall protect its inhabitants at that time.

Only by such protection as God and The Land itself provide will the name of Israel be remembered. As 2 Bar. 3:4–5 expresses it:

What, therefore, will there be for these things [that is, at the end]? for if thou destroyest thy city and deliverest up thy land to those who hate us, how shall the name of Israel be remembered?

In concurrence with the "active" role ascribed to The Land itself in 2 Bar., in 4 Ezra The Land becomes "holy" or sanctified in the last days because Yahweh draws especially near to it. The Israelites will escape from the dangers and terrors of the end through no merit of their own. Their only guarantee of salvation will lie in their actually dwelling in The Land, which Yahweh will save for his own sake alone, as his own possession. 4 Ezra 9:7–9 makes this clear:

And everyone shall survive from the perils aforesaid and shall see salvation in my land, and within my borders which I have sanctified for myself eternally.

Even in 1 Enoch (first century C.E., at 90:20, cosmic and supraterrestrial as are its visions of the future, at the end it is in the pleasant Land of Israel that the throne of Yahweh is finally to be erected.

The Qumran Writings

The high evaluation and significance of The Land is also present in the documents from Qumran. In these The Land is understood as Yahweh's own possession. In *IQS* 1:5, we read that the members of the sect are "to practice truth and righteousness and justice *in the land*." The council of the community is characterized as follows in *IQS* 8:3:

In the council of the community (there shall be) twelve laymen and three priests who are perfect in all that is revealed of the whole Torah, through practicing truth and righteousness and justice and loving devotion and walking humbly each with his fellow *in order to maintain faithfulness in the land* with a steadfast intent and with a broken Spirit [emphasis added].

Further in *IQS* 8:4b–7 we read:

When these things come to pass in Israel, the Council of the Community will have been established in truth:
As an eternal planting, a holy house for Israel,
A most holy institution for Aaron,
Witnesses of truth concerning judgment,
And the chosen of grace to atone for the land
And to render to the wicked their desert [emphasis added].

The council of the community is to be "accepted to make atonement for the land" (*IQS* 8:10). The life of the community, in accordance with its own understanding of the Law, is designed to achieve what the sacrificial system had in vain sought to accomplish, the acceptance of The Land by Yahweh. *IQS* 9:3 ff. reads:

When these things come to pass in Israel according to all these regulations, for a foundation of a holy spirit, for eternal truth, for *a ransom for the guilt of transgression and sinful faithlessness, and for acceptance for the land* [emphasis added].

Part of the purpose of the community is to restore a land made unclean to acceptance. There is an "order" of The Land which the Law recognizes and which is to be observed in human habitations (*CDC* 9:6b). The tribal organization of The Land is assumed (*IQM* 2): even in war the Jubilee of The Land is to be honored (*IQM* 2). The relationship between human conduct and The Land, which we so often discover in the Tanak, is assumed throughout the Scrolls. Sin leads Yahweh to hide his face from The Land (*CDC* 2:9–11) and causes The Land to

become desolate (*CDC* 4:10). One significant mark of sin is the re-
moval of the boundaries of The Land, which, as we have seen, were
regarded as set by Yahweh himself (*CDC* 1:16; 8:1). But, however
deep the consciousness of the corruption of The Land through sin, it
is of the very genius of the Qumran community that it recognizes that
the condition of The Land is not totally hopeless, because a "remnant"—the sect itself—has been spared to atone for it. The awareness
of the peculiarity of Israel, and its stance against other lands, is clear:
Israel stands against the nations. In the last days, warriors from its
tribes are to go out against the Gentile lands (*IQM* 2). For the author,
at the time of the return of the exiles from the desert of the peoples
(Col. 1:3, compare Ezek. 20:35), the sect, the true Israelites, would
occupy The Land, according to their tribes, and institute an offensive
war against those outside. With The Land as its base, this was to be
a holy war, much more intense and widespread than those conceived
in the Tanak, which were usually defensive. What concerns us here is
the centrality of The Land of Israel in the thought of the author, in
line with Isa. 2:1-5 and especially Ezek. 38 ff.

Our brief survey of the Apocrypha, Pseudepigrapha, and Qumran
writings reflects the comparative infrequency of references to The
Land in these sources. This must, however, be qualified. After the
Exile, the sentiment concerning The Land became concentrated in
Jerusalem and the Temple, references to which in the sources used are
very numerous. The absence of direct references to The Land can,
therefore, be misleading, because The Land is implied in the city and
the Temple, which became its quintessence. (See, e.g., Tob. 13:13, 17;
and especially 14:5, which looks forward to a future Temple to which
the exiles will return as to a rebuilt house; at the same time, 14:7 claims
that all the children of Israel shall dwell forever in The Land of Abraham
in safety, and it shall be given over to them.) Moreover, brief as it is,
our treatment has brought into focus two factors. First, the difference
between the approach to The Land in the Apocrypha and Pseudepigrapha and that in the Qumran writings, which we shall enlarge upon
and seek to explain below, and, secondly, the relationship between
historical events and the approach to The Land. We saw in dealing
with the Hexateuch how *D* and *P* reacted to the collapse of the state
in the sixth century B.C.E. The same reaction is traceable mutatis
mutandis in 2 Bar. and 4 Ezra where, after C.E. 70, there emerges an
almost desperate concentration on the efficacy of life in The Land.
Indeed, these documents seem to go farther than *D* and *P*. There are
passages in the Tanak where The Land expels unworthy inhabitants:
in 2 Bar. and 4 Ezra, as we have seen it acts, not only negatively, but
positively on behalf of "Israel." Such a note could only emerge out
of desperation, which was probably more typical of apocalyptic circles
than of the rabbinic ones, to which we turn next.

The Rabbinic Sources

In many apocalyptic and "sectarian" groups, then, the question of The Land remained a living issue up to the first century. Such groups, as we saw above, have often been claimed to be outside the dominant Pharisaic stream of Judaism, so that their concern with The Land might be discounted by some as a mark of insignificant currents. But such an approach to first-century Judaism is no longer possible. The customary picture of first-century Judaism before C.E. 70 as dominated by the Pharisees, who constituted the representatives of what has been called normative Judaism, is not tenable: differences of emphasis there were between apocalyptists and Pharisees, but no cleavage. We shall find that, on the question of The Land, the Pharisees largely shared the views of the groups referred to.

In fact, Pharisaism so cherished the view that there was an unseverable connection betwen Israel and Yahweh and The Land, that this view has been especially connected with the devastation of The Land by the Romans in the war of C.E. 66–70. Conditions in Palestine after C.E. 70 were economically difficult. As a result, there developed an increasing tendency for Jews to emigrate from Palestine to neighbouring countries, especially to Syria. This became so serious that it threatened to depopulate The Land. The need to encourage Jews to remain in it was so urgent that the Pharisaic leaders after C.E. 70 adopted a policy of extolling the virtues of The Land and encouraging settlement. Conservative sages, such as Rabbi Eliezer the Great or ben Hyrcanus (C.E. 80-120), in order to protect Palestinian agriculture wanted to subject Syrian agriculture to all the requirements of tithing and the sabbatical year so as to check the emigration of farmers to Syria. R. Gamaliel II (C.E. 80–120), while he opposed such extreme measures, also shared in this purpose. The following passage from Mishnah Hallah iv: 7-8 is instructive:

7. If Israelites leased a field from gentiles in Syria, R. Eliezer declares their produce liable to tithes and subject to the Seventh Year law; but Rabban Gamaliel declares it exempt. Rabban Gamaliel says: Two Dough-offerings [are given] in Syria. But R. Eliezer says: One Dough-offering. [Beforetime] they accepted the more lenient ruling of Rabban Gamaliel and the more lenient ruling of R. Eliezer, but afterward they followed the rulings of Rabban Gamaliel in both things.

8. Rabban Gamaliel says: Three regions are distinguished in what concerns Dough-offering. In the land of Israel as far as Chezib one Dough-offering [is given]: from Chezib to the River [Eastward; to the Euphrates] and to Amanah, [Northward, to the river Amanah (2 Kings 5:12), which rises in the Antilebanon and flows through Damascus] two Dough-offerings. . . . From the River and from Amanah, inwards, two Dough-offerings [are given].

Legislation thus affected Syria. R. Akiba's rule, "the like of whatsoever is permitted to be done in the land of Israel may be done also in Syria," implies much discussion of this point. Akiba died in 132 C.E. But it is not necessary to emphasize economic factors exclusively in this connection, important though they are. The roots of the emphasis on The Land are deep in the Tanak, as we have seen: it was the land of milk and honey (Exod. 3:8, etc.), Israel's lasting resting place (Deut. 12:9), and God's own Land (Josh. 22:19, etc.). After the horrors of wars in the first and second centuries, and their subsequent dispersion, it was natural for rabbis to idealize the old life in The Land before the wars. The Tannaitic and other rabbinic sources, building on the Scriptures, point to the significance of The Land in the most unambiguous way, even if stimulated by economic and political realities. There is a kind of "umbilical cord" between Israel and The Land. It is no accident that one-third of the Mishnah, the Pharisaic legal code, is connected with The Land. Nine-tenths of the first order of the Mishnah, *Zeraim* (Seeds), of the fifth order, *Kodashim* (Hallowed Things), and of the sixth order, *Toharoth* (Cleannesses), deal with laws concerning The Land, and there is much of the same in the other parts of the Mishnah. This is no accident, because for the rabbis the connection between Israel and The Land was not fortuitous, but part of the divine purpose or guidance, as was the Law itself. Consider the following passage, ascribed to a rabbi flourishing between C.E. 140 and 165, from Lev. Rabbah 13:2:

> R. Simeon b. Yohai opened a discourse with: "He rose and measured the earth" [Hab. 3:6]. The Holy One, blessed be He, considered all generations and he found no generation fitted to receive the Torah other than the generation of the wilderness; the Holy One, blessed be He, considered all mountains and found no mountain on which the Torah should be given other than Sinai; the Holy One, blessed be He, considered all cities, and found no city wherein the Temple might be built, other than Jerusalem; the Holy One, blessed be He, considered all lands, and found no land suitable to be given to Israel, other than the Land of Israel. This is indicated by what is written: "He rose and measured the earth—and He released nations" [ibid.].

The choice of Israel and the Temple and of The Land was deliberate, the result of Yahweh's planning; R. Simeon b. Yohai's thought goes back to the beginning of things and finds Yahweh's purpose at work then. The connection between Yahweh, Israel, The Land, Sinai, the Temple is primordial: it is grounded in a necessity of the divine purpose and is, therefore, unseverable. And it is no wonder that the rabbis heaped upon The Land terms of honor and endearment. For them, The Land of Israel is called simply *Hâ-'âretz,* The Land; all countries outside it are *ḥûtz lâ-'aretz,* outside The Land. In *BT* Berakoth 5a we read: "It has been taught: R. Simeon b. Yohai [C.E. 140-65] says: The Holy One, blessed be He, gave Israel three precious gifts, and all of them were given only through sufferings. These are: The Torah, the Land of Israel, and the World to Come."

We have seen that behind the glorification of The Land stood passages in the Scriptures. But, in addition to this, two factors could not but unceasingly stamp The Land upon the consciousness of Israel. The first is that the Law itself, by which Jews lived, was so tied to The Land that it could not but recall The Land. As we have already stated, one-third of the Mishnah deals with The Land and all the agricultural laws in it—like those of Scripture itself—do so. Consider the following passages: Lev. 19:23 (*H*); 23:10 (*H*); 23:22 (*H*); 25:2 (*H*); Deut. 26:1. These passages make it clear that the agricultural laws are to apply "in The Land." Further, only in Palestine could there be cities of refuge, which were so important in the civil law (Num. 35:9 f.; Deut. 4:41 f.; 19:1 f.). True, there are laws not contingent upon The Land; and the distinction between these and their opposite was clearly recognized. But the reward for the observance of the laws was "life in The Land," as is implied in Mishnah Kiddushin 1:9–10.

9. Any religious duty that does not depend on the Land (of Israel) may be observed whether in the Land or outside of it; and any religious duty that depends on the Land may be observed in the Land [alone]; excepting the laws of *Orlah*-fruit and of Diverse Kinds. E. Eliezer says: Also the law of new produce.

10. If a man performs but a single commandment, it shall be well with him and he shall have length of days and shall inherit the Land; but if he neglects a single commandment, it shall be ill with him and he shall not have length of days and shall not inherit the Land. He that has a knowledge of Scripture and Mishnah and right conduct will not soon fall into sin, for it is written, "And a threefold cord is not quickly broken." But he that has no knowledge of Scripture and Mishnah and right conduct has no part in the habitable world.

The Law itself, therefore, to use current terminology, might be regarded as an effective symbol of The Land: it served as a perpetual call to The Land.

But, secondly, precisely because it was The Land to which the Law most applied, The Land gained in sanctity. Consider the following passages from Mishnah Kelim 1:6–9.

6. There are ten degrees of holiness. The Land of Israel is holier than any other land. Wherein lies its holiness? In that from it they may bring [the offerings of] the omer [sheaf], the firstfruits, and the two loaves, which they may not bring from any other land.

7. The walled cities [of The Land of Israel] are still more holy, in that they must send forth lepers from their midst; moreover they may carry around a corpse therein wheresoever they will, but once it is gone forth [from the city] they may not bring it back.

8. Within the wall [of Jerusalem] is still more holy, for there [only] they may eat the lesser holy things and the second tithe. The Temple Mount is still more holy, for no man or woman that has a flux, no menstruant, and no woman after childbirth may enter therein. The Rampart is still more holy, for no gentiles and none that have contracted uncleanness from a corpse may enter therein. The Court of the Women is still more holy, for none that had immersed himself the selfsame day (because of uncleanness) may enter therein, yet none would thereby become liable to a sin-offering. The Court of the Israelites is still more holy, for none whose atonement is yet incomplete may enter therein, and they would thereby become liable to a sin-offering. The Court of the Priests is still more holy, for Israelites may not enter therein, save only when they must perform the laying on of the hands, slaughtering, and waving.

9. Between the Porch and the Altar is still more holy, for none that has a blemish or whose hair is unloosed may enter there. The Sanctuary is still more holy, for none may enter therein with hands and feet unwashed. The Holy of Holies is still more holy, for none may enter therein save only the High Priest on the Day of Atonement at the time of the [Temple] service. R. Jose said: In five things is the space between the Porch and the Altar equal to the Sanctuary: for they may not enter there that have a blemish, or that have drunk wine, or that have hands and feet unwashed, and men must keep far from between the Porch and the Altar at the time of burning the incense.

In each case—in the reference to The Land, the walled cities of The Land, the wall of Jerusalem, the Temple Mount, the Rampart, the Court of Women, the Court of the Israelites etc.—it is the connection with an enactment of the Law that determines the degree of its holiness. And, for our purposes especially, it is noteworthy that it is the applicability of the Law to The Land in 1:6 that assures its special holiness. The implication is that Jewish sanctity is only fully possible in The Land: outside The Land, only strictly personal laws can be fulfilled, that is, the moral law, sexual law, sabbath law, circumcision and dietary laws, etc. Of necessity, outside The Land, the territorial laws have to be neglected. Exile is, therefore, an emaciated life, even though, through suffering, it atones. A passage in *BT* Sotah 14a expresses this point of view in dealing with Moses' failure to enter The Land.

In the light of the above, it is not surprising that both the gift of prophecy—the gift of the Holy Spirit, and the gift of resurrection of the dead—were by some connected with The Land. Mekilta Pisha 1 both affirms Israel as the only land fit for prophecy and the dwelling of the Shekinah, and reveals the efforts made to deal with the difficulties such a position confronted; for example, the fact that Yahweh had appeared outside The Land.[11]

Again, in the view of some rabbis, the resurrection was to take place first in The Land, and the benefits of The Land in death are many (see Gen. Rabbah 96:5). Some urged that those who died outside The Land would not rise: but even an alien (Canaanitish) slave girl who dwelt in The Land might expect to share in the resurrection (see *BT* Ketuboth 111a). At the end of the second century, Rabbi Meir, at his death, required that his remains should be cast into the sea off the Palestinian coast, lest he be buried in foreign soil. There is no space or necessity here to enlarge further. The desire to die in The Land, to possess its soil, to make pilgrimages to it, all these manifestations of attachment to The Land history attests. The archaeological and literary evidence that Jews from the Diaspora frequently arranged to be buried in Eretz Israel is clear for both the Tannaitic and Amoraic periods.[12]

Throughout the centuries, beginning with the fall of Jerusalem in C.E. 70, the conscious cultivation of the memory of The Land, concentrated in Jerusalem and the Temple, has continued in Judaism. The rabbis at Jamnia, in demanding that the Eighteen Benedictions (the Tefillah or Shemoneh Esreh) should be said three times a day—morning, afternoon, and evening (Mishnah Berakoth 4:1 ff.), had in mind, among other things, the perpetual remembrance of Jerusalem and The Land. The Shemoneh Esreh for the morning and afternoon service corresponded to the morning and afternoon daily whole-offerings in the Temple. There was no time fixed for the evening Shemoneh Esreh, but on sabbaths and festivals, the Shemoneh Esreh was to be said four times (there being demanded an additional Tefillah corresponding to the "additional offering" presented on those days in the ancient

---

11. To the materials in *GL*, add a passage pointed out to me by Mr. Dale C. Allison from Pseudo-Philo (see M. R. James, ed., *Liber Antiquitatum Biblicarum*, p. 95):

4. And before all of them will I choose my servant Abram, and I will bring him out from their land, and lead him into the land which mine eye hath looked upon from the beginning when all the dwellers upon earth sinned before my face, and I brought on them the water of the flood: and then I destroyed not that land but preserved it. Therefore the fountains of my wrath did not break forth therein, neither did the water of my destruction come down upon it. For there will I make my servant Abram to dwell, and I will make my covenant with him, and bless his seed, and will be called his God for ever.

See also N. Avigad and Y. Yadin, eds., *The Genesis Apocryphon;* and Genesis Rabbah 33:6-7 on Gen. 8:10.

12. See Eric M. Meyers, *Jewish Ossuaries*, pp. 72–79. He also cites passages indicating resentment against second burials in Eretz Israel.

Temple). Three times daily, then, the Jew was required to pray; among other things, he was required to repeat the 14th Benediction (dated by Dugmore to 168–65 B.C.E.), the 16th (possibly pre-Maccabean), and the 18th (C.E. 40–70). These read as follows (they are modified in later Jewish prayer books):

Benediction 14

Be merciful, O Lord our God, in Thy great mercy, towards Israel Thy people, and towards Jerusalem Thy city, and towards Zion the abiding place of Thy glory, and towards Thy temple and Thy habitation, and towards the kingdom of the house of David, Thy righteous anointed one. Blessed art Thou, O Lord God of David, the builder of Jerusalem.

Benediction 16

Accept [us], O Lord our God, and dwell in Zion; and may Thy servants serve Thee in Jerusalem. Blessed art Thou, O Lord, whom in reverent fear we serve [or, worship].

Benediction 18

Bestow Thy peace upon Israel Thy people and upon Thy city and upon Thine inheritance, and bless us, all of us together. Blessed art Thou, O Lord, who makest peace.

That there was a deliberate concern with Jerusalem appears from the text in Mishnah Berakoth 4:1 ff., where the rules concerning the Shemoneh Esreh, indicated above, are set forth, and where Mishnah Berakoth 4:5 states that, according to R. Joshua (C.E. 80–120),

If [a man] was riding on an ass [when the time for the prayer is upon him] he should dismount [that is, to say the Tefillah]. If he cannot dismount he should turn his face [toward Jerusalem]; and if he cannot turn his face, he should direct his heart toward the Holy of Holies.

The centrality of The Land is clear. The same is also emphasized in Num. Rabbah 23:7 on Num. 34:2. The deliberate recalling of the Temple and, thereby of Jerusalem and The Land, in the liturgy also appears from the Mishnah Rosh-ha-Shanah (the Feast of the New Year) 4:1–3. There were other ways by which the same purpose was achieved (see *BT* Baba Bathra 60b).

Other elements in the Jewish liturgy also commemorate the destruction. For three weeks of sorrow, ending on the ninth day of Ab, the fifth month of the Jewish calendar (July 8–August 7 to August 6–September 5), which is entirely given over to fasting, Jews annually recall the devastation of their Land and of Jerusalem. So much has that event become the quintessence of the suffering of Jewry that the 9th of Ab is recognized as a day on which disasters again and again struck the Jewish people. The essential feature of the liturgy for the 9th of Ab (which is the only essential twenty-four-hour fast, apart from the Day of Atonement) was the reading of lamentations and dirges. Later, on the fast of the 9th of Ab, an addition which concentrates on Jerusalem still further was made to the service. The prayer, as used today, begins with the words:

> O Lord God, comfort the mourners of Zion;
> Comfort those who grieve for Jerusalem.

It ends with:

> Praised are You, O Lord, who comforts Zion
> Praised are You, who rebuilds Jerusalem.

The reference to the festival of Ab leads naturally to the significance of the Jewish calendar for our purposes. That sabbaths and festivals and the rites of the faith should be accurately observed according to the Torah was a serious matter with cosmic consequences, because of the relation between the cultus and the cosmos; hence the importance of the Jewish religious calendar. Ideally, the sabbaths and the festivals should everywhere be observed at the same time, because there could only be one proper, ordained time. But this created problems. The communities in Babylonia or Asia Minor, for example, could not know—in the absence of communication systems such as our present ones—whether the month of Ellul had been declared hollow or full in Palestine. The ripening of barley did not come at the same time in Egypt, Babylonia, and Palestine. The Jewish religious calendar did not take into account the differences of time between Palestine and other countries.

This difficulty was recognized as early as 124 B.C.E. (2 Macc. 1:9). The authorities in Jerusalem tried to synchronize the dates of festivals in Jerusalem and the Diaspora. Messengers were sent to the Diaspora to this end (1 Macc. 1:9). Fires were used as signals from one region to another to indicate the incidence of the new moon in Jerusalem. Moreover, with the exception of the Day of Atonement, the sages doubled every festival day in the Diaspora to ensure against a margin of possible error. By such means, Jews in the Diaspora could believe that the prayers offered by them went up to heaven at the same time as those in The Land. That the effort to observe the same calendar outside The Land as in The Land involved religious Jews in incongruous and sometimes bizarre situations is familiar.

The religious calendar of Jews everywhere, then, was governed by that observed in The Land. But so, too, was the physical structure of the Jewish institution which was next in importance to the Temple and which after 70 C.E. came to replace the Temple, the synagogue. To this day, those who pray in a synagogue turn towards Jerusalem. In the synagogues of Galilee, in order to pray towards Jerusalem, one had to turn around. In other parts of Palestine in the first century, synagogues had three entrances on the side facing Jerusalem (although synagogues in the Golan Heights had no uniform arrangement). Later, the recess for the Ark of the Torah was placed in the wall facing Jerusalem, and in the Byzantine period the apses of synagogues were built to face Jerusalem.[13]

So far, we have mostly adduced materials from the Haggadah and the liturgy of rabbinic Judaism. There was also a more specifically halakic approach to the question of The Land. We can here only refer to two items. In the Jerusalem Talmud, in Kilayyim 7:5, there is a law which is quoted as giving to Israel a legal right to The Land. This is translated by Lieberman as: "Though soil cannot be stolen, a man can forfeit his right to this soil by giving up hope of ever regaining it." The argument is that the people of "Israel" "never for a moment gave up hope of regaining the soil of Palestine. Never did they renounce their right to Palestine and never have they ceased claiming it in their prayers and in their teachings. It is on this foundation," adds Lieberman, "that [Jews] now claim that Eretz Israel belongs to [them]."[14] Not unrelated to this law is that of *ḥazâkâh* (prescription) in which the legal right of Israel to The Land was sought. How early such attempts were, and how significant in the discussion of the relationship between Israel and Eretz Israel in the period of our concern, we cannot determine. The history of the halakic understanding of that relationship lies beyond the scope of this study.

Be that as it may, it is in the Haggadah and the liturgy that the full force of the sentiment for The Land is to be felt. It cannot properly be seen except through Jewish eyes, nor felt except through Jewish words, such as those so powerfully uttered by Abraham Heschel in *Israel: An Echo of Eternity,* a book which is more a lyrical outburst than a critical study, and by André Neher in a moving essay, "Israël, terre mystique de l' Absolu," in his *L'Existence Juive.*

THE LAND IN SECONDARY SOURCES

So far, we have referred to the evidence of the classical sources of Judaism. The same theological conviction that there is an unseverable connection among Israel, The Land, and its God continued to be cherished throughout the medieval period and down to the modern.

13. On the synagogue, see F. Hüttenmeister and G. Reeg, *Die antiken Synagogen in Israel.*
14. S. Lieberman, "Response," p. 287.

A rough division has been drawn between two periods. The first stretches up to the last revolt of Jews in the Roman empire in the hope of reestablishing a Jewish state. This followed upon the imposition of harsh anti-Jewish statutes under Justinian (483–565 C.E.), and later the brief reign in Jerusalem of Nehemiah, a messianic figure, from 614 to 617 C.E. It is legitimate to recognize, up to that time, a living, if intermittent, hope for, and sometimes violent activity directed towards, the actual return of The Land politically to Israel. After the Arab conquest of The Land in 638 and the building of the Mosque of Omar, which was to be a center of Islamic faith, on the site of the Temple in 687–91, there was, it has been suggested, a change. From then Jewish devotion to The Land for a long period expressed itself not so much in political activity for the reestablishment of the state of Israel as in voluntary individual pilgrimages and immigrations to The Land.

But the division suggested between the two periods indicated must not be viewed as watertight. On the one hand, in the earlier period the Tannaitic and Amoraic sages were wary of political attempts to reestablish the kingdom of Israel in its own Land. On the other hand, in the Middle Ages, there was much activity aimed at such a reestablishment: the history of this has been largely lost, so that its full strength must remain conjectural. The extent to which apocalyptic messianism persisted, to break out finally in Sabbatianism in the seventeenth century, is only now being recognized, under the influence particularly of the great work of Gershom Scholem. It fed into the Zionist movement of our time. What we can be certain of is that Eretz Israel, as an object of devotion and intense and religious concern, continued to exercise the imagination of Jews after the fall of Jerusalem in 70 C.E. and after the Arab conquest: it remained part of the communal consciousness of Jews.

In this connection, two facts need to be borne in mind. First, the devotion to The Land to which we refer is not simply to be equated with the imaginative notions of other peoples about an ideal land—such as the Elysium of Homer, the Afallon of Celtic mythology, or the Innisfree of Yeats. Rather, it was concentrated on an actual land with a well-known history, a land known to be barren and rugged and to offer no easy life, although it was transfused with an unearthly glory because chosen to be Yahweh's own, and Israel's as an inheritance from him. Secondly, the influence of the familiar or customary division of history at the advent of Christ into two periods, B.C. and A.D., has often tended to create the unconscious assumption among Gentiles that after the first century, Jews *as a people* ceased to have a common history. No less a scholar than Martin Noth saw Israel's history as having come to a ghastly end with the Bar Kokba revolt.

But the Jews continued not simply as a conglomerate of individuals but as a people. The Talmud, the primary document of Judaism in the Middle Ages and afterwards, up to the present time, concerns itself with the way in which the people of Israel should "walk. " The Talmud has a communal national reference in its application of the Torah to the actualities of the Jews' existence. Its contents, formation, and preservation presuppose the continuance of the self-conscious unity of the people of Israel. It is this that explains the character of the Talmud: it adds Gemara to Mishnah, and Rashi (1040–1105 C.E.) to both, to make the tradition of the past relevant to the present. It is realistically involved with the life of the Jewish people over a thousand years of history.

In the devotional life of the Jewish community, the relationship to The Land also remained central. To trace the various expressions of devotion to The Land among Jews across the centuries is beyond our competence. The most noteworthy is, perhaps, that of pilgrimage. The Law demanded that every male Israelite should make a pilgrimage to Jerusalem three times a year, at Passover, the Feast of Weeks, and Tabernacles (Exod. 23:17; Deut. 16:16). During the Second Temple period, even Jews of the Diaspora sought to observe this demand. (See, for example, Mishnah Aboth 5:4; Mishnah Taanit [Days of Fasting] 1:3; Jos., *Wars* 6.9.) After the destruction of the Temple in 70 C.E., pilgrimages especially to the Wailing Wall became occasions for mourning: there were pilgrimages throughout the Middle Ages to other holy places. Individual Jews witness to this, a most famous expression coming in the works of the "God-intoxicated" or "God-kissed" Jehudah Halevi (ca. 1075–1141 C.E.), a Spanish physician and philosopher born in Toledo. At the age of fifty, he left his beloved Spain on a perilous pilgrimage to Zion. Possibly he died before reaching Jerusalem, but not before expressing his love for The Land and Zion in unforgettable terms such as:

My heart is in the east, and I in the uttermost west—

How can I find savour in food? How shall it be sweet to me?

How shall I render my vows and my bonds while yet

Zion lieth beneath the fetter of Edom, and I in Arab chains?

A light thing would it seem to me to leave all the good things of Spain—

Seeing how precious in mine eyes it is to behold the dust of the desolate sanctuary.[15]

15. *Selected Poems of Jehudah Halevi,* ed. H. Brody, p. 2. Professor Diez Macho of Madrid has pointed out that Halevi was not an isolated figure, but part of a tendency—if not a movement—in his day. Because of his profound yearning for Zion, Halevi has been called the father of Zionism or the first of the Zionists. For him, the prophet, not the philosopher, is the highest type of human being, and prophecy can only be experienced in Eretz Israel.

It was not only single, individual pilgrims who sought The Land, but groups of communities, as in the case of Rabbi Meir of Rothenburg, who in 1286 C.E. sought to lead a great number of Jews from the area of the Rhine to Israel. Later, in 1523, a messianic movement which aimed at a return to The Land was led by David Reuveni and attracted the interest of communities in Egypt, Spain, and Germany. The living Jewish concern to establish an earthly kingdom in Jerusalem in part probably prompted the seventeenth article of the Confession of Augsburg of 1530. The justification for such a reaction was made luminously clear in the astounding response to the Sabbatian movement from the Yemen to Western Europe.[16]

These data to which historians point us cannot be ignored. The relative weight which should be given to the purely *religious* interest in The Land which led individuals and groups to journey to Israel out of a desire to experience its mystical or spiritual power, as against a political concern to escape and to right the wrongs of exile, we are not competent to assess. Certainly, many pious Jews had no directly political concern: their sole aim was to recognize that in The Land a relationship to the eternal was possible as nowhere else. A striking illustration of spiritual concentration on The Land is provided by Rabbi Nahman of Bratzlov, who journeyed to Israel in 1772–80. He asserted that what he had known *before* that journey was insignificant. *Before* there had been confusion; *after* "he held the Law whole." But all he had desired was simply direct contact with The Land. This he achieved by merely stepping ashore at Haifa. He desired to return immediately. (Under pressure, he stayed and visited Tiberias, but never even went up to Jerusalem.) Again, the celebrated Maharal of Prague (Rabbi Yehuda Liwa of Loew—Ben Bezalel, 1515–1609) understood the nature and role of nations to be ordained by God, as part of the natural order. Nations were intended to cohere rather than to be scattered. Nevertheless, he did not urge political reestablishment of a state of Israel in The Land: that he left to God. Exile, no less than restoration, was in His will: the latter *would* come in His good time, but only then. The promise of The Land would endure eternally: return was ultimately assured (Lev. 26:44–45).

16. The pertinent part of Article 17 of the Augsburg Confession of 1530 reads as follows:

[The churches, with common consent among us] condemn the Anabaptists who think that to condemned men and devils shall be an end of torments. They condemn others also, who now scatter Jewish opinions, that, before the resurrection of the dead, the godly shall occupy the kingdom of the world, the wicked being everywhere suppressed [the saints alone, the pious, shall have a worldly kingdom, and shall exterminate all the godless]. [P. Schaff, ed., *Creeds of Christendom, III, Evangelical Creeds,* p. 18.]

At no time since the first century has The Land of Israel been wholly without a Jewish presence, however diminished. The figures throughout the centuries have been very variously estimated, but James Parkes rightly insists that Jews in Palestine across the centuries have been forgotten by historians. It is certain that in the nineteenth century, first under the influence of Rabbi Elijah, Ben Solomon Salman of Vilna, known as the Vilna Gaon (1720–97), a number of parties of Jews, soon to be joined by many others, went to Safed in 1808 and 1809. These sought not simply contact with The Land, of which they claimed that "Even in its ruins none can compare with it," but permanent settlement. Regarding themselves as representatives of all Jews, they assumed the right to appeal to other Jews for aid and reinforcement. Some—as in the case of Rabbi Akiba Schlessinger of Pressburg (1837–1922)—were driven to go to The Land, where alone the good life was fully possible, by the realization of the increasing impossibility of living according to the Torah in Western societies which were becoming more and more secular. For such, The Land became an escape and a refuge from modernism and secularism, a bulwark for the preservation of the religious tradition. After these early settlements, there were other efforts by religious Jews to reenter The Land, whose history cannot be traced here. Suffice it to note that the Zionist movement, despite its strongly "nationalistic," socialistic, and political character, is not to be divorced from this devotion to The Land.[17] We shall deal with this later.

17. This remains true. But the concentration on The Land among religious Jews who revered and even went to Eretz Israel has also to be distinguished from the purely historical, geographical, and archaeological interest of many Zionists (see, especially, D. Vital, *The Origins of Zionism*, pp. 6 ff.). Here we are dealing with Judaism and The Land, not with Jews and The Land. But the impression must not be given that these two themes can—or should—be effectively separated. R. J. Werblowsky illustrates the problem. He points out that in the nineteenth century assimilationist Jews were fascinated and blinded by the Enlightenment. In their enthusiasm for assimilation, they shed both their religious and national identities. But they soon discovered the falsity of their hopes of being fully integrated and "normalized" in Western society. In disillusioned reaction to the society that had erstwhile been so seductively attractive to them, they turned again to the tradition they had shed. But for "enlightened" and "assimilationist" Jews to rediscover and to return all at once to both their religious and national identities was hardly possible: the rediscovery of *one* element of their tradition was traumatic; to have discovered *both* at the same time would have been too overwhelming. So it was that the "enlightened" Jews who saw the futility of assimilation turned, under the influence of the intellectual climate of the nineteenth century, first to "nationalism," socialism, and romanticism: they rediscovered themselves as be-

longing to the people of Israel, to a "national" tradition, not necessarily to the religion of Israel, which they still found it easy to regard as a fossilized survival. Even Werblowsky seems able to think of liturgical practice somewhat in these terms, writing of the belief in the relationship between Israel and The Land: "Très souvent, il était à la fois vivant et 'gélé,' comme dans une chambre froide, par les prières chaque jour répétées, les formules liturgiques et le rappel des promesses prophetiques" ("Israël et Eretz Israël," p. 377).

All this helps to explain the insensitivity of some of the leaders both before and in the Zionist movement to the strictly religious dimension of the relation to The Land. Of the Zionist leaders, Werblowsky writes: "Beaucoup d'entre eux ne pouvaient faire qu'une seule découverte a la fois" (ibid., p. 388). For secular Jews in the nineteenth century, religious devotion to The Land symbolized all that was particularistic, "scandalous," and nonassimilable in Judaism, even when they themselves ultimately became Zionists.

2
An Undeniable Historical Diversity

Whoever goes up from Babylon to the Land of
Israel transgresses a positive commandment, for it
is said in Scriptures, *They shall be carried to
Babylon, and there they shall be, until the day that I
remember them, saith the Lord.* Ketuboth 110b–111a
(Babylonian Talmud)

We have sought in the preceding pages to do justice to the theological
role of territory in Judaism. Jewish theology, as revealed in its major
witnesses, points to The Land as of the essence of Judaism. In strictly
theological terms, the Jewish faith might be defined as "a fortunate
blend of a people, a land and their God." But in any blend, an ingredient
may be submerged, and in this formula, it has been claimed, the
essential and distinctive significance of The Land may be lost sight of.
As the personal identity of each member is carefully preserved in
discussions of the Trinity, and not simply "blended," so, too, in our
understanding of Judaism, the distinct or separable significance of The
Land must be fully recognized. Judaism held to an election of a people
and of its election to a particular land: Werblowsky rightly speaks of
"une vocation, spirituelle á la géographie."[1] But like Christian, Jewish
theology has had to find ways of coming to terms with history.

1. R. J. Werblowsky, "Israël et Eretz Israël." In "Réflexions sur la pensée
nationale juive moderne," Nathan Rotenstreich emphasizes the newness of
Zionism or modern Jewish nationalism. It is, for him, discontinuous with
traditional Jewish religious thought: "It attempts to create a new Jewish unity
with living institutions rooted in the present rather than surviving to the
present" (p. 5). He therefore connects Zionism with the collapse of the foundations of traditional Jewish life, which succumbed to the attack on the traditional authorities, grounded in a suprahistorical authority, of the Enlightenment (pp. 3–4). One can hardly agree that Zionism is so utterly newborn.
As will be clear from the presentation, Zionism is in this book viewed as
"twice-born," in the sense that it was preceded by a long tradition of concentration on The Land. (On its religious dimension, see Rolf Rendtorff, "Die
religiösen und geistigen Wurzeln des Zionismus.") This does not mean that

37

JEWISH PLURALISM

In the first place, the term "Judaism" itself cannot be understood as representing a monolithic faith in which there has been a simplistic uniformity of doctrine—whether demanded, imposed, or recognized—about The Land, as about other elements of belief. Certainly this was so at all periods and in all sections of the Jewish community before 70 C.E. To substantiate this point, we shall appeal to: (a) the role of the nomadic ideal of the desert in the Tanak; (b) the nature of the revolts in the Maccabean period and in the first century C.E.; (c) the place of Abraham in the Tanak; (d) Israel as a covenanted community; (e) the universal emphasis of many postexilic writers; (f) individualism; and (g) The Land as a symbol of the transcendental.

(a) As we have already seen, the rightness of Israel's conquest of Canaan did not go unquestioned. But the cruelty of the conquest apart, the antipathy which is endemic and universal between those who follow a nomadic way of life and those who "indulge" in the sedentary, agricultural way is evident in the Tanak. In Gen. 4:1–17, for example, Cain, the tiller of the soil, who first built a city, is at a disadvantage against Abel, who was simply a keeper of sheep, not a full nomad. The offering of the firstlings of the flock is held to be more acceptable than that of the fruits of the soil. While it is doubtful whether the patriarchs were strictly nomadic, they did represent the classic simplicity of the ideal human life.

The role of the wilderness in the history of Israel has to be carefully noted. There are verses (Hos. 9:10; Ezek. 16:5; Jer. 31:2; and, less clearly, Deut. 32:10) where the wilderness period, as such, seems to be regarded as the decisive phase of that history—that is, the period of Israel's election. But usually the "wilderness" is inextricably bound up with the Exodus, the events at Sinai, and the wanderings. In the wilderness, Israel had experienced danger in obeying God's word and help in that danger (Exod. 13:17–14:31; 19:4, etc.): there, according to *J* and *E*, the revelation of God's name had been received (Exod. 3:13 [*E*]; Exod. 3:1 [*E*]; Exod. 33, 34 [*J*]), on the knowledge of which depended the possibility and validity of Israelite worship. There also the covenant had been established and the Law given, the foundations, along with the revelation of the name, of Israelite religion and Judaism. Through the covenant in the wilderness, with which the Law was inextricably bound up, Israel became the people of Yahweh (see Deut. 27:9 f.).[2] The desert is, therefore, the place of revelation and of the

---

the precise forerunners of Zionism can be easily categorized (see Jacob Katz, "The Forerunners of Zionism," pp. 10–21). For a balanced and thorough treatment, see Ben Halpern, *The Idea of the Jewish State,* pp. 3–19, 55–94, and especially 95–130.

2. See also W. D. Davies, "Reflections on the Spirit in the Mekilta."

constitution of "Israel" as a people: there she was "elected" (Exod. 4:22 f.).

It is not surprising, therefore, that prophets looked back to the period in the wilderness for inspiration, as did Elijah (1 Kings 19:4–8). The time in the wilderness was regarded with nostalgia. Redemption was to be preceded by a return to the wilderness, where the old status of love and trust, broken by the "harlotry" of life in The Land, would be restored. (Hos. 2:14–15; cf Heb. 2:16–17). The return to the wilderness is a return to the grace of God. Such a return is not envisaged by Jeremiah, but he also regards the time of the wilderness as one of mutual love between Israel and Yahweh (Jer. 2:1 f.). The time of the wilderness was one in which Israel had found grace (Jer. 31:2; cf. Exod. 33:12 f., 16 f.). There is also an appeal to that time as the norm against which to judge the corruption of the sedentary life, a corruption that was bound up with cultus that had evolved in The Land (Amos 5:25 and Jer. 7:21–23). In Isa. 63:10-14, the time in the wilderness had been marked by the presence of the Spirit. But, more important still, the response to the challenge of Canaanite religion to Yahwism in some circles took the form of a complete rejection of settled agricultural life as the will of Yahweh for his people. This was the position of the Rechabites, who appear as a vital group as late as the sixth century B.C.E. They would not grow cereals, cultivate the vine, or live in houses. True, they did live in Judah, but the Hebrew text at Jer. 35:7 makes it clear that they regarded themselves merely as sojourners who had no original rights in The Land. That they lived in tents, not in houses, marks them as deliberately nomadic: the tent is the nomadic abode, a symbol of nomadic opposition to sedentary culture, which was deemed to be unmanly and degrading (compare the attitude revealed in the story of the blessing of Jacob and Esau in Gen. 27:11: Esau is a hairy man and Jacob a smooth man). The Rechabites' total abstinence from wine was not so much a moral protest against drunken Canaanite orgies connected with fertility rites (although such a protest is not to be excluded) as an affirmation of the nomadic life, in which wine was not drunk. There are counterparts to the Rechabites among the Nabataeans.

By the time of Jeremiah, although, in the prophet's view, admirably active, the Rechabites had dwindled to a few: the prophet could invite them all to meet him in a chamber in the Temple (Jer. 35:2). There is meagre evidence that they did survive the Exile, but it is more likely that they increasingly succumbed to the ways of the majority in Israel. There are no traces of them in the New Testament itself.

It is not impossible, however, that the Rechabites stood in some connection with the Nazirites, about whom we do read in the New Testament. The origins and purposes of the Nazirites are obscure. But they have been understood as representatives of the opposition to the

Canaanization of the cult of Yahweh. The Nazirite avoidance of wine was possibly bound up with a suspicion of the land of the vine, the symbol of the agricultural as against nomadic life (Amos 2:11–12; Num. 6). However, the requirement of the presentation of a cereal offering in Num. 6:17 on the completion of the Nazirites' time of separation should warn us against pressing this point. And, in any case, the significance of the Rechabites and Nazirites should not be overemphasized. They were few in number, and at no time did they represent the mind of Israel. Jeremiah's commendation of the Rechabites (35:18–19) referred not to their way of life as such, but to their fidelity to that to which they were committed: he cherished a like fidelity for Israelites generally to the commandments to which *they* were committed.

The attempt to claim, on the basis of the material we have presented above, and of other factors which we cannot consider here, that Israel had a nomadic ideal of life must be rejected. To begin with, the passage from Amos which has been taken to suggest this has been otherwise explained. Thus, Amos 5:25 does not necessarily mean that Amos questioned the Mosaic origin of the sacrificial system, and probably does not involve any idealization of the period in the wilderness.

This alternative interpretation of Amos 5:25 affords a convenient point of transition to other passages which present the time of the wilderness and the wilderness itself in a cold light, without any idealization. We find a clear-eyed recognition of the wilderness period as marked by rebellion. It was a time of "murmuring." The long and dangerous journey through the wilderness had not been the free choice of Israel, but the outcome of a command by Yahweh (Exod. 3, 4): it had not been voluntary, simply a matter of obedience. In the course of it, there were trials to Israel's faith—Pharaoh and his army (Exod. 14:10 f.), lack of water (Exod. 15:24; 17:2), of bread (Exod. 16:2 f.), and the giants barring entrance to The Land (Num. 14:2 f.). These all led to disobedience to Moses, the leader; to Aaron, his mouthpiece; and to Yahweh himself (Exod. 15:24; 16:2; 17:2; Num. 14:2): Israel tired of the wilderness life (Num. 21:5). The "murmuring" reached its culmination in the worship of the golden calf (Exod. 32), the significance of which is manifold. The bull or calf is a prominent image of Canaanite fertility worship: the seduction of the latter, so we are to understand, had already exerted itself in the wilderness. By the worship of the golden calf, Israel revealed her preference for many gods (Exod. 32:4) and practically revoked her covenant with Yahweh. The election of Israel was all but annulled (Exod. 32:10) and was preserved only by the renewal of the covenant in Exod. 34. The point is that the wilderness was as much a scene of sin as of election.

In Deuteronomy, the time of the wanderings is used for purposes of exhortation, as in Deut. 8:2–5. Here there is no idealization of the time in the wilderness. Rather, it was then that Yahweh had tested, disciplined, and humbled Israel, leading her to the knowledge that she lived solely by his word and to the humility springing from this. There is no glorification of the simple nomadic life and the wilderness in themselves. Rather, a *time* is remembered which, as Deut. 8:7 ff. makes clear, prepared Israel for life in The Land.

Emphasis on the time in the wilderness as one of terrible punishment and discipline and warning appears in the Psalms. That time is seldom referred to—as surely might be expected in view of Yahweh's providential succour, guidance, and election—in psalms of praise and thanksgiving. Where it is referred to in the latter, the generation of the wilderness is the supreme example of sinfulness. Psalms 78, 95, and 106 are particularly instructive.

The connection between the period of the wilderness and the Exile is also made in Ezek. 20:23. The prophet goes so far as to claim that at that time, in order that Israel might know that he was the Lord, Yahweh had given her "statutes that were not good and ordinances by which they could not have life" (20:25): He had deliberately defiled and horrified his people (20:26). And in Ezekiel there is also an echo of Deuteronomy's view of the time of the wilderness as a painful preparation for life in The Land. For him, in the future, before the redemption of Israel, the wilderness is to be the place of judgment, as it had been in the past (see Ezek. 20:33 ff.). We have previously noted in Hosea the notion of a return to the wilderness as a condition of renewal before entry into The Land. There a return to the time when Israel enjoyed filial status with Yahweh is signified: it provided a "door of hope." In Ezekiel, as we have seen, the wilderness is a place of judgment: the infidelity of the people in the period of the wanderings is reiterated unsparingly. But in Ezekiel the return to the wilderness is also a prelude to life in The Land and is, in this sense, a sign of hope. The way to The Land is through the wilderness. And this motif persisted.

In Deutero-Isaiah, the return of the dispersed to The Land is to be through a wilderness, the difficulties of which have been smoothed (Isa. 40:3 f.; 35:1 f., 6 ff.; 41:18 f.; 49:9 ff.): a way will appear through the wilderness (40:3; 43:19; 49:11). There is to be a new exodus, incomparably greater, even though the counterpart of the first. This notion later emerges in 1 Enoch 28:1, 29:1; and The Martyrdom of Isaiah 2:8–12. That it was understood not merely oratorically or metaphorically is clear from three sources.

First, the Dead Sea Scrolls. The community of the new covenant, by the location of its headquarters at Qumran in the desert, a location dictated by the text of Isa. 40:3; by its organization—into tribes, thousands, hundreds, fifties, and tens, which parallel the subdivision of Israel under Moses; and by the regulation of its life in camps (compare 1QM 7:3–7 with Num. 5:1–4) showed its concern to "return" in repentance to the wilderness in preparation for the redemption that would lead it to the purified Land. Secondly, in Josephus certain groups who *may* have had messianic pretensions, since they promised to repeat the "signs" or miracles of the first exodus, went into the desert to prepare for a coming redemption. So, too, a prophet from Egypt; Theudas; and a weaver, Jonathan, all had recourse to the desert to prepare for their assault on Jerusalem. And, in the last desperate hours of the war against Rome, the Jews asked for permission to leave the Temple for the desert with their wives and children, probably because they expected the final deliverance to be inaugurated there. In the light of the Dead Sea Scrolls, it seems clear that a retreat to the desert could easily be understood as a preparation for the messianic age. Finally, this is indicated in the New Testament itself by John the Baptist's preparatory ministry in the wilderness, and explicitly in Matt. 24:26.

It is of the utmost importance that the new covenanters at Qumran, John the Baptist, and the figures mentioned by Josephus, did not go into the wilderness because they valued it as such, but because they were thereby fulfilling what had become a kind of eschatological "dogma" that a time in the wilderness would precede the end. Their "return" to the wilderness was *not* governed by a rejection of "cultured" life in The Land in favor of a more simple nomadic existence in the desert, or by a geographic preference for the wilderness over The Land, but by an eschatological schema; not by considerations of space, but of time; not by the cult of the primitive, but by the observation of the times.

There is thus no justification for positing a nomadic ideal in the Tanak. Efforts to do so on the grounds of an idealization of the desert cannot be substantiated. The other grounds for doing so do not carry conviction, for reasons which cannot be set forth here. Our rejection of a nomadic ideal in the Tanak can be carried over into Judaism. True, the wilderness reappears in the eschatology of Judaism, in terms, among other things, of a new exodus which would witness a new Moses and the return of the manna, etc. But in that eschatology also, the wilderness is not the goal but a stage on the way to The Land, the glorification of which we have already illustrated from rabbinic sources.

(b) Most of the exiles in Babylon did not choose to return to The Land when Cyrus (538 B.C.E.) made this possible. Moreover, while the leaders of the returned community were from Babylon, clearly The Land as such had little appeal for them. It was not the returned exiles whom Haggai and Zechariah called upon to rebuild the Temple, but native Israelites. And it should be emphasized that, after the return from the Exile, Jews in Palestine itself were a "dispersion." During the period after Nehemiah (432 B.C.E.) and before Alexander's conquest in 332 B.C.E., the district of Judaea consisted simply of Jerusalem and a small area, about thirty-five miles long and twenty-five to thirty miles broad, surrounding it. Both within this tiny area and outside it, Jews came to be surrounded by Hellenistic influences. The temptation to assimilate was real and ubiquitous. What was the attitude to The Land in this period among Palestinian Jews thus exposed? Had it been of vital significance, it is surprising that so little of a direct appeal to The Land was made in the Maccabean revolt, particularly since The Land itself had been so reduced. No preeminence was given to Abraham and the promise. It was the commandments of the Law, not the occupation of The Land, that concerned the dying Mattathias, who had initiated the revolt. It was so throughout his life. His rallying cry was simple: "Whosoever is zealous for the Law and maintaineth the covenant, let him come forth after me." And it was in this spirit that the volunteers, "a company of Ḥasidim," who have been regarded as the fathers of the Pharisees, offered themselves. The absence of an appeal to The Land is striking because of the vividness of the awareness of the unity of the People of Israel in 1 Macc. It agrees with this that, when appeal is made to history, it is not to the promise to Abraham, but to the Exodus, the event that gave birth to the people. Later on, territorial considerations did enter into the Maccabean movement, but these were motivated more by political ambition than by religious concern with the promise.

But the matter is even more puzzling, because there was a direct threat to confiscated Jewish lands under the Seleucids. The rural Jews, especially, would have been sensitive to the threat to their Land, and not only they, but all Jews in Judaea. This makes it all the more difficult to understand the absence of an appeal to The Land as such in our sources.

We note, in the second place, that a similar phenomenon—absence of a direct appeal to The Land—confronts us when we turn to the revolt against the Romans, culminating in the fall of Jerusalem in C.E. 70. There is a baffling lack of any direct appeal to the promise of The Land and to The Land itself. There are a few passages where appeal is made to the "laws of the country" or "of The Land," but it is religious loyalty and social, economic, and political pressures which spurred the rebels of the first century C.E., like those of the second century B.C.E., not an explicitly territorial concern. Is this to be interpreted as an indication that The Land as such was not a primary focus of concern? The argument from silence is precarious, however, for several reasons.

During both the Maccabean and Roman revolts, the people of Israel were dwelling in The Land, so that preoccupation with any conquest or occupation of it was not their immediate concern. Rather, it was the terms on which they were to live in The Land. What were these to be? Two desiderata had to be met to satisfy those in Israel who were "zealous."

First, it will be clear from what we have said before that Israel, as the covenant people, could only occupy The Land securely if the commandments were observed. The occupation of The Land presupposed loyalty to the Torah, which was a form of loyalty to The Land. Torah and Land are, if not inextricable, closely related. The threat to the Torah was in a tangible, though indirect, sense a threat to The Land. And when Israel actually dwelt in The Land, as in the Maccabean and Roman periods, the explicit concentration was naturally on the former, the Torah.

Secondly, The Land was involved in any threat to the Temple. Life in The Land was regarded as integrally related to the cultus at Jerusalem. Changes in that cultus were particularly resented by the farmers in the rural areas, for whom the productivity of the soil was compromised by changes in Temple worship. It is no accident that the leadership in the Maccabean revolt was from the rural priesthood. They believed that on the observance of the Law, which included the observance of the festivals and Temple ritual, depended the well-being of The Land. It follows that, in periods when Israel actually dwelt in The Land, it was at the point of observance of the Torah and reverence for the Temple that concern for The Land expressed itself, albeit indirectly. This explains the centrality of Torah and Temple in the Maccabean and Zealot revolts, which in the minds of the rebels assumes the essentiality of The Land.

But what most threatened the loyalty due to Torah and Temple, through which the covenant people could enjoy life in the promised Land, was an alien occupying power. So long as the Seleucids or the Romans—or, indeed, any other power—ruled The Land, which belonged to Yahweh, so long would observance of the Torah and reverance for the Temple be precarious. It is in the light of this fact that the description of "the fourth philosophy," the Zealots, is to be understood in Josephus (see *Antiquities* 18. 1. 6).

History had taught the Jews in the Maccabean period, as in the Roman, that a foreign ruler could disrupt the conditions under which alone the covenant people could live in the promised Land. Even Josephus, despite his hatred of the Jewish nationalists, had to admit that they were very like the Pharisees. That is, although Josephus presented them in terms of "madness," they revered the Law and the Temple. Their peculiar emphasis (which doubtless the Pharisees shared *in principle,* although *in practice* they urged patience and long-suffering) that God alone was to be their ruler and Lord, sprang from the bitter history of Israel and clear-eyed recognition that they could only dwell securely in the promised Land when it was not occupied territory.

The story of the conquest and occupation of The Land under Joshua was vivid in the Maccabean mind and in that of the nationalists of the first century. The would-be return to the wilderness in both revolts points to this. Touched upon only briefly in 1 Macc. 2:29–30, the theme is noted in far more striking circumstances in Josephus's account of the fall of the Temple. After suicidal resistance, and finally the rejection of Titus's offer to enter into negotiations, the rebels wanted only "permission to pass through his line of circumvallation with their wives and children, undertaking to return to the desert and to leave the city to him." What is the explanation of this strange request? In all probability, the rebels were governed by the eschatological belief that before the final redemption, even after the Temple itself had been forsaken by the Lord, the Lord himself would not forsake his people, but continue his presence with them in the wilderness to lead them again into the promised Land. Like the Maccabees who withdrew to the wilderness, the Zealots also in their final request showed how the story of the conquest of The Land informed their thinking and activity.

Moreover, in the Maccabean period, at two points in Daniel, the interest in The Land may be claimed to break through indirectly. First, in Dan. 7:25–26, as part of the description of the Fourth Beast, who is to be identified with Antiochus Epiphanes, the saints of the Most High are to endure the domination of the Fourth Beast "for a time, two times, and half a time." The process of thought by which this notion of three and a half years, or a very brief period, arose has eluded commentators. But a suggestion by Bickerman is convincing. In three and a half years, the enemy of the saints of the Most High would be "consumed and destroyed to the end." On this Bickerman comments: "Three years and a half is a half of the Sabbatical period. According to the Law, the land of Israel had to have a solemn rest every seven years and lie fallow. In Leviticus (26:34–43) the desolation of the land under foreign domination appears as reparation for the lack of the sabbatic rest under national rule. The Jews will have to suffer a half of a sabbatic septennium in payment for their disobedience of God's law."[3] If this suggestion be followed, the awareness of The Land, its reactions and demands, was alive in the Maccabean period. This is also implied in another passage in Dan. 11:14—12:4. Here that Land is "the fairest of all lands" (NEB, Dan. 11:16; compare 8:9). There is no doubt that at the end The Land, "the fairest of all lands," remains central, despite the cosmic horizons of Daniel. Antiochus Epiphanes was to meet his doom, apparently, "between the sea and the holy hill"—that is, between Jerusalem and the sea (11:45), which Ezekiel (38:14–16; 39:2–4) had foretold as the scene of the climax of all things. And it was in The Land that the resurrection would take place (Dan. 12:1–3).

How, then, shall we assess the role of loyalty to The Land in the Maccabean and Zealot revolts? Despite the silence of the sources, it

3. E. Bickerman, *Four Strange Books of the Bible,* p. 101.

cannot be doubted that that loyalty was a primary axiom for the rebels—our deepest axioms or assumptions are often most unexpressed. But it was unexpressed, too, because in both revolts it took a religious form, so that in the sources it is loyalty to the Torah and the Temple that is stressed.

The essence of the Maccabean revolt is clear. It was not a popular revolt of the whole people, the majority of whom seemed to have been ready to assimilate: The Land cannot have been primary for them. The revolt was the work of a small minority of enthusiasts for the Law and, implicitly, for The Land, who were as incensed by the apostates among their own people as they were with Antiochus. It seems that the majority of the tiny Jewish political unit around the city of Jerusalem, as well as the Jews in the rest of Palestine, who were surrounded by a sea of Hellenistic influences, cannot have been moved by loyalty to The Land. And as for the Ḥasidim who joined the Maccabean revolt, it is a familiar, but for our purposes a highly significant, fact that as soon as the religious aims of the revolt had been achieved, that is freedom to observe the Law, they withdrew from further participation. They had no territorial ambitions.

So also in the revolt against Rome in the first century. Josephus doubtless isolates the extremist leaders of the revolt against Rome too much in their ideology and activity. But it cannot be doubted that they constituted a minority, as did the Maccabean rebels. First-century Judaism is the creed of Hillel and Rabbi Johanan ben Zakkai—lovers of peace—no less than of the Zealots.

But the situation in Israel between the Exile and the first century was even more complicated than we have indicated. Let us return to the sectarians at Qumran, who demonstrate a concentration on The Land and the need for its purification. As we have seen, the Maccabees and the Zealots hardly ever refer to The Land directly, whereas the sectarians regarded it as part of their very purpose to "atone for The Land." This difference probably has deep roots. Those who returned from Babylon, when Cyrus made this possible, were not a monolithic group. For many among them, the return to The Land and the rebuilding of the Temple signified Yahweh's favor. His judgments against Israel had now run their course. The restored community, devoted to the Law and the Temple, could count on his blessing. Life in The Land was the seal of divine favor. To the early days of the return belong those psalms which emphasize Jerusalem as the dwelling place of Yahweh, the centre of the theocracy of Israel.

Among those who thought in this way were the core of the Maccabean and later first-century rebels. They do not refer to The Land: they silently assume its importance and their right to it. They are not troubled by any sense that the people of Israel themselves had been

responsible for defiling it. The Land needed no purification or atonement, only defence, when the Torah and its Temple were threatened
from outside.

But there were others in postexilic Israel who differed. For these,
although Israel had been given the opportunity to resettle in The Land,
divine displeasure had not been exhausted. They still anticipated a
dread future of further judgment upon Israel before the end should
come. (For the way in which vengeance against sinful Israelites is often
associated with the concept of The Land, see Jub. 15:28; 20:4; 21:22;
36:9; 50:5; and 2 Bar. 66:2, 5.) In postexilic Israel, those for whom
Israel was a theocracy, which had "arrived," coexisted with those for
whom it was still under the shadow of eschatology.

It is in the light of this discussion that the difference between the
Maccabean and later nationalist movements and the sectarians at Qumran is to be understood. Let us recall the sectarians' understanding of
themselves and of those around them. They were governed by their
memory of the Exile, in which they found the model or parallel to
their own experience. In that first exile in a foreign land, Yahweh had
spared a remnant which had confessed its faults and returned to The
Land under Ezra and Nehemiah. But the community which had since
developed in The Land had not remained true to the demands of the
covenant revealed by them: it had forsaken the revelation given to the
remnant in and from Babylon. The Land had become polluted or
defiled. Loyal to the commandments of the covenant of the remnant
from the Exile, the sectarians, who continued that remnant, viewed
the life of their countrymen, the sanctuary, and the priesthood at
Jerusalem, with horror. Separation from Judah and Jerusalem became
imperative. They must go into "exile." Exile was preferable to life in
the defiled Land. Ephraim, in exile, became a revered prototype.
The sectarians chose to leave Judah to go to "the land of Damascus"—
into exile.

It is best to interpret "the land of Damascus" as referring to Qumran,
not to Babylon. But Qumran was not simply a geographic centre. In
fulfillment of Zech. 11:1 and Amos 7:15 "the land of Damascus" was
a symbol of the land of deportation, "the land of the north." There
Yahweh now had his sanctuary, not at Judah or Jerusalem: there he
now gave his revelation and, there, in the end of days, a star, a leader,
was to appear to lead the remnant back to Jerusalem purified through
punishment. Through "the diaspora," "the exile" of the sectarians,
salvation would come for The Land. The sect called itself "the exile,"
and saw Judah and Jerusalem, The Land, as profaned and in dire need
of atonement. And this atonement was to come not from Jerusalem
but from outside it. The true community of God was an exile through
which alone The Land was to achieve atonement.

It is not impossible that those Jews who were still geographically
exiles in the time of the sectarians influenced them. Not all had returned

to The Land from Babylon. Were those who remained there influenced by the words of Jeremiah and Ezekiel as to the positive aspects of life in the Exile? Was it they who retained the traditions and thought of Baruch and Ezra? Some of them were of Davidic descent, some were priests of ancient lineage. They continued from afar to infuse new blood into Palestinian Judaism right down to the first century and much later. What was their attitude to the developments in Judah and Jerusalem after the return? We know that they regarded the Second Temple as tainted, and the question becomes inevitable whether there were continuing connections between the sectarians at Qumran, who regarded themselves as "exiles," and those others exiled in Babylon and elsewhere in the Diaspora. (In the "War of the Sons of Light and the Sons of Darkness," there is a clear indication of the sectarians' very wide range of concern [IQM 1:1–7; 2:1 ff], the exiles in Babylon being included in the final war.) Was it to such connections that the sectarians owed the Iranian elements which their documents reveal? And was it to Babylon that those regulations in CDC which seem to envisage a foreign country apply? Were there Essenes in Babylon also, and did they share in a theology which perceived life outside The Land as making possible the emergence of a remnant to atone for The Land?

One thing may be regarded as certain. The uncritical, and assumed or implicit devotion to The Land which emerged in the Maccabean and Zealot mind was not unchallenged. True, for the sectarians also, especially as their mind is revealed in the Temple scroll, life in a purified Land and a purified city and Temple was the final goal, but they clearly saw that, in their present state, Land and city and Temple were defiled.

(c) The comparative paucity of references to Abraham and The Land in the Maccabaean and Roman revolts incites a prior question. Does the Tanak itself support the ascription of a controlling significance to the promise to Abraham? One serious difficulty is this: in the Tanak, outside the Pentateuch, the promise to Abraham as such is seldom referred to. Is it likely, therefore, to have played a significant, reassuring part in the faith of Israel?

The same paucity marks the Apocrypha and Pseudepigrapha.[4] We previously noted that the sources dealing with the Maccabees seldom refer to Abraham, and then not in connection with the promise of The Land. The same is true of the Apocrypha and Pseudepigrapha in general. Surprisingly, the same must be asserted even of the rabbinic sources. In the Mishnah there are hardly twelve references to Abraham, and among the early Midrashim, apart from Genesis Rabbah, where discussion of Abraham is inevitable, the patriarch is rarely discussed. It agrees with this that the covenant itself—because of the emphasis

4. The Apocalypse of Abraham (80–100 C.E.) and the Testament of Abraham (early first century C.E.) do not concentrate on the promise of The Land.

upon it in Christianity?—was seldom directly treated in early rabbinic sources. The covenant with Abraham was at the foundation—assumed and unexpressed—of the people of Israel. Like the foundation of a building, it was often hidden from view and not actively discussed. It is erroneous to claim that Abraham and the covenant were a preoccupation of the Judaism revealed in the classical sources.

(d) The people of Israel were essentially a covenanted community, but in the strictly religious sense. Our treatment of the relationship of the Law and The Land may have created the impression that Israel in the Tanak is to be understood as a community bound to a land and governed by a law, much as a modern national state might be so tied and governed. But one thing has emerged clearly from studies on law in the Hebrew Scriptures. The laws were not related primarily to the political organization of a state, but rather to a community of people in which the common allegiance to Yahweh was the constitutive element. The context or setting in life in which Israel had received the Law was the covenant, a sacral act, and the communication of the Law was connected with the celebration of the covenant which bound Israel to its God. To maintain the validity of this covenant—of which the proclamation of the Law was an essential part—Israel celebrated or commemorated it in regular feasts. In this religious act lay the foundation of Israel. "The Israelite nation, then, had its true existence apart from and prior to the erection of their political, social and economic order in Canaan."[5] The community is to be understood as a corollary of the covenant.

It is this that explains why it is difficult, if not impossible, to discover any Israelite idea of the state. The Israelites did not imitate the Canaanite principalities which they ousted. These principalities were made up of fortified cities surrounded by small territories: they were under a king, often of foreign birth, who led an army drawn from his own people and from mercenaries. But Gideon refused to be a king (Judg. 8:22 f.) (the kingdom of Abimelech, based on non-Israelite elements, was short-lived [Judg. 8:31; 9:1 f.]). In Canaan, Israel at first formed a federation of twelve tribes: these owed a common loyalty to Yahweh and shared a common law. But, to go by the Book of Judges, they had no organized government. The judges themselves were charismatic figures called by Yahweh for specific missions: they were not rulers of all Israel. In time, the Israelite federation became a national monarchical state under Saul. But such a state was not unopposed. The attitude toward the monarchy was divided. To some it was initiated by God: to others it was due to a reprehensible desire on Israel's part to be like other nations. Nevertheless, under David and Solomon, unity was achieved between Israel and Judah: the two areas were

5. R. B. Y. Scott, *The Relevance of the Prophets*, p. 189.

subsumed under one sovereign. But this state of affairs lasted only for two generations. On Solomon's death, Israel and Judah separated, and two kingdoms emerged. Sometimes they were allies: sometimes enemies. What is significant is that they acted independently, and that other nations treated them as two distinct powers. Political unity, a single statehood, eluded the people. At the same time, throughout the separation of the monarchy, the *religious* idea of the unity of the people, of the federation of the Twelve Tribes, remained. And the prophets, as we have seen, looked forward to their reunion. "Israel" and the political organization or organizations of its people are to be distinguished.

After 587 B.C.E., when Jerusalem fell, the idea of a state declined. The Jews became again mainly, if not purely, a religious community: in time priests came to rule them under God. Israel is the people of Yahweh alone. In Ezra and Nehemiah, the primary, if not the only, concern is that the people should obey the Law. If we follow the traditional view of the origin of the Hasidim, Pharisees, and Essenes, it was loyalty to the Law alone that governed them, and initially it was this that moved the Maccabees also. After the Exile, religious Jews became a people of the Torah. The history of Pharisaism is necessarily concentrated much more on the Torah than on the political control of The Land.

The messianic ideas of Judaism, which have persisted from biblical to modern times, for example in Sabbatianism, have retained a political dimension, and one aspect, the national state, has remained central to them. But those ideas have often been spiritualized and transcendentalized and made symbolic. Without further elaboration, we shall assume here that the doctrine of the unseverability of The Land from Yahweh and his people is not to be too easily equated with the eternal connection of any state with the people and with Yahweh.

And yet, despite the data to which we have referred above and Scholem's apparent distinction between the political and the religious (see below), caution is necessary. There is the question which forcibly came to the surface among European peoples, not to be reinterred, in 1848: Can a people fully be itself without political self-expression or the right to self-determination (two concepts not usually distinguished), that is, without being allowed to be a nation? Is the distinction between a people living in The Land of Israel and the nation of Israel ultimately a false one? Does not its full life in The Land demand that the people of Israel control its own land? And there is the problem posed by the exact interpretation of the Jewish evidence. Usually the best guide to the inner life and meaning of a religious community is its liturgy. If so, in the most familiar and central prayer of Judaism, the Shemoneh Esreh, the distinction between life in The Land and "national" control of The Land is not recognized. The 14th Benediction, which is usually dated from the Maccabean period, reads: "Be merciful, O Lord our God, in Thy great mercy, towards Israel Thy people, and towards Jerusalem Thy city, and towards Zion the abiding place of Thy glory, and towards Thy temple and Thy habitation, and towards the kingdom of the house of David, Thy righteous anointed one. Blessed art Thou, O Lord God of David, the builder of Jerusalem." The reference to the kingdom of the house of David is unambiguous. For religious Jews, we must conclude, The Land is ultimately inseparable from the state of Israel, however much the actualities of history have demanded their distinction.

In this work, we are concerned not with the role of a Jewish state, but with that of The Land as such—that is, the promised Land. But we must issue the *caveat* that the distinction, although often necessarily recognized in Jewish life and thought, and therefore unavoidable in this discussion, is in the final analysis alien to the Jewish faith. To religious Jews, the separation of The Land and the state is the abortive product of Jewish history, not of Jewish religious consciousness and intent. And yet, despite the vicissitudes of Jewish history, the sacred documents on which religious Jews have based themselves—the Tanak, the Mishnah, the Midrashim, and the Talmud, the liturgies they have constantly celebrated, and the observances which they have kept across the centuries, all point to "The Land" itself, not, primarily at least, to any state, as an essential aspect of Judaism. We shall see that the leaders of Judaism were compelled by the experiences of their history to emphasize the religious, not the political, aspects of their faith; their covenantal status, not their aspirations to statehood.

(e) In many documents of the Tanak, the precise dating of most of which is difficult, but all of which are postexilic—Job, Proverbs, Ecclesiastes, the Song of Songs, Esther, Jonah, and even part of Daniel—The Land of Israel as such hardly plays any part. This is noteworthy. Especially in the postexilic period, when Jews inhabited The Land, the loss of political control in their country might have been expected to lead to a living concern with, if not concentration upon, the territorial doctrine if it had been very significant among them. To judge from the literature to which we have referred, however, this did not happen. Instead a concern with broad human problems, rather than specifically Israelite ones, is more in evidence.

The broad human concerns in the postexilic writings to which we have referred are not necessarily to be understood as precluding attachment to The Land. The postexilic period witnessed the work of the priestly "school" which formulated *P*. This certainly concentrated on Temple and Land, as had Ezekiel (although it is to be recognized that in Ezekiel and *P* there is also traceable a tendency to deny that the presence of Yahweh is to be associated with any single place). The Psalms bear witness to the love of The Land, and the author of 1 and 2 Chronicles enlarged the role of David (1 Chron. 17:14; 28:5; 29:23).

But the fact remains that in the literature of the postexilic period there is an undeniable relocation of interest away from The Land to the broadly human. This is surprising at first, but fits in with another, frequently noted, development in the postexilic period.

(f) In that period there emerged, not a new, but a deepened awareness of the dimensions of specifically personal religious experience. The spiritual pilgrimage of the individual as such, not only as a member of the group, gained in significance. Jeremiah had prepared the way for this at the cost of the loneliness of his ministry: he seems to have felt at times that "the whole cause of Yahweh in the world hung on his individual life."[6] Ezekiel had come to recognize that, however much a part of the group, each Israelite stood alone. And in Deutero-Isaiah an interesting phenomenon already begins to confront us. The vocabulary of entry into The Land—that is, the vocabulary of national promise begins to be applied to the just man, the saint, as in Isa. 57:13b; 65:13–16. The Wisdom literature, on the one hand, has, as we should now put it, a curiously "international" flavor (and, indeed, draws upon Egyptian and other non-Jewish sources). On the other hand, it applies appeals and warnings uttered by the prophets to Israel as a whole to the individual Israelite. It is not only that the fate of the individual is bound up with that of his people, but that the experience of Israel, as a people, is reproduced, on an appropriate scale, in that of the individual Israelite (see Prov. 1:24–28).[7]

Later still, in the Maccabean period, the martyrs further imprinted the significance of the individual Israelite on Judaism. The martyrs in the Book of Daniel and elsewhere stand to the majority of their own people, whom they regarded as "apostates," in a relationship comparable to that in which Israel as a whole had often been thought to stand to the Gentile nations. The singularity of the people of Israel in the midst of the nations is now experienced by the martyr in the midst of Israel. The triumph of the individual martyr demanded the doctrine of the resurrection of the dead. Here, as in every sphere, Judaism preserved both a communal and an individual emphasis (see Wisd. Sol. 5:1–2, which describes the triumph of the righteous in the resurrection and the discomfiture of the wicked). But the individualization and internationalization of religious concern could not but lead to a relocation of emphasis. And this was furthered by the influence of the Dispersion or, more accurately, of the Exile.

6. J. Skinner, *Prophecy and Religion*, p. 223.

7. Cf. Isa. 65:2, 12; 66:4 with Prov. 1:24; Isa. 66:4 with Prov. 1:26b; Isa. 64:13–14 with Prov. 1:27c; Isa. 65:24 with Prov. 1:28. On the relation between individualism and disconnection from immediate surroundings, as in exile, see the quotation from A. N. Whitehead in *GL*, pp. 218–19. The former is often born out of the latter.

(g) As indicated in both Hellenistic and Palestinian sources, The Land became, in some quarters, a symbol for a transcendent order, or for the age to come. Such sources can be divided into two kinds: those in which The Land retains its geographic dimension and yet is given a moral and transcendental connotation (Philo's works and a section in the Mishnah) and those in which The Land is wholly transcendentalized (the Testament of Job).

Philo hoped for a restoration to The Land in the messianic age, but the emphasis in his thought is not on The Land. In the messianic age, other nations will enjoy their own lands: what Philo is concerned with is that they should recognize and accept the Law. It is in its possession of the latter that the peculiarity of the people of Israel lies, not in its connection with The Land (Philo *Moses* 1.279). Similarly, Philo recognized that the root of anti-Judaism lay in the laws observed by his people.

Moreover, although Philo retains the actuality of the messianic hope for The Land, he can also interpret The Land symbolically. In his *Questions on Genesis,* he does not deal directly with Gen. 12:1–3, but does offer comments on Gen. 15:7, 8. In these, the promised Land becomes "fruitful wisdom." (See also Philo's comment on Gen. 15:18–21.) It does not come as a surprise, therefore, when we find The Land spiritualized in Pharisaism itself. In Mishnah Sanhedrin 10:1, we read: "All Israelites have a share in the world to come, for it is written, Thy people also shall be all righteous, they shall inherit the land for ever; the branch of my planting, the work of my hands that I may be glorified" (Isa. 60:21). To "inherit the land" is equated with having a share in "the world to come." The phrase "the world to come" may sometimes be equated with the messianic age. Here, however, the context makes it clear that it refers to the final age beyond the resurrection of the dead. The Land is no longer territorial: it has become a symbol of the life of the age to come, what the Fourth Gospel refers to as "eternal life." This symbolism appears with a different connotation in the *gemara* on M. Sanhedrin 10:3, where The Land is interpreted not as Palestine, but as "this world," and where the holy mount of Jerusalem is the equivalent of the future world, the age to come. (See also *BT* Sanhedrin 110b.)

The Land seems to be wholly transcendentalized in the little noticed and examined Testament of Job, which Kohler traced to pre-Christian Essene circles, finding its eschatology and messianic belief to be Jewish.[8] It is difficult to agree with Kohler's understanding of the eschatology. The traditional eschatological terms—throne, kingdom, glory—do appear, but the hope expressed in the Testament of Job suggests more the immortal world of souls than the resurrection of

---

8. K. Kohler, "The Testament of Job."

the dead. Job looks forward to an eternal order, beyond this world, where he and his children will enter into glory. In one manuscript—probably the most authentic—this eternal order is described as "the holy land," a term used in parallelism with "the imperishable world" (see Test. Job 33).

The same anticipation of a life in a world to come emerges in Job's reaction to the request of his wife, Sitis, that the bones of his children be disinterred and rendered proper, decent burial. Job's words, when the kings gave order that this should be done, are:

Do not go into the trouble in vain, for you will not find my children, since they have been taken up into [the] heavens by their lord and king (Test. Job 39).

On the protest of his friends, Job replied:

"Raise me that I may stand." And they raised me, lifting up my arms on both sides. Then standing I made confession to the Father: And after my prayer I said to them: "Look up with your eyes to the east and see my children crowned alongside the glory of the Heavenly One."

And the reaction of Sitis was to fall on the ground and exclaim: "Now I have known that the memory of me remains with the Lord." That Sitis died without proper burial (a greatly emphasized aspect of Judaism) is of no consequence: she is remembered by God. So, too, Job, who had set his hope, not on earthly things and an unstable earth, but on the living God, was not concerned to hand on to his daughters earthly or worldly well-being, and so gave them "three-stringed girdles" which transformed their existence from the earthly to the heavenly. And the worst fate that can befall Elihu, as all men, is that he should not be remembered by God or His holy ones or by the living. The reality of the supernal world is the ground of all hope and the reality of God's remembrance of us in that world.

All this is set in a discussion between Job and his friends, and they regard him as mad. Doubtless we hear the echo here of the way in which Sadducees and Samaritans, and perhaps even Pharisees, responded to those who were openly receptive to Hellenistic ideas and prepared to mythologize "The Land" or to turn it into a symbol of the transcendental. This process has been also traced in the Book of Wisdom and in 4 Maccabees (see Wis. 3:1–4; 4 Macc. 9:21 f.).

There is another development in the first century and later which has a bearing on our theme. It cannot be sufficiently emphasized that in Judaism two entities were indissolubly linked to The Land: Jerusalem and the Temple. But during the first century and later there was more and more concentration on the transcendental heavenly Jerusalem and heavenly Temple, whose origins are much earlier than those of their earthly analogues. Along with this, in the eschatological thinking of

Judaism, there persisted the expectation of a new creation. This development—that is, the spiritualization and transcendentalizing of The Land in terms of the heavenly Jerusalem and the heavenly Temple against the background of a new creation—raises acutely the question of how far in the course of time the expectations engendered by the promise to Abraham were so transmuted that the hope of occupying The Land in history became a hope for an order beyond history. How far did The Land become a symbol for a transcendent order, the promise of territory being absorbed, and thereby annulled, in the yearning for the future "age to come" and "new creation"?

In the postexilic period, the life of Jewry was mainly centered in Jerusalem and in the area surrounding it, so that it was probably inevitable that the city should gather to itself the hopes of Israel. Geographic actualities demanded this, but it was even more rooted in the history and religion of Israel.

Pre-Israelite Jerusalem need not concern us, and a detailed account of the development of the mystique of Jerusalem in the Tanak would take us too far afield. Suffice it to say that the city became the political and religious centre of Israel in the reign of David, who introduced the Ark, the symbol of Yahweh's presence, into it. A covenant—the covenant at Sinai, adapted to changing circumstances—was formed between Yahweh and David. Through the latter, Jerusalem became the political centre of the people of God; through the Ark, the religious and historical traditions of that people were preserved and grafted on to Jerusalem, as their repository. That the traditions referred to were focused in the Ark in part explains why the prophet Nathan opposed the building of a temple. But although the spiritual centrality of Jerusalem for Israel was thus originally conditioned by the presence of the Ark within its walls, in Solomon's reign a temple was built there. This was acceptable to Yahweh, the God of Sinai, as a fit abode for his glory, and served, therefore, to increase still further the religious significance of the city.

This significance survived events which might be expected to have diminished it. It survived the division of the kingdom (Jer. 41:5); it survived the decline of the dynasty of David; it even survived the loss of the Temple and of the Ark in 587 B.C.E. Why? Although the preexilic prophets had linked Jerusalem to the dynasty of David, they had preferred, like the Psalmists, to think of the city not as the city of David, but as that of Yahweh: they referred to it as Zion, the archaic name of the Jebusite acropolis that had *become* the city of David (2 Sam. 5:7). It is, therefore, not altogether surprising that the fall of the Davidic dynasty did not loosen the religious hold of the city. And although no preexilic prophet states that Yahweh had chosen Jerusalem, Isa. 14:32 does assert that He had founded it (and so was its creator). There, in the Temple, Yahweh dwelt (Amos 1:2; Isa. 2:2; 8:18; 31:9), seated on his throne, the Ark (Isa. 6:1; cf 1 Sam. 4:4; 2 Sam. 6:2). The destruction of the Temple and the disappearance of the Ark could not but, therefore, have been traumatic experiences for the people of God. And yet Jerusalem remained its religious centre. How could this be?

It could be only because, as Jeremiah and Ezekiel make clear, apart from the Ark and the Temple, Jerusalem itself was believed to be peculiarly related to Yahweh. Jeremiah envisages the whole of Jerusalem as the throne of Yahweh in the future; he mentions no temple. In Jer. 3:16–17, Yahweh's presence, it is implied, has become independent of the Temple, as of the Ark. This divorce of Yahweh from "holy space," centered in the Temple, is evident also when we compare Isa. 2:2 with Isa. 27:13 and 66:20. The "mountain of the Lord's house" of the first passage has in both the latter become simply "the holy mountain of Yahweh." True, Ezekiel and Zechariah do see a temple in the future restored Jerusalem. But for Ezekiel, at least, the heart of that city is the presence of Yahweh himself. Its name will be: "Yahweh is there" (Ezek. 48:38). Ark and Temple might pass away, but the presence of Yahweh in the city is still assured.

But for Israel, the year 587 B.C.E. was traumatic in another way. Jerusalem itself was then reduced to ruins. This event was traumatic because of the belief that the city, as the city of Yahweh, was inviolable. The origins of this belief need not detain us. Isaiah and the Psalms point to it. Though Isaiah did not wholly endorse it, and Micah and Jeremiah rejected it, its reality for the majority of Israel cannot be doubted (Lam. 4:12; 3:31–33). (See further Ezek. 43:1–5; Deut.-Isa. 40:1–2; 49:16; 52:1; 52:8.) Yahweh cannot forget Jerusalem: "Behold, I have graven you on the palm of my hands, your walls are continually before me" (Isa. 49:16). Deutero-Isaiah pictures the dispersed Jews from many lands returning to the city (40:11; 41:17 ff.; 43:5 f). Jerusalem will be greatly enlarged and exceedingly beautiful (49:19 ff.; 54:1–3, 11–12; 60:13–18). Haggai asserts that, "The latter splendour of this house [the rebuilt Temple] shall be greater than the former, says the Lord of hosts" (Hag. 2:9). Zechariah is assured that Yahweh "will again choose Jerusalem" (2:12; see also 1:14b, 17; 3:2) and describes the future glories of that city (8:3–8). The nations will flow to a city rebuilt and elevated miraculously above the earth (14:10 ff.). The hope for such a city in the future reaches full tide in Isa. 60–62.

The promise of a new earthly Jerusalem is stressed in many sources. We cannot pursue the evidence in detail; suffice it to refer to Tobit (ca. 200 B.C.E.), where in 1:4 we read that Jerusalem is "Chosen from among all the tribes of Israel, where all the tribes should sacrifice and where the temple of the dwelling of the Most High was consecrated and established for all generations for ever." Cf. Ecclus. 36:11–14; 51:12 (ca. 180 B.C.E.); Ps. Sol. 17:22 f. (ca. 70–40 B.C.E.); Sib. Or., passim (ca. 140 B.C.E.–C.E. 70); Test. Levi 10:5. In 3 Macc. 2:9–10 (first century B.C.E.) Jerusalem is elect from creation; in 4 Ezra (first century C.E.) it is connected with the election of the people of Israel itself (4 Ezra 5:24 ff.); cf. Num. 3:2. In Pharisaic sources, the hope for the restoration and the glorification of Jerusalem is vivid. Written well before C.E. 70, the 14th Benediction in the Shemoneh Esreh, cited above, makes this clear. (See further *BT* Megillah 17b–18a, and especially Aboth de Rabbi Nathan 35.) While the earthly Jerusalem stood, and after it had again fallen in C.E. 70, the hope for a New Jerusalem persisted.

The city had been connected with Mt. Sinai in Isa. 2:1–5 The same connection occurs in Ps. 68:15–17. But these two passages also connect Jerusalem with a conception found in Canaanite mythology—that of the mountains of the gods, of which Bashan and Zaphon and the north (Isa. 14:12–13) are examples. There is a reference to Bashan as envious of Mt. Zion in Ps. 68:15–17, but in Ps. 48:1–3 Zion is identified with Mt. Zaphon. Jerusalem has become the place of the highest mountain. The view reemerges in Ezek. 20:40; 40:2. In the latter passage, the prophet sees the future Jerusalem opposite "a very high mountain" in The Land of Israel.

The theme of the mountain reemerges in a group of psalms which are preoccupied with Zion (the psalms of Korah, 42–49; 84–85; 86–88). According to the authors of these, Yahweh dwelt exclusively in Zion. There was the house and dwelling place of God (42:4); from "the holy hill" came forth the light and truth of God (43:3). The mountain of God is mentioned in 48:2; 87:1. With this mythological motif are combined those of paradise (46:4) and of the conflict with chaos (46:2 ff.). The city is endowed with the riches of mythology to give it a cosmic significance. No wonder that those born in Jerusalem are especially blessed (Ps. 87:5). A day in the courts of her temple is better than a thousand elsewhere (Ps.84:10).

One of the most direct testimonies to the continuing vitality of the veneration of Jerusalem appears at column 22 in *11QPsᵃ*, a document discovered at Qumran. The literary affinities between this column, generally referred to as the Apostrophe to Zion, and Isa. 54:60–62; 66, and other passages in the Tanak, have been pointed out. It has also been suggested that we have here a distinct stage in the theology of Zion—the application to the city of terms usually applied to God Himself: the glorification of Zion could hardly go further!

In the passages hitherto appealed to, it would seem that Jerusalem is still *in* The Land, but so transformed and idealized that it must be asked whether it is still *of* The Land. This question is especially posed by the section in Isa. 60–62, in which we claimed above that the hope for Jerusalem had reached full tide. Does it warrant the view that already in the Tanak, the city has become a transcendental entity, "mystic, wonderful," so that the earthly Jerusalem is subsumed in a heavenly city? R. de Vaux does not hesitate to claim that in Isa. 60–62 the dazzling description of the city "has no longer any connection with earthly realities: Jerusalem transcends history; in her is summed up the whole history of salvation."[9] Although in most of Isa. 60–62 the earthly city is surely envisaged, in Isa. 60:14–20 at least, we are pointed beyond the boundaries of time and space. But not all have found a transcendent reference here. The above passage may be taken as only metaphorical, and there are certainly mundane verses in Isa. 60 in which Jerusalem is envisaged as a very earthly city, to which the wealth of the nations is brought (Isa. 60:3, 5 ff., 10, 13).

If we reject the view that the belief in a heavenly Jerusalem is already present in Isa. 60:19–20, it probably first occurs in 1 Enoch 90:28–38, where, although the express phrase "heavenly Jerusalem" does not occur, its existence is presupposed. Here the "new house" is implied to exist already before it is set up in what 1 Enoch 90:20 calls "the pleasant land." It is conceived in very enlarged proportions to contain those beasts and birds—the dispersed and apostates—who desire to enter it. But the meaning of "new house" is ambiguous. Usually it has been taken, without discussion, to refer to the new Jerusalem; but it might be interpreted as the new Temple. This ambiguity of interpretation suggests what is frequently found in the sources, and is illustrated in quotations which follow—the interpenetration or the identification of the city and the Temple, and the indiscriminate transition from the one to the other. However, the magnitude of the "new house" contemplated suggests that the whole city, not merely the Temple, is in view, so that we may, though not with complete certainty, find an implicit reference here to a heavenly Jerusalem. But notice: this heavenly Jerusalem is to come down to The Land. It does not remain "in heaven": however "heavenly," it is to become earthly.

A more unambiguous reference to a preexistent city appears in the Syriac Baruch (2 Bar.) at 4:1–7. Probably written within forty years of the destruction of the second Temple in c.e. 70, and purporting to deal with visions of destruction of the first Temple and the city in the time of Jeremiah, this work makes a clear distinction between the earthly temple and another. Here again we note the transition, without warning, from the city to the Temple. The city, no less than the Temple, existed before creation: a vision of it was granted to Adam, but withdrawn after the Fall, only to be renewed to Abraham, the father of the eschatological faith of Israel, and later to Moses. The vision of the city is granted to Abraham "by night among the portions of the victims." The reference is to Gen. 15:9–21. A vision of the city—not referred to in that text—is mentioned rather than the promise of The Land: has it taken the place of the latter in the author's mind?

9. R. de Vaux, "Jerusalem and the Prophets," p. 296.

The same belief in a "heavenly Jerusalem" emerges in 4 Ezra, also written after C.E. 70. Most interesting here is that the city and The Land are placed in parallelism and, thereby, perhaps equated (4 Ezra 7:26). This explains, perhaps, why in 3:13, 14 the promise of The Land to Abraham is not mentioned, but is subsumed under his vision of "the end of the times." Among the future glories of the redeemed, there is no mention of the Land, but there is of the city. 4 Ezra 8:52–53 asserts of the seer, who is among the saved:

> For you
> is opened Paradise,
> planted the Tree of Life;
> the future age prepared,
> plenteousness made ready;
> a city builded . . .
> and in the end the treasures of immortality
> are made manifest.

This passage is significant. Here, unmistakably, the "city builded" is classified with a future order which wholly transcends the historical one.

But no passage makes the existence of a heavenly Jerusalem—the city of 4 Ezra 8:52–53—clearer than the tantalizing section dealing with "The Vision of the Disconsolate Woman" in 4 Ezra 9:38–10:57. Here, despite the complexities of the text, the distinction between the earthly Jerusalem (the Son) and "the (heavenly) pattern of her" (the woman) is unmistakable. The "wholly other" character of the heavenly pattern is emphasized, especially in the section which explains why the vision had only been granted in a field: it had to be placed in a fresh setting. How important the vision of the heavenly city was for the author of 4 Ezra appears from the frequency with which he refers to it (see 7:26; 13:35 f.).

In the rabbinic sources, discussion of the heavenly Jerusalem centres on two themes. First, its exact location in the heavens—for example, is it in the third heaven or the fourth? Apart from the materials to which we have referred, the New Testament also, for example, at Rev. 21:2, 10, makes it clear that such speculation prevailed in the first century, although most of the rabbinic material dealing with it is of later origin. One text, Gen. Rabbah 69:7, places the heavenly Jerusalem eighteen miles above the earthly (so Simeon ben Yohai, C.E. 140–65). The same rabbi in Gen. Rabbah 55:7, on Gen. 22:2, finds that, on earth, Moriah corresponds to the heavenly Temple. In *BT* Hagigah 12b, Resh Lakish (Rabbi Simeon b. Lakish, C.E. 279–320) thinks that the heavenly Temple is situated in *zᵉbûl* (the fourth of the seven heavens). (*Zᵉbûl* is that in which "[the heavenly] Jerusalem and the Temple and the altar are built, and Michael, the great prince, stands and offers up thereon an offering"; reference is made to 1 Kings 8:13 and Isa. 43:15, where *z*ᵉ*bûl* is referred to as the habitation of God.) Secondly, how was this heavenly city to be made manifest? There is a sharp division between the earlier rabbinic sources and the latter at this point. That there was a correspondence between the structure of the heavenly Jerusalem and the earthly was generally recognized. But none of the earlier texts suggests that the heavenly Jerusalem will descend to earth to replace the earthly: the heavenly city remains transcendent. The descent of the city envisaged in the Pseudepigrapha, referred to above, seems to be rejected. The Jerusalem on earth will be rebuilt with human hands; the heavenly Jerusalem remains above. But the two cities *are* connected, as in *BT* Taanith 5a. The argument here is that the words *sheḥûbᵉrah* (joined, compacted), implies that Jerusalem has a *ḥᵉbûrâh* (companion) in heaven: both earthly city and heavenly prototype are located opposite each other. And again in Mekilta, Beshallah, the assumption seems to be that "Jerusalem" existed at the time of the Exodus. Since the Jerusalem on earth did not then exist, the reference must be to the heavenly Jerusalem. A preexistent heavenly Jerusalem seems also to be implied elsewhere in the same passage: "Israel" and "Jerusalem" seem to be regarded as having been designated to be in the presence of God "from the time of the six days of creation." According to R. Eliezar Jacob, a contemporary of the destruction of C.E. 70, "Jerusalem is destined to keep rising aloft until it reaches the throne of glory" (Pesikta de Rab Kahana, end of section 20). Does this mean that the earthly Jerusalem is ultimately to be united with the heavenly one—that is, to become wholly transcendent—or simply that there is no fundamental difference between the earthly and the heavenly Jerusalem? This question must remain unanswered. Was Philo of Alexandria's understanding of the tabernacle built by Moses that it only *resembled* its heavenly prototype *(Moses* 11.74 ff.)? "The tabernacle, then, was constructed to resemble a sacred temple in the way described," we are told *(Moses* 11.59). How much beyond Philo the rabbis went in connecting the earthly and the heavenly city remains problematic.

At no point should the doctrine of the promise of The Land be separated from that of Yahweh as Creator of the universe. And, in the eschatology of Israel, that promise must more and more be understood in a larger context, against the eschatological doctrine of a new creation. Only the bare structure of this doctrine need be given here. Already in Isa. 11:6, a passage usually referred to as messianic, the end is conceived of as the restoration of the beginning: a return to the paradisal conditions existing before the fall of Adam. By the time of Trito-Isaiah, the belief that cosmic changes will mark the end becomes explicit: "For, behold, I create new heavens and a new earth" (Isa. 65:17). There are parallels in both Isa. 66:22 and Deut.-Isa. 51:6, the latter passage contrasting this passing material world with God's salvation, which is to be for ever.

Later sources reveal a bewildering variety of views on the end: in most, it will be by fire, the final destruction by fire corresponding to the initial destruction by the flood; it will occur sometime after the messianic age, or before the final judgment of God. If there is to be a "place" for salvation, where is that to be, in heaven or on earth after it has been scorched? What is meant by the "new heaven"? Is the old earth to be undone and then remade out of a new substance? Or is the earth in its present material form to undergo a transformation? Or is it, without undergoing dissolution, to be purified? Or is "the new" to be wholly unrelated to the old? Such questions are reflected in the Apocrypha and Pseudepigrapha, the Qumran writings, and the rabbinic sources. And speculation about the end also occurs in another frame of reference, in Hellenistic sources, which also reveal that the future may lead to a fiery end of all things.

The promise of The Land, cherished as we have seen it to be, must be considered in the framework of such speculation, which could not but have depressed the doctrine of The Land to a less central position than it would otherwise have occupied. The flames of the end, feeding on a cosmos afire, would tend to diminish interest in The Land as such.

EXILE AND DISPERSION

In the preceding section, historical and theological data from the Tanak and later sources were presented which inhibit the simplistic ascription of a single territorial doctrine to Judaism. We now turn to another very critical aspect of Jewish history which militates against any uncritical elevation of The Land in Judaism. The condition and distribution of Jews outside The Land in the postexilic period deserves attention. Few of the exiles in Babylon chose to return to The Land when Cyrus (B.C.E. 538) made this possible. For a thousand years after Cyrus, there continued in Babylon a well-organized Jewish community, which eventually gave the Babylonian Talmud to the world. The Jews had early spread to the west also. As is made clear in the Elephantine papyrii, there was a colony of Jewish soldiers in the city of Yeb (Elephantine) in Egypt at the beginning of the sixth century B.C.E. Alexander the Great stimulated the spread of Jews, and throughout the Greek and Roman periods various reasons contributed to further this. Already around 168–65 B.C.E., the Jews had built a temple at Leontopolis in Egypt, in which they had offered sacrifices. Although in contravention of the Torah, the sages in Palestine seem to have accepted this. Jews in Sardis in Asia Minor under John Hyrcanus II established their own cult (Josephus *Antiquities* 14. 10. 24). Josephus quotes Strabo, the geographer (ca. 40 B.C.E.–C.E. 24): "This people has already made its way into every city, and it is not that easy to find any place in the habitable world which has not received this nation and in which it has not made its power felt" *(Ant.* 14. 7. 2). Few have written as perceptively on this dispersion as Bickerman, who notes the continued attachment of the Diaspora Jews to Jerusalem:

> The post-biblical period of Jewish history [that is, that following Nehemiah]
> . . . is marked by a unique and rewarding polarity: on the one hand, the
> Jerusalem center and, on the other, the plurality of centers in the Diaspora.
> The Dispersion saved Judaism from physical extirpation and spiritual inbreed-
> ing. Palestine united the dispersed members of the nation and gave them a
> sense of oneness. This counterpoise of historical forces is without analogy in
> antiquity. . . . The Jewish Dispersion continued to consider Jerusalem as the
> "metropolis" (Philo), turned to the Holy Land for guidance, and in turn,
> determined the destinies of its inhabitants.[10]

But the experience of living outside The Land could not but tend to detach Jews from it. In this sphere, as in others, absence made the heart grow fonder, but the Babylonian exiles chose not to return to The Land, and those at Leontopolis were apparently content to be settled there. Later, the Jews of Alexandria opposed the Sicarii,[11] and the Dispersion everywhere on the whole refused to cooperate in the war against Rome in C.E. 66–70. They had their own life to live outside The Land, and a form of religious association appropriate for such a life, the synagogue, had already almost certainly emerged, if not in the Babylonian exile, at least by the third century B.C.E., and developed throughout the dispersion to supply Jews with a rallying point other than the Jerusalem Temple. In time, the dispersion, which had been regarded as a punishment for sin, could be justified by at least two rabbis. Rabbi Eleazer of Modiim (C.E. 120–40) said that "God scattered Israel among the nations for the sole end that proselytes should wax numerous among them." And although his was apparently a lonely voice, it is not without significance: separation from The Land could be regarded as a not unmitigated evil. Philo came to regard the dispersion as under the providence of God *(Flaccus* 45). In the late Middle Ages, the Lurianic Qabbala came to give a profound meaning to the Exile of the Jewish people, which it explained in subtle mythical terms.

Vital rightly notes that "exile" has been the distinctive characteristic of Jewish life.[12] It has been ineluctable and extraordinarily rich and

10. E. Bickerman, *From Ezra to the Last of the Maccabees,* pp. 3 f.
11. Philo Judaeus, *Embassy to Gaius.*
12. D. Vital, *The Origins of Zionism,* p. 1.

creative in Jewish history. Certain historical facts are fundamental. The Land of Israel was not the birthplace of the Jewish people, which did not emerge there (as most peoples have on their own soil). On the contrary it had to enter its own Land from without; there is a sense in which Israel was born in exile. Abraham had to leave his own land to go to the Promised Land: the father of Jewry was deterritorialized. Paradoxically, on reaching The Land, he did not possess it; he roamed in it and dug wells. He did not chase the Canaanites out of it. On discovering that The Land could not maintain them both, he divided it with his cousin Lot (Gen. 13:6). That is, there was a "territorial concession" on his part. According to some, so little did Abraham "possess" The Land that he had to "buy" a grave for his wife at Machpelah.[13]

As for the spiritual history of Jews, its heroic periods have often been outside The Land. The Torah itself, the heart of Judaism as we shall urge, was given outside The Land, in the desert, in "no-man's-land," at Mount Sinai. Much of the Tanak, and the Talmud itself in its Babylonian form, were redacted outside The Land. It is surprising that, until late in the Middle Ages, Judaism did not produce a developed theology of exile (although such a theology can be extracted from Jeremiah and Ezekiel, as T. M. Raitt has shown in his recent study of these prophets).

The fact that since the Babylonian Exile there have almost certainly been more Jews outside than in The Land, so that even today Israelis are only a fraction of world Jewry, cannot but have diminished the centrality of The Land among many Jews and influenced their attitudes towards the doctrine concerning it. The prominence of the state of Israel in our time can easily hide the significance of the Exile for Judaism throughout most of its history. But the theological preeminence in Jewish history of Jews outside The Land needs no documentation. Apart from all else, their significance in the very survival of Judaism must be recognized. The loss of the Temple and The Land, the centres of Judaism, could be sustained only because there were organized Jewish communities scattered elsewhere. Disaster at the centre did not spell the end of Judaism but could be, and was, offset and cushioned by its existence elsewhere. From this point of view, exile may be regarded as having been the historical condition for the survival of Judaism and Jewry. (That this did not mean a radical decline of the significance of the primary centre we shall show later.)

13. See J. W. Bowman, *Which Jesus?* p. 68. Bowman's appendix 4, "Did God Give the Holy Land to Abram and His Descendants?" pp. 166–68, deserves serious attention, but we are not convinced that his interpretation of Gen. 23 is to be followed. For another interpretation of this purchase, see *GL*, p. 222, n. 17.

Such considerations explain the long discussion on the role of Exile and Diaspora among Jews. There have always been large numbers of Jews in the Diaspora who have accepted the territorial doctrine as such. The literal acceptance of the doctrine is best exemplified, perhaps, in Sabbatianism and among those Jews who settled in Palestine long before the emergence of the state of Israel. For reasons previously elaborated, Zionism cannot be equated with a reaffirmation of the eternal relation of The Land, the people, and the Deity, except with the most cautious reservations, since it is more the expression of nationalism than of Judaism. But many Jews in the Diaspora have sought other ways to deal with the particularity of The Land. Some insist that The Land is still *central* for Judaism but not *primary*; others in the Diaspora express the matter in terms of *centre* and *periphery,* or of an ellipse with two poles, claiming that The Land is not always necessarily central. At first encounter, such views appear merely face-saving: certainly the distinction between the central and the primary, it might be argued, is a distinction without a difference. Is it not simply a tacit admission that the doctrinal claims for The Land have become an embarrassment? In fact, the view is another expression of a pro-longed concern in the Diaspora to transcend the theological distinction between Palestinian and Diaspora Judaism, and to find a raison d'être for the Diaspora which gives it that significance which its dominating actuality seems to demand. In modern times, these views are associated with such names as Moses Mendelssohn (1729–86), Samuel Holdheim (1806–60), Abraham Geiger (1810–74), and Hermann Cohen (1842–1918). The attitude to which we refer gives to the Diaspora (not here understood as "exile") an independent spiritual raison d'être, and finds in it the very self-fulfillment of Judaism. This theology of the Diaspora has been summarized by André Neher as follows:

The *Shekinah* resides with every exiled fragment of the Jewish people. In every particle of land trodden by a Jew the presence of God is revealed. Far from being an outward road leading the chosen People farther and farther away from their election, the exile is for Israel a mission, each stage of which strengthens the bonds between the Jew and the God who accompanies him. . . . The universe would be lacking in shape unless Israel were omni-present, making the divine sap pulsate through the organism of the cosmos like the blood through the body. . . . In each field of his exile the Jew places the seeds which will one day bring forth the divine harvest.[14]

14. Cited in 'Abd Al-Tafāhum, "Doctrine," p. 374, from Neher's *Moses and the Vocation of the Jewish People,* p. 162. 'Abd Al-Tafāhum also refers to the views of Franz Rosenzweig and Hans Joachim Schoeps, but these are not directly related to the question of The Land by him. See, however, T. Dreyfus, "The Commentary of Franz Rosenzweig to the Poems of Jehudah Halevi."

In order to justify the claim of an independent religious viability and dignity for the Diaspora, appeal has been made not only to the theology described by Neher, but to history. Emphasis is laid on the fact that the Diaspora was born as much out of deliberate departures from The Land as out of necessity—through wars, enslavement, expulsion. Largely voluntary, the Diaspora was well established before the tragic events of the first century C.E., and must not be regarded as predominantly a consequence of these. Outside The Land, Jews have developed a religious life of their own, respecting the authorities of The Land, but not dominated by them. As indicated before, rabbinic Judaism recognized a distinction between commandments which only could be, and had to be, practised in The Land and those which could and had to be practised outside The Land. The logical outcome of this was that in time it came to be affirmed that the Jews were religiously bound to abide by the civil law of the countries where they dwelt. To what degree and how long Palestinian authorities controlled the Diaspora after 70 C.E. is a matter of debate. E. E. Urbach has dealt with this problem in terms of the relation between The Land as centre and the Diaspora as periphery. After a survey of various treatments of the theme, and an illuminating examination of the evidence from the period of the second Temple and the centuries following its destruction, he concludes that without the precondition of Jewish sovereignty and independence in The Land, "any attempt to prove its continuance as a Jewish center cannot succeed, and all concepts of center and dispersion in Jewish history are merely reconstructions without basis in fact."[15] For him only the self-determination of the Jewish people in its own Land could and can make The Land the centre of Jewish existence. Certainly after the period to which Urbach appeals, many Jews, religious as well as secular, have come to regard the Diaspora as capable of maintaining an authentic Jewish way of life in any locality and independently of any central authority in The Land. Theological considerations have given way to historical actualities and necessities.

And this adaptation has been justified by a second historical consideration. A doctrine that was theologically and socially appropriate immediately after the collapse of the revolt in the late first century, and even for the greater Diaspora which developed after 70 C.E., it is implied, cannot reasonably be expected to be uncritically endorsed after twenty centuries of growth of the Diaspora throughout the world.

For the notions of centre and periphery and of Jewish existence as an ellipse between Jerusalem and Babylon or Russia and America, etc., see P. Nave, "Zentrum und Peripherie im Geschichte und Gegenwart." On "the mission of Israel," see also J. J. Petuchowski, *Zion Reconsidered*, pp. 120–23.

15. E. E. Urbach, "Center and Periphery in Jewish Historic Consciousness."

After so many centuries of life outside The Land, religiously, culturally, and otherwise, most Diaspora Jews would find such an endorsement hard to support. Not only have time and change taught them new duties, but the undeniable creativity of Diaspora Jews, religiously as well as otherwise, makes their claim to authentic Jewish existence impossible to ignore, and any uncritical acceptance of the continuance of The Land as *the* Jewish centre unrealistic. After the Six Day War of 1967, the claims of The Land came to be felt with renewed force. A Jewish scholar, asking what attitude Jews should take to The Land, could nonetheless express the view that, while taking note of the existence of the state of Israel as a country largely inhabited by Jews, the Diaspora should "then proceed with the business in hand." It might recognize the state of Israel a s Judaism's "show case" to the world at large, but it would also maintain that Judaism has become sufficiently independent of geography so that the Jewish religious problems of New York and of London can be, and have to be, settled in New York and London—and not in Tel Aviv or Jerusalem. There can be a "full-blooded Judaism which is in no need to hope and to pray for a messianic return to Palestine."[16]

For E. E. Urbach, only an independent sovereign Jewish state in The Land can make of The Land the centre; for J. J. Petuchowski, under the present significant preponderance of the Diaspora, even such a state cannot justify this. For Urbach, the centrality of The Land depends upon its independent political vitality; for Petuchowski, the Jewish existence outside The Land already has such vitality that it can relegate The Land to secondary—even insignificant—status. But on one very significant point both scholars are alike. They make no reference in their conclusions to the territorial theological tradition with which we have here been concerned. If we understand him aright, Urbach conditions even the significance of The Land, primarily at least, on its political power. As for Petuchowski's view, it seems virtually to reduce the suggested distinction between a central and a primary role for The Land to a triviality, and the momentous efforts of many Jews to achieve a life in The Land to a "show case to the world at large."[17] The doctrine of The Land, so tenaciously held across centuries and at such cost, seems to end, for the one scholar, in *Realpolitik,* and for the other in a worthy advertisement. However, such a statement does not do justice especially to Urbach's view or the several treatments of the question elsewhere, as U. Tal makes clear in "The Land and the State of Israel in Israeli Religious Life." Both Urbach and Petuchowski, moreover, reveal the pressure to come to terms with the actuality of the Diaspora, movingly expressed—as is the mystique

---

16. J. J. Petuchowski, "Diaspora Judaism—An Abnormality?" p. 27.
17. Petuchowski, *Zion Reconsidered,* p. 132.

of The Land—in words penned in New York City, *centrum mundi,* by Dr. Louis Finkelstein, in a description of his understanding of his own work:

We at the Seminary regard ourselves and American Jewry neither as one of the foci of a great ellipse nor the center of a circle with only mystic connections with a similar circle surrounding Jerusalem. We recognize that we stand on the periphery of Jewish inspiration; and if we are content with our position, it is only because we believe that the service we can render God, Torah, and mankind from this stance is one to which we have been called and which we cannot neglect. Yet always we turn to Zion not only in prayer but also in the hope of instruction. We gladly assume the role of amanuensis to our brethren who have been given the superior privilege of serving God and studying Torah in the land in which both were uniquely revealed. If the experiences we have garnered in our efforts to weave the tapestry we have mentioned may prove of use, they are at the disposal of our masters and teachers in Israel and Zion.[18]

Not all Diaspora Jews have shared this veneration for The Land, however. Many have succumbed to one extent or another to the blandishments of life outside its borders, or come to terms with it in other ways.

THE WITNESS OF HISTORY: THE CLASSICAL RABBINIC ATTITUDE

Judaism survived and came to terms with the loss of The Land in C.E. 70, catastrophic as it was, with dignity and comparative speed. It did so because Pharisaism, after C.E. 70 the dominant element in Judaism, was politically and otherwise prepared to adjust to the absence of The Land, as to the loss of other symbols of its faith. This is not as surprising as at first encounter. The relations of the Pharisees to the Maccabees had foreshadowed their reaction to the fall of Jerusalem. Commenting on the estrangement of the Pharisees from the Maccabean dynasty, Bickerman writes:

to them [the Pharisees] it must have appeared that a foreign domination respecting Jewish autonomy and recognizing the Torah as the binding law of Judaism would offer less hindrance to their work of education. Precisely because it was foreign, and hence concerned only for the prompt payment of tribute and for civil order, they assumed that the internal life of the people would remain outside the range of its interest.

. . . The Pharisees might justly expect foreign rulers scrupulously to follow the opinions of the scholars in all such [legal] matters whereas a Jewish King,

18. L. Finkelstein, "Israel as a Spiritual Force," p. 16.

as was the case with the Maccabees, would desire to shape even the internal and religious life of the people according to his own notions and not always according to the recommendations of the teachers of the law. In point of fact, it was the Roman rule which made possible and facilitated the development of Pharisaic Judaism to a high degree, until the great conflict between the two unequal powers set in. In this conflict the Jewish people lost its land, in order to win a historic continuity such as was vouchsafed to no other people of antiquity, not even to their conquerors, the Romans.[19]

It was the Pharisaic understanding of Judaism that made this continuity possible—an understanding that placed Torah above political power and control of The Land. That the Pharisaic position had much to support it is clear. According to the Torah itself, the possession of The Land was to be subordinated to obedience to the Torah. The promise was not of a continued possession of The Land, but of a possession conditioned by observance. Although possession of The Land had been promised, it was not necessarily perdurable or without interruption. But, as a corollary, the loss of The Land did not necessarily have to mean the end of the people. And the history of Israel had abundantly confirmed this.

This brings us to the reorganization of Judaism by the sages at Jamnia after the fall of Jerusalem in 70 C.E., when they formulated the liturgy and the canon and codified the Torah. The question is whether it was their aim and achievement so to reinterpret Judaism that it could persist without The Land, Jerusalem, and the Temple. Nineteenth-century scholars thought that it was. But the issue is not to be settled so simply. The ambiguity of the rabbinic position has to be recognized. The rabbis at Jamnia did deliberately seek to establish a sentiment for Torah (and ipso facto for the synagogue) which would *comfort* Israel for its loss of The Land, the city, and the Temple. But this sentiment for Torah was not to be a final *substitute* for the latter triad. The Pharisees after 70 C.E., no less than in the Maccabean period, were realists. In the latter period, they came to recognize that the Maccabees would not act in accordance with the law as they, the Pharisees, desired and therefore withdrew their support from them. In the Roman period, also, they recognized political realities, and after 70 C.E., while by no means abandoning ultimate hope for The Land, the city, and the Temple, sought comfort in devotion to the Torah, with all that this implied for their personal and communal life. The fact that Rabbi Johanan b. Zakkai claimed for Jamnia the prerogatives of the Temple at Jerusalem (Mishnah Rosh Hashanah 4:1; *BT* Rosh Hashanah 29b), and followed the policy of excluding former Temple officials from authority, meant that "place" could be transcended. Some

---

19. Bickerman, *From Ezra to the Last of the Maccabees*, pp. 3 f.

have argued that Johanan was trying to free Judaism from connection with Jerusalem and the Temple. But this is untenable. Johanan did not reject the Temple: he merely sought to provide an "interim" form for religious life. (In Jewish history that interim has been variously understood as preceding a return to The Land or the end of all things.)

The passages to which appeal can be made in support of the ambiguity to which we refer are very numerous. Here we shall merely note those which indicate how the rabbis came to terms with their new situation after the fall of Jerusalem. Some denied that the Shekinah (the Divine Presence) had ever rested on the second Temple at all (Pesikta Rabbati 160a), others asserted that the Shekinah is everywhere and therefore could not be confined to the Temple, but might be present in the humblest synagogue (Exod. Rabbah 2:5; Deut. Rabbah 7:2; Lev. Rabbah 4:8; *BT* Berakoth 10a). Some claimed that mercy, and not sacrifice, was important (Aboth de Rabbi Nathan 6; Deut. Rabbah 5:3). Above all, it came to be urged that study of Torah ensures the presence of the Shekinah; it replaces sacrifice, and is more important than the rebuilding of the Temple (Mishnah Aboth 3:2; Pesikta de Rab Kahanah 60b; *BT* Megillah 16b; *BT* Shabbath 119b). Some held that "if one repents, it is imputed to him as if he had gone up to Jerusalem, built the Temple, erected an altar and offered upon it all the sacrifices enumerated in the Torah" (Lev. Rabbah 7:2).

These passages reveal that the Temple and the city—and, we may presume, The Land—could be spiritualized even while the hope for their restoration was retained. It was its ability to detach its loyalty from "place," while nonetheless retaining "place" in its memory, that enabled Pharisaism to transcend the loss of its Land. Nor was it unique in this. The same spiritualization of the *realia* of their faith had previously emerged among the sectarians at Qumran. They interpreted the community itself as the Temple: the presence of God shifted for them from a physical building to the "spiritual" domain of the community itself. The spiritualization went further. At Qumran, as in Pharisaism, obedience to the Torah became the true sacrifice of the new Temple (*IQS* 3:11–12; 4:21; 5:5 ff.; 8:4–11; 9:3–6; 4Q Flor. 1:6 f.). At the same time, as among the Pharisees, so among the sectarians, the hope for a new and restored Temple and cult at Jerusalem remained strong. Religion, like philosophy, has its antinomies and paradoxes.

In the preceding pages we have pointed to attitudes and historical realities which make it clear that there was before 70 c.e., and immediately after in the early Tannaitic period, no uniformity of territorial doctrine. And despite the overwhelming dominance of the rabbinic form of Judaism since then, the history of the Jews, although not to the same degree, reveals the same fissiparous, amorphous, and unsystematized doctrinal character. The concept of an adamant, uniform "orthodox" Judaism, which was not stirred by dissident movements and ideas or by the mystical, messianic yearnings which expressed themselves outside of, or in opposition to, the main, strictly rabbinic, tradition, is no longer tenable. To define the place of Eretz Israel in Judaism requires recognition that that place has changed—or, more accurately, has received different emphases among various groups and at different times. However persistent some views of, and attachments to, The Land have been, and however uniform the testimony of the classical sources, there has not been one unchangeable, essential doctrine universally and uniformly recognized by the whole of Judaism. In the Middle Ages, a controversy which circled around Maimonides (1135–1204) is illuminating. In his *Dalālat al-Hā'irīn* (translated into English as *The Guide of the Perplexed)*, the Great Eagle never concerned himself directly with "The Land." Although he did so in his commentary on the Mishnah, his silence about The Land in the *Guide* caused dismay and dispute among the rabbis. It led Naḥmanides (1194– 1270) to criticize the Great Eagle by insisting that there was a specific *mitzwah to* settle in The Land, a *mitzwah* which Maimonides had ignored. In modern times, reform Judaism in the United States, anxious to come to terms with Western culture, has been careful to avoid any emphasis on particularistic elements in Judaism that would set Jews apart from their Christian neighbors. Until very recently, when external and internal pressures made themselves felt, the doctrine of The Land tended to be ignored or spiritualized. It was an embarrassment.

The demotion of The Land and the messianic idea, with its disturbing potentialities, was no less evident in the liberal Judaism of nineteenth-century Europe. How far the confused and confusing embarrassment with The Land went there, even among Jewish theologians, appears from Hermann Cohen. In 1880 he claimed that Judaism was already in process of forming a "cultural, historical union with Protestantism." It is not surprising that he could write:

> *The loss of the national state is already conditioned by messianism. But this is the basis of the tragedy of Jewish peoplehood in all historic depth.* How can a people exist and fulfill its messianic task if it is deprived of the common human protection afforded by a state to its people? And yet, just this is the situation of the Jewish people, and *thus it must needs be the meaning of the history of the Jews,* if indeed this meaning lies in messianism [emphasis added].[20]

Cohen was concerned with the state and Judaism; by implication, however, he here questioned the messianic destiny of Israel in its own Land. Even if he still recognized that destiny as a reality, he so domesticated it in the context of his Western Europe that it bore little

---

20. H. Cohen, *Die Religion der Vernunft aus den Quellen des Judentums,* pp. 311–12.

resemblance to the dynamic messianism expressed in previous Jewish history. Cohen's "messianism" eradicated the Davidic Messiah and the hope of a kingdom of God on earth—and with this any hope for The Land. That reform and liberal Judaism in the United States and Europe have recently reintroduced an emphasis on The Land, in response to contemporary events which they could not ignore, cannot obliterate their earlier nonterritorial or antiterritorial attitude. Not unrelated to this discussion in reform and liberal Judaism, though not directly connected with those movements, is the insistence of such figures as Aḥad Ha'Am (1856–1927) that Jews first need to devote themselves to spiritual renewal, not to the occupation of a territory. Aḥad Ha'Am founded a select and secret society in 1899 "dedicated to the notion that moral and cultural preparation had to precede the material salvation of the Jews."[21]

All this means that, at first sight at least, the witness of history can be taken as suggesting that Eretz Israel has not been of the essence of Judaism to the extent that the literary sources and liturgies and observances of pious Jews, and even the political activity of nonreligious Jews, would seem to suggest. Certain aspects of that history are pertinent. We have elsewhere indicated that, although it was assumed, there was no explicit appeal to the doctrine of The Land in the Maccabean revolt or that against Rome in C.E. 66. This is striking. Even more overlooked have been the protests expressed in the Maccabean period against the Hasmonaean rulers who had created an independent state. These protests made the later attitudes of the Pharisaic leaders in coming to terms with Roman rule and in declaring the laws of The Land, wherever Jews dwelt, to be Law, less innovative than has customarily been recognized. And, at this point, the nature of the rabbinic attitude across the centuries must be fully recognized. That the doctrine of The Land remained honored among the rabbis cannot be doubted. But, despite the facts referred to in the preceding pages, after C.E. 70, and Bar Kokba and Rabbi Akiba in the second century C.E., until very recent times it was a doctrine more honored in word than in deed. After C.E. 70, the powerlessness of Jews against the Roman authorities left the rabbinic leaders no choice other than submission and acquiescence to their divorce from "The Land." This submission and acquiescence were to persist and mold the life of the majority of Jews up to the present century and enabled the rabbis to come to terms with the loss of their Temple, City, and Land. As we have seen, protests in various forms against exile did not cease. The Lurianic Qabbalah, for example, was a magnificent attempt to confront the curse of exile, and Sabbatianism in its historical context can be regarded as a desperate lunge at the kingdom of God, which would lead to a return to Eretz

21. Vital, *Origins of Zionism,* p. 156.

Israel. But very widely, both in orthodox Judaism (by which is here meant the rabbinic mainstream) and in reform Judaism in the United States and Western Europe, the question of The Land was postponed to the age to come, either as an unacknowledged embarrassment or as a last, or ultimate, hope. Across the centuries, most Jews have lived at the whim of the Gentile world: they have not been able to afford to risk alienating their Gentile rulers by giving practical expression to their visions of a territorial return to Eretz Israel: for most Jews, despite some brilliant exceptions, such visions were a luxury of Sabbath reading, dreams to be indulged in, but not actively realized in daily life. Instead, the rabbis emphasized that the Torah itself was to become a "portable land" for Jews: it could be obeyed everywhere, and could and would constitute the centre of Jewish religious identity everywhere. The Mishnah is a map without territory.[22] Generally, orthodox

22. In "Map Without Territory," Jacob Neusner sets the Mishnaic system of sacrifice and sanctuary in its historical context. After 70 C.E., the city of Jerusalem was in ruins; and after 135 C.E., the locus for the cult was inaccessible—the cosmic centre of Jewry was gone. "The problem confronting all Israelites in the ten decades from 70–170," Neusner observes, "is to work out a way of viewing the world, of making sense of a cosmos which, having lost its center, is nonsense" (p. 110). The sages meet this problem by drawing up a map of a never-never land which does not and cannot exist, a map which ignores territory. This map, the Mishnah, is a work of imagination amazingly irrelevant to its own day. In one sense, the Mishnah is locative (see p. 121) and organizes the world around the themes and topics of the Temple. But what does it say to a world which cannot have a temple? The Mishnah mediates the old world, which had the Temple, to a new world that has none: it refers backward, but also forward—now to a community. "Now the focus will be upon a people, not place; anywhere, not somewhere. . . . In the world of disaster and cataclysmic change, Mishnah stands as a statement of how the old is to be retained. It defines the conditions of permanence amid change" (p. 122). "What Mishnah does by representing this cult, laying out its measurements, describing its rite, and specifying its rules, is to permit Israel in the words of the Mishnah to experience anywhere and anytime that cosmic center of the world described by Mishnah: *Cosmic center in words is made utopia*" (p. 125; italics in original), "Mishnah is mobile. Memorizing its words is the guarantee of ubiquity" (p. 125). Neusner rightly connects this with the "anthropologization" of the cosmos which was taking place at the end of the classical period. The masters of the Mishnah are counterparts of the "holy man" who emerged at the end of the classical world at the expense of the Temple. (Neusner quotes Peter Brown, *The World of Late Antiquity*, p. 102, and J. Z. Smith, *Map Is Not Territory*, on this.) Although the Mishnah never says so (p. 119), Neusner is careful to note that the hope is that the centre— the geographic centre—will once more be regained (p. 125). One might suggest

Judaism has refused to indulge in political speculation and activity which might further a return to The Land, and has accepted instead an attitude of quietism. In one of the paradoxes of history, rabbis and apocalyptists were here at one: they have preferred to wait for Divine intervention, usually postponed to an indefinite future, to produce the return. From a different point of view, as we saw, the reform, in order to accommodate its faith to the nineteenth century and to make it comparable and compatible with Christianity, also preferred to refuse to give to "The Land" a special overwhelming significance. In brief, in most rabbinic writers up to the twentieth century, and in some orthodox circles even up to the very present, the significance of The Land, though never denied, has been transferred to the "end of days." Paradoxically, "The Land" retained its geographic character and actuality, and was not always transcendentalized, although it was largely removed de facto from the realm of history altogether. In the reform, again in some circles even up to very recent times, "The Land" was conveniently relegated to a secondary place; its geographic actuality was either sublimated or transformed into a symbol of an ideal society not necessarily located in Eretz Israel. Historically then, out of necessity since C.E. 70, and Bar Kokba and Rabbi Akiba, the doctrine of The Land as a communal concern (it was often cherished by individual Jews) has been largely dormant or suffered benign neglect in much of Judaism.

What happened is apparent. In their realism, the rabbis at Jamnia had triumphed over the Zealots of Masada. They recognized that the power of Rome was invincible: for them, Jewish survival lay in sensible—because unavoidable—political submission, and in obedience to the Torah in all aspects of life where this was possible. The law of the country where Jews dwelt became law. (The principle was *dînâ' de-malkûtâ' dîna'*: see *BT* Nedarim 28a; *BT* Gittin 10b; *BT* Baba Kamma 113a-b; *BT* Baba Bathra 54b.) The paradigmatic figure was Joḥanan ben Zakkai, who had asked of Vespasian only permission to found a school where he could teach and establish a house of prayer and perform all the commandments—a spiritual center which accepted political powerlessness. For most of the rabbis after C.E. 70, exile became an accepted condition. For them, discretion was the better part of valor. That it is to their discretion that Judaism owes its existence since C.E. 70 can hardly be gainsaid.

THE IMPACT OF ZIONISM

So far we have mainly dealt with the sources and past history of Judaism. It is necessary to recognize, however, that the very discussion

---

that despite the suspicion of false apocalyptic hopes among the sages, hope for The Land underlay their activity. The "anthropologization" and "communalization" (to use these ugly shorthand words) were probably less conscious than Neusner's treatment allows.

of this theme in this volume would probably not have been evoked were it not for the pressure, both conscious and unconscious, of the Zionist movement. The ascribing of a theological concern with The Land to Jews who entertain no definable Jewish theology, or even reject the tradition of their fathers, has become insidiously easy because of the Zionist climate within which so much of modern Jewry lives.

Neat dichotomies between the religious and political factors in Zionism are falsifications of their rich and mutually accommodating diversity. To read Gershom Scholem's autobiographical pages is to be made aware of this. The Zionist movement can effectively be dated to the Congress of Basel in 1897. It grew until, after almost twenty centuries abeyance, the state of Israel emerged in 1948. But the role of Jewish territorial doctrine and sentiment in the movement has to be carefully assessed: it can easily be exaggerated. Certainly the territorial theology of Judaism should not be *directly* ascribed (the qualifying adverb is important) to the many nonreligious Jews who played a most significant part in Zionist history. At first it was possible for some of the leading Zionists to contemplate the establishment of a state outside The Land altogether—in Uganda, in Argentina, in newly conquered Russian territories in Asia, in Asiatic Turkey, and in North America.[23] The often silent but almost ubiquitous presence of the religious tradition, with its concentration on Eretz Israel, caused such to change their minds, however, and made the choice of the Jewish homeland inevitable. Herzl, like other Zionist secularists, was compelled to recognize this.

But Zionism remained an expression not only—and probably not even chiefly—of the theological territorial attachment of Judaism, but even more of the nationalist and socialistic spirit of the nineteenth century. In this sense, it is a typical product of that century. An examination of the history of Zionism makes its specifically religious motivation less significant than an uncritical emphasis on territorial theology would lead one to expect. In reply to an article by Yeuda Bourla, a novelist who died in 1970, Gershom Scholem wrote:

I . . . am opposed, like thousands of other Zionists . . . to mixing up religious and political concepts. *I categorically deny that Zionism is a messianic movement and that it is entitled to use religious terminology to advance its political aims.*

The redemption of the Jewish people, which as a Zionist I desire, is in no way identical with the religious redemption I hope for the future. I am not

23. The notion of "territorialism" unrelated to Eretz Israel—that is, the belief that the precise place possessed was not important, so long as Jews had a place—is associated especially with Y. L. Pinsker (1821–91), whose pamphlet *Auto-Emancipation: Mahnruf an seine Stammesgenossen von einem Russischen Juden* was published in 1892 (see Vital, *Origins of Zionism,* pp. 338–89).

prepared as a Zionist to satisfy political demands or yearnings that exist in a strictly nonpolitical, religious sphere, in the sphere of End-of-Days apocalyptics. The Zionist ideal is one thing and the messianic ideal is another, and the two do not touch except in pompous phraseology of mass rallies, which often fuse into our youth a spirit of new Sabbatianism that must inevitably fail. The Zionist movement is congenitally alien to the Sabbatian movement, and the attempts to infuse Sabbatian spirit into it has already caused it a great deal of harm.[24]

It seems that Scholem would here largely recognize Zionism as comparable with other nationalistic movements such as those of Italy and many other countries in the nineteenth century. In a summary of forces which led to the triumph of Zionism, Scholem writes with greater fullness as follows:

If Zionism triumphed—at least on the level of historical decisions in the history of the Jews—it owes its victory preeminently to three factors that left their imprint on its character: it was, all in all, a movement of the young, in which strong romantic elements inevitably played a considerable role; it was a movement of social protest, which drew its inspiration as much from the primordial and still vital call of the prophets of Israel as from the slogans of European socialism; and it was prepared to identify itself with the fate of the Jews in all—and I mean all—aspects of that fate, the religious and worldly ones in equal measure.[25]

This admirably balanced assessment is as significant for what it does not contain—i.e., apocalyptic territorial messianism—as for what it does. Scholem, while recognizing the role of the religious tradition, does not make it the dominant factor. To him Zionism was essentially a sociopolitical protest. In the judgment of many Jews, the Congress of Basel was important not primarily because it gave expression to a strictly religious hope for The Land, living and creative as that was, but to a concern for the actual economic, political, and social distress, and often despair, of Jews in Europe; it was a response not so much to a crisis in Judaism and to an endemic territorial theology as to the plight of the Jewish people.[26]

---

24. "With Gershom Scholem: An Interview," in Scholem, *Jews and Judaism in Crisis,* ed. W. J. Dannhauser, p. 44.

25. Ibid., p. 247.

26. See Vital, *Origins of Zionism,* p. 375. Vital's excellent treatment concludes with the claim that what kept Zionists together and their institutions intact was that the terrible "social reality was always stronger than the disputes about it." The misery of the Jews' condition in the Pale of Settlement, Galicia, and Rumania could not wait for relief—it outweighed "both the force of inertia

To understand the secular character of Zionism and to overemphasize its undeniable religious dimensions is to lay oneself open to the temptation of giving to the doctrine of The Land a significance which in much of Judaism would be a distortion.[27]

---

and of religious teaching." To this was added anti-Semitism in the West.

One can agree with Vital's emphasis, but when he sets the force of "religious teaching" against the need for relief, one hesitates to concur. His conclusion at this point ignores his own opening chapter, which points to the pervasive religious substructure of all Jewish thinking about The Land. The misery of Jews would not in itself have been creatively dynamic had it not been sustained by hope, however variously expressed. Misery alone breeds despair. Did not the endemic hope for The Land, even when denied its religious character, provide the light at the end of the tunnel which helped to sustain Jews? The history of movements of social reform, and of revolutions, sufficiently indicates that total misery in itself merely leads to inertia. Such movements have usually been born out of an element other than misery itself.

27. The position indicated in our treatment of Zionism is reinforced in a private communication from Mr. Abba Eban, which he has allowed us to publish. A question that has frequently puzzled me is why the founders of the state of Israel agreed to the creation of a state in which the areas significant in Jewish religious tradition were not included, that is, Judah and Samaria, the West Bank, and the totality of Jerusalem itself. I posed this question to Mr. Abba Eban, who responded as follows:

The founders of political Zionism regarded the Bible as a general source of legitimacy for reestablishing a Jewish state. At no time, however, did any of them, including the religious parties, consider themselves to be committed to the ancient distributions of Jewish population within Eretz Israel. The League of Nations' mandate recognized the right of the Jewish people to reconstitute its national home "*in* Palestine." A Zionist text calling for the "reconstitution of Palestine as the national home of the Jewish people" was rejected by the international community. Thus, there is a partitionist implication inherent in the development of Jewish statehood from the very moment when that statehood became a concrete political prospect.

The settlement policy of the Zionist movement was based on the aim of avoiding any conflict with existing demographic realities. The idea was to settle Jews where Arabs were *not* already in firm possession. Thus, instead of settling in Jaffa with the aim of outnumbering the Arabs, the early Zionists established their own separate city of Tel Aviv. In agricultural settlement, they looked for areas which were empty of Arabs. Since the main concentrations of Arab population were in areas associated with the ancient Jewish kingdoms, it followed that modern Jewish settlement was destined to concentrate itself elsewhere, namely the land of the Philistines in the coastal plain, as well as in the valleys of Jezreel and Esdraelon, which Arab populations had avoided because of insalubrious conditions. In other words, the principle for Jewish settlement and land purchase was always empirical and contemporary, never religious or historical.

In the United Nations' discussions leading to Israel's membership of the UN, we relied on the general premise of a historic connection, but made no claim whatever for the inclusion of particular areas on our side of the Partition boundary on the grounds of ancient connection. Since Hebron was full of Arabs, we did not ask for it. Since Beersheba was virtually empty, we put in a successful claim. The central Zionist thesis was that there existed sufficent room within Eretz Israel for densely populated Jewish society to be established without displacing Arab populations, and even without intruding upon their deeprooted social cohesion.

In *The Idea of the Jewish State,* Ben Halpern presents a rather more complicated picture (see, especially, pp. 41, 47). I have unfortunately not, as yet, been able to locate the works of A. Ruppin, to which Mr. Eban refers.

3
The Contradiction Resolved?

So far we have pinpointed what appears to be a contradiction: much of the theology and history of Judaism in its main expressions points to The Land as of its essence: the history of Judaism, however, seems also to offer serious qualifications of this. Can this contradiction be resolved? We suggest that the Jews' understanding of their own history sought to come to terms precisely with this contradiction and tried to resolve it in life, *solvitur ambulando*.

We have appealed to history in support of the claim that exile as much as, if not more than, life in The Land has significantly marked Jewish history. The force of that appeal must in no way be belittled. Taken in isolation, however, it is misleading, because in the Jewish experience, both religious and secular, exile has always coexisted with the hope of a return to The Land. It might well be argued that the Jewish people would probably have gradually disintegrated and ceased to be without that hope. Here the distinction between exile *(galûth)* and simple dispersion is important: the two terms are easily confused.[1]

1. The incidence of these terms is significant. It is interesting to note that *diaspora* never translates the Hebrew words *gôlâh* or *galûth,* which denote the process of deportation and the state of those deported. These terms are rendered in LXX by *aichmalôsia* (captivity); *apoikesia* (emigration); *metoikesia* (deportation); and *paroikia* (sojourning). These pejorative terms were abandoned in turn in favor of *diaspora.* The reason for this, according to F. Rendtorff and K. L. Schmidt, was a desire to give expression to the benefits as well as the disadvantages of the Diaspora for the Jewish people. (See K. L. Schmidt, "Diaspora.") The terms *galûth* and *diaspora* demand further research. A beginning is made on *galûth* in R. E. Price, "A Lexiographical Study of *glh, šbh* and *šwb* in Reference to Exile in the Tanach."

For various approaches to history among Jews, see Lionel Kochan, *The Jew and His History* (reviewed by U. Tal in *Journal of Jewish Studies* 31 [Autumn 1980]: 252–57). For attitudes to The Land and The State in present-day Israel, see a clear summary statement by Michael Shashar, "The State of Israel and the Land of Israel," *The Jerusalem Quarterly* (Fall 1980); and also by Yeshayahu Leibowitz, "State and Religion," *ibid.* (Winter 1980). Particularly noteworthy is "The Land and the State of Israel in Israeli Religious Life," by U. Tal in

Statistics cannot be supplied, but many Jews throughout the centuries have voluntarily chosen to live outside The Land, and many still do. The dispersion of such is not exile. But, in most periods, most Jews have had no choice, and ultimately owe their place in the various countries of the world to the enforced exile of their ancestors. It is with these "exiles"—not simply the "dispersed"—that we are here concerned. That Jews outside Palestine conceived of their existence not simply as a dispersion meant that, wherever they were, they were still bound symbolically, theologically as well as historically, to their home base, to Eretz Israel: they were not simply scattered. The Diaspora maintained the notion of its existence as a *galûth,* exile.

The Jews have been sustained, as a people, largely by the way in which they have traditionally interpreted their own history as revealing a recurring pattern of exile and return to Eretz Israel. In the various countries of their abode, they have understood their existence as essentially transient or pilgrim, always en route to The Land. The Scriptures point to the patriarchs in search of The Land; the settlement of The Land is followed by the descent—in this case an economically necessary "exile"—into Egypt, followed by a return thence and resettlement in The Land. Later there is another exile to Babylon, this time enforced, and again a return in the time of Cyrus. The Hellenistic period saw the rise of a vast dispersion, both voluntary and forced, and the first-century revolt against Rome was followed by an exile which continued right down to this century, again leading to a return. Jews have constantly been conditioned by the harsh actualities of their history to think of return. Even the so-called "nonexilic" exile of Jews in Moorish and Christian Spain, where Jews for long enjoyed virtual integration into the societies in which they lived, ended in disaster and a fresh dispersion. The pattern of exile and return has been historically inescapable, and has underlined the belief that there is an unseverable connection between Yahweh, His people and His Land. History has reinforced theology to deepen the consciousness of Jews that The Land was always "there"—whether to be wrestled with in occupation or to return to from exile. As Professor Edmund Jacob has written in a brilliant lecture: "En effet, toute l'histoire d'Israël peut être envisagée comme une lutte pour la terre et avec la terre, comme le combat de Jacob était une lutte avec Dieu et pour Dieu."[2]

Proceedings of the Rabbinical Assembly, 76th Annual Convention, (Grossinger, N.Y.: Rabbinical Assembly, 1977) 38: 1–40. See also Tal's paper "Historical and Metahistorical Self-Views" in *Religious Zionism,* University of Tel Aviv Press, 1981; and also an interview with Tal on "The Nationalism of Gush Emunim in Historical Perspective" in *Forum on the Jewish People, Zionism and Israel,* no. 36 (Fall/Winter 1979), published by the World Zionist Organization, Jerusalem.

2. E. Jacob, *Israël dans la perspective biblique,* p. 22.

The implication of the acceptance of exile in the Tanak and by the rabbis is, moreover, that the relation between Israel and The Land is not simply to be understood in terms of occupation or possession of it, and that the destruction of The Land should not, and does not, spell the destruction of the people. Israel has no perpetual, inalienable right to The Land; it can lose possession of it. The Land, in turn, is not an end in itself, but a means whereby the people of Israel are the better to fulfill their destiny—that is, to fulfill the demands of the Torah. Possession of The Land depended on fulfillment of the commandments (Deut. 11:14). Israel's relation to The Land was highly dialectical, holding in tension the need to possess The Land and the recognition that it could always by its infidelity be exiled from it— though exiled only to return.

In Jewish tradition, return could be conceived of in two ways. Nonreligious Jews in every age could interpret it as a political event— that is, as simply the restoration to Jews of political rights in their own land denied them after the collapse of the Jewish revolts in 70 and 132-35 C.E. (unrealistic as it must have often seemed to non-Jews). Such Jews have often understood exile and return in secular political-economic terms. In principle, so did many of the sages. The rabbinical leaders never recognized that the conquest of Eretz Israel by a foreign power could be legitimized: the Romans were usurpers, their agents thieves. The Land belonged to Israel because Yahweh had promised it to her. So in the Mishnah it is implicitly regarded as legitimate to evade Roman taxes (Mishnah Nedarim 3:4). The ruling powers were to be given obedience, but not cooperation—even in the interest of law and order. To the rabbis, the return would involve control of The Land.

But, again to the frequent astonishment of non-Jews, much more was involved than this to the sages and their followers, who perceived the dimensions of the question as primarily spiritual. To them, just as exile was conceived of as the outcome of the wrath of God, so too the return was to be the manifestation of His gracious purpose for them despite their past disobedience. From this point of view, the return was to be a redemption. What to non-Jews was primarily, if not always exclusively, of political significance, for religious Jews was of theological significance.

But this neat division between religious and non-religious Jews, like all such divisions, is misleading. Neither category was watertight; they interacted and were mutually stimulating, as well as being highly variegated. The concepts of the one permeated those of the other to make for infinite complexity. Although the secular thought in terms of return, and the religious in terms of redemption, ultimately, because of the nature of the Tanak, upon which, whether consciously or unconsciously, they both drew, the two points of view often dissolved into each other. In the Zionist movement, secular, socialistic Jews constantly found themselves "at home" with the religious elements in the movement, who did not share their political views but provided a common ambit of thought on, or sentiment for, The Land. Nevertheless, just as with seeing the return in terms of the restoration of political rights, seeing it in terms of redemption has certain consequences. If the return were an act of divine intervention, it could not be engineered or forced by political or any other human means: to do so would be impious. That coming was best served by waiting in obedience for it: men of violence would not avail to bring it in. The rabbinic aloofness to messianic claimants sprang not only from the history of disillusionment with such, but from this underlying, deeply engrained attitude. It can be claimed that under the main rabbinic tradition Judaism condemned itself to powerlessness. But recognition of powerlessness (rather than a frustrating, futile, and tragic resistance) was effective in preserving Judaism in a very hostile Christendom, and therefore had its own brand of "power." True to the paradoxical realism of Judaism, moreover, "orthodoxy" did not allow the belief that the return depended upon Divine initiative to prevent it from always holding in principle that a fully dedicated obedience to the Torah could bring about that initiative. In the Lurianic Qabbalah, for example, this connection was particularly active.

For the purpose of this essay, the significance of the attitude towards their existence in foreign lands and towards the hope of return which we have ascribed to religious Jews is that despite their apparent quietism in the acceptance of the Torah as a portable land—and this, it must be emphasized, is only in an interim ethic—the hope for a return to Eretz Israel was never far from their consciousness. They remained true "in spirit" to the territorial theology of the Tanak and of the other sources of their faith. Except perhaps in modern Germany, where they often thought themselves to be "at home," religious Jews generally, especially those of the most traditionalist persuasion, have regarded any existing, present condition outside The Land as temporary. If not always pilgrims to it in a literal sense, they have always set their faces towards The Land. This fidelity has, in turn, strengthened the continuing belief in the "umbilical," eternal connection between the people and its Land and helped to preserve for that Land its "sacredness." In the experience of Jews, theology has informed the interpretation of history, and history in turn has confirmed the theology.

In reflecting on the answer finally to be given to the question presented to us in the light of the evidence so inadequately set forth here, an analogy from Christian ecclesiology suggests itself. In Roman Catholicism and High Church Anglicanism, the distinction has often been drawn, in discussions of the apostolic episcopate, between what is of the *esse* and what of the *bene esse* of the Christian Church. That episcopate is claimed by some to be constitutive of the Church—that is, to be of its essence, so that where there is no "apostolically" ordained bishop, there can be no true Church. To others, it is simply a means of securing the well-being of the Church. Is this distinction applicable to the way in which the mainstream of Judaism has conceived of The Land? Judaism has certainly been compelled by the actualities of history to accept exile as a permanent and major mark of its existence and as a source of incalculable benefit. Has it, then, by implication, recognized—despite the witness of most of its classical sources and, indeed, it might be argued, in conformity with much in them—that while life in The Land is of the *bene esse* of all Jewish religious existence, it is not of the *esse?* Moses desired to be in The Land so that he might have the possibility of achieving greater obedience to the Torah: that he did not enter it was a very great deprivation. But it was not fatal to his existence as a Jew (*BT* Sotah 14a). The greatest blessing is to live in The Land, but this is not absolutely essential. A Jew can remain true to his Judaism, however inadequately by the standards set by the sources, as long as he is loyal to the Torah. He can continue in his faith outside The Land, but not outside the Torah. Is not The Land, but the Torah is the essence of Judaism? It is its very relation to the Torah that endows the Land with holiness. It is highly significant that the capture of Jerusalem by King David is not commemorated in any special festival. Comparably, the feast of Ḥannukah commemorates the victory of the Maccabees not because they captured Jerusalem but because they were victorious in a war in defence of the Torah. No less significant is the fact that the Torah is not called the Torah of Israel, but the Torah of the Name (i.e., God). Neither is The Land called The Land of Israel—which is the people of God and of the Torah. From this point of view, The Land is of the *bene esse,* not of the *esse* of the Jewish faith: to give any absolute or final significance to The Land would be a denial of Judaism. There is no little danger in using such terms as *terre mystique de l'Absolu* if the term "Absolute" is transferred to The Land itself.

Yet one is uneasy about the analogy, and that not only because the Torah itself and the Mishnah are so overwhelmingly concerned with The Land. The antithesis between *esse* and *bene esse,* conceptually valid as it may seem to be, does not do justice to the place of The Land. We suggest that the way in which the question of The Land was originally posed—that is, in terms of the essence of Judaism—may itself, in fact, be misleading and result in a misplacement in our answer. The term *essence* suggests the impersonal, and is as inadequate in dealing with The Land in Judaism as it is in dealing with Christianity, as for example it was used by Feuerbach and Harnack in the notion of the "essence of Christianity." Neher[3] and Lacocque[4] have pointed to the

3. A. Neher, *L'Existence Juive.*
4. A. Lacocque, "Une Terre qui découle de lait et de miel."

personification of The Land in Judaism in feminine terms. They perhaps go too far in ascribing to simile and figurative language an actual personalism. But it is well to recognize that The Land was called _Beulah_ (the betrothed), and exaggerated as their claims may be, they do guard us against impersonalism in understanding the role of The Land. As F. W. Dillistone would put it, The Land is not space but a place.[5] It evokes immense and deep emotion among religious Jews. it presents a kind of personal challenge and offers a personal anchorage. The sentiment (a term here used in its strict psychological sense) for The Land is so endemic among religious Jews (we are not here directly concerned with others) and so constantly reinforced by their sacred sources, liturgies, and observances that to set life in The Land against life outside The Land as _esse_ against _bene esse_ is to miss the point. It is better to put the question in another way and ask: does The Land lie at the heart of Judaism? Put in this more personal manner the question answers itself.

The intensely "personal" nature of the relationship between the people and The Land becomes clearest in the use of feminine marital terms to describe it. Martin Buber[6] did not hesitate to speak of the sacred marriage between The Land and the people of Israel, and that The Land is the spouse of Yahweh appears in many passages of the Tanak (Hos. 2:5–23; Jer. 3:19–20; Isa. 62:4; and the Song of Songs have been so understood).[7] This is related to the Baal worship of Canaan, but it recalls to us also the question of the existence of a Hebraic mother-goddess or goddesses. The issue is pointedly raised by Richard Rubenstein when he urges that "the rediscovery of Israel's earth and the lost divinities of that earth" enables the Jews of today to "come into contact with those powers of life and death which engendered man's feelings about Baal, Astarte, and Anath. These powers have again become decisive in our religious life".[8] Along with The Land's role in the promise, and as the centre of the earth, Edmund

5. F. W. Dillistone, _Traditional Symbols and the Contemporary World_, ch. 6.

6. Martin Buber, _Israel und Palestine_, p. 11. It is significant that the word _'eretz_ can be both masculine and feminine. The plural form is feminine, _'arâtzōth_.

7. These passages are not unambiguous. In taking them to refer not only to the people of Israel as married to Yahweh but also to The Land as so married, I follow Jacob, _Israël dans la perspective biblique_.

8. Rubenstein, _After Auschwitz_, p. 106. See, also, J. Z. Smith, _Map Is Not Territory_, p. 106, on the subject. Not all agree that the rediscovery to which Rubenstein refers is to be welcomed. Some look upon it as a retrogression to the territorial gods of ancient paganism (see J. J. Petuchowski, _Zion Reconsidered_, pp. 84–85). Clearly "paganism" can crouch at the door ready to leap in even in Judaism.

Jacob has rightly identified the conjugal myth of the marriage of the people with The Land as the governing source for the doctrine of The Land in Judaism.[9] The mythological expressions which, in liturgy and in song, express the significance of The Land as such are unmistakably personal and powerful. Into the discussion of this question, reopened by Rubenstein, we are not competent to enter. We merely recognize that the doctrine of The Land has age-old mythological roots, not to be limited to the soil of Israel.

Just as Christians recognize "the scandal of particularity" in the incarnation, in Christ, so for many religious Jews (though their particular doctrine is not so central as is the incarnation of Christ for Christians) there is a scandal of territorial particularity in Judaism. The Land is so embedded in the heart of Judaism, the Torah, that—so its sources, worship, theology, and often its history attest—it is finally inseparable from it. As J. Juster insisted, "Il faut . . . ne pas essayer de diviser des choses indivisibles."[10] However, all this being recognized, it remains to emphasize one thing. If by a territorial religion is meant, as is usually the case, "a cult whose constituency is a territorial group identified by common occupation of a particular land area, so that membership of the cult is in the final instance a consequence of residence and not kinship or ethnic designation,"[11] then Judaism is not a territorial religion: The Land is *not* the essence.

9. E. Jacob, "Les Trois Racines d'une théologie de la 'Terre' dans l'A.T."

10. Quoted in G. F. Moore, *Judaism*, 1, 234.

11. J. M. Schoffeleers, *Guardians of the Land: Essays on the Central African Territorial Cults*, p. 1.

4

Reflections on the Doctrine of The Land

What are we, finally, to make of this doctrine of The Land which gives theological significance—as it has been crudely put—"to a piece of real estate"? Certain 'disaffected' Jews, no less than Gentiles, have dismissed it as a bizarre and anachronistic superstition, unworthy of serious consideration. To many rationalists, and even humanists, especially since the Enlightenment,[1] in a rational universe the doctrine is an affront. This response is generally coupled with the assumption that the doctrine is simply an aspect of that other doctrine of "chosenness" or "election" that—so it is claimed—has irrationally and arrogantly afflicted (a verb chosen advisedly) the Jewish people, the particularism of The Land being, in fact, an especially primitive expression of the unacceptable particularism of the Jewish faith.

Even when sponsored by such as Martin Buber, however, the claim that the doctrine of The Land is altogether unique is now recognized to be hard to substantiate.[2] Mutatis mutandis, historians of religion, especially, have discovered similar, if not identical, attitudes towards their particular lands among other peoples. The Jews' interpretation of The Land as an enclave in the wilderness, and as the pillar and centre of the cosmos, and their experience of separation from The Land as an exile of devastating chaos, find parallels in other traditions. However much a mark of "primitive" Jewish particularism, the doctrine has its roots in what seems to be a universal human need.[3]

It is not surprising, therefore, that recently the deep concern with The Land in Judaism has been approached afresh. Some interpret it psychologically: the doctrine is simply the communal or societary expression of the psychological need of every child or person to be

---

1. See Arthur Hertzberg, *The French Enlightenment and the Jews*, passim.

2. In the view of J. Weston Le Bar, Distinguished Professor of Anthropology, Duke University, Judaism is unique in its insistence on The Land as "chosen" and "promised" (oral communication). But the notion of "manifest destiny" in American history, for example offers at least a parallel.

3. Professor D. Daube, in a private communication, urges this. In his judgment this psychological fact gives a profound meaning and universal ground for the attachment to The Land.

"rooted" in his or her own home or space, to cling to accustomed ground. Others have emphasized its biological roots. Robert Ardrey has urged that, in insisting on their eternal relationship with The Land, the Jews are simply obeying what he calls "a territorial imperative," which governs human no less than animal behavior.[4] "Territory" is in essence a psychological expression, and the possession of a territory serves the purposes of security, stimulation, and identity.

We have elsewhere subjected Ardrey's position to criticism.[5] Certain of his historical data are questionable, and he fails to do justice to the specifically religious dimensions of Israel's relation to The Land of Yahweh. That relation was not simply territorial, in Ardrey's sense, but also theological. So, too, the role of the Law cannot be explained solely in terms of the hostility to outside pressures to which Ardrey refers. The commandments were not so much a fence around the Jews, as he insists, as they were around the Torah itself. I also understand that many scientists qualified to examine his concept of the territorial imperative find it untenable.

But Ardrey's insistence on the importance of territory and its loss for a people can hardly be gainsaid. Aspects of Jewish history confirm him in this. Apart from psychological consequences of deterritorialization too obvious to need discussion, there are deep cultural deprivations. The character of Yiddish illustrates how "unnatural," in the strict sense, are the results of the radical divorce from The Land in the literature of the deterritorialized. That language was the product of generations of Jews who lived in ghettoes in various countries in Europe, but understood their homeland to be elsewhere. In general, for example, the ghetto Jew knew the flora and fauna of Palestine better than he did those of Poland or Russia. In *The World of Scholem Aleichem,* Maurice Samuel holds that:

Yiddish is a folk language, but unlike all other folk languages, it has no base in nature. It is poor, almost bankrupt, by comparison with other languages in the vocabulary of field and forest and stream. . . . Yiddish has almost no flowers . . . the very words for the common flowers which are familiar to city dwellers everywhere are lacking in Yiddish. Yiddish is a world almost devoid of trees. . . . The animal world is almost depopulated in Yiddish . . . the skies are practically empty of birds. . . . There is likewise a dearth of fish . . . there are no nature descriptions to be found anywhere in Yiddish prose or poetry. . . . All these expressions and perceptions were lacking because their material was withheld from the Jews. There were large areas of what we generally call folk self-expression to which the Jews were forever strangers.[6]

4. See GL, appendix 3, pp. 405–8, on Ardrey's *The Territorial Imperative.*

5. Ibid. For a severe critique of Ardrey, see also Ashley Montague, "The New Litany of Innate Depravity, or Original Sin Revisited."

6. M. Samuel, *The World of Scholem Aleichem,* pp. 194–96.

This needs no comment. Language is the life-blood of a culture. It is not surprising that many Jews have seen in the amazing renaissance of Hebrew in modern Israel a sure sign of the messianic character of that state.

Then again, there are the political deprivations incurred in deterritorialization. Hannah Arendt rightly emphasized the degeneration suffered by Jews denied political self-expression and control of their own land—in her view the most tragic of all denials.[7] The American Indians leap to mind. And one has simply to ask, by way of a parallel example, what "the Southland" (a significant term: one does not speak of "the Northland" although one does speak of the North and the South) would have developed into had not Southerners been allowed to reenter the mainstream of the political life of the United States, to appreciate something of the degree of the deprivation that deterritorialized Jews have suffered over the centuries, and the overwhelming intensity with which the emergence of the Jewish state was acclaimed. From one angle age-long adherence to the doctrine of The Land can be understood as a protest against deterritorialization. In varying degrees, however, we are all now children of the Enlightenment, a movement which searched for universals in every sphere,[8] and recognized no particularism or uniqueness, least of all of a geographic-religious kind. The Enlightenment still predisposes us to pass by, and often to scorn, the notion of a particular Land for Judaism. The very words "Chosen People," "Chosen Land" strike an unsympathetic chord. Christian and even Jewish thinkers (under the influence of the former) have preferred to deal with Judaism in conceptual categories derived from Christian theology instead of in terms of the geographic and other data provided by the earlier faith itself, and have in particular concentrated on time to the neglect of space.[9] For example, it is only

7. See Hannah Arendt, *The Jew as Pariah*.

8. See Hertzberg, *Enlightenment and the Jews;* also J. A. Sanders, "Text and Canon," pp. 27–28.

9. See *GL*, p. 66, n. 4; also, typically, Martin Buber, ed., *Jüdische Künstler,* p. 7: "The Jew of antiquity was more an audient than a visual being and felt more in terms of time than of space," Buber writes. André Neher is more balanced: "Mais Israël en découvrant le temps a aussi découvert l'espace qui est cet espace réduit de la terre d'Israël, couronné par Jerusalem" (*Rencontre,* p. 78). This book has concentrated on territory and bypassed the question of time. My insistence on the recurring pattern of exile and return in Jewish history may be taken as being more in accord with a cyclical view of time (usually associated with the Greeks) than with the dominant view of time in the Bible, which has often been taken as linear (see, especially, O. Cullman, *Christ and Time*). But the recurring "fulfillment" pattern coexists with a search for the transcendent, and there *is* a dénouement to the recurring pattern in

very recently that attempts have been made to ask how the writers of the New Testament, the foundation document of Christianity, reacted to the doctrine of The Land. The reasons for this tardiness are not only that the earliest Jewish Christians have left so few documents, and that the early Christian movement quickly became predominantly Gentile, so that the New Testament is largely concerned with non-Jews, to whom the question of The Land was not primary. Beginning with the New Testament, and certainly since St. Augustine, Christianity in its major expressions has substituted for the holiness of place—The Land, Jerusalem, the Temple—the holiness of Christ. The Land—although called Holy in Christianity—is ultimately incidental in Christian affection and faith. Life "in Christ" replaces life "in The Land" as the highest blessing, so that the traditional Jewish doctrine of the unseverability of Land, people, and God is not upheld.[10]

---

rabbinic Judaism and Christianity—in the former in the map without territory, the portable Torah, and in the latter in the advent of Christ, although both religions also retain hope for the ultimate future. (In much of Zionism, the dénouement comes to be regarded as politically achieved in the emergence and creation of the state of Israel.) See, further, *GL*, p. 36, where I quote G. von Rad, *The Problem of the Hexateuch*, p. 297: "Promises which have been fulfilled in history are not thereby exhausted of their content but remain as promises on a different level." Contrast Freedman pp. 103–104 below.

10. No effort is made here to deal with the specifically Christian responses to the territorial doctrine of Judaism. The evidence for these in the New Testament was examined in *GL*, pp. 161–376. The achievement of a largely unexpressed consensus among the main bodies of Christians was long in emerging (see, for example, R. J. Vair, "The Old Testament Promise of the Land as Reinterpreted in First- and Second-Century Christianity"). Mutatis mutandis, there has continued to be a degree of literal adherence to the territorial dimension of Judaism, especially among certain fundamentalist sects and the Mormons (see W. D. Davies, "Israel, Mormons, and The Land," pp. 80–92). In its dominant expressions, however, Christianity has demanded the deterritorialization of the theological tradition it inherited from the people of Israel. But such deterritorialization does not conflict with the positive aspects of the doctrine of The Land expressed here. In "Judaïsme et Christianisme," a response to Professor David Flusser's review of *GL*, for example, Father Pierre Benoit observed:

[Le Professeur Flusser] reproche aux Chrétiens de réclamerdes Juifs qu'ils cessent d'être des Juifs, et deviennent des Gentils dans le Christ. Je réponds à ce grief par une distinction. Le dilemme énoncé par Flusser est ambigu: il parle du Juif devenant chrétien "sans abolir le caractère et le mode qui lui sont propres, et sans renoncer aux promesses spéciales qu'il a reçues de Dieu," ou au contraire "en abandonnant le caractère spécial et les prétentions spéciales du Juif." L'alternative est mal proposée dans le mesure oú elle ne

But all this has been at a price. In understandably insisting that the territorial doctrine has been transcended in the Gospel, Christianity has often failed to do justice to the cultural and historical dimension which that doctrine preserved. Judaism's insistence that the people of Israel needed a land through which and within which fully to express its identity, that that people had to have a "space" which it could turn into its own "place," probably points to a truth about all people, ultimately even for nomadic people, who, where opportunity offers, tend to seek a place in which to settle. Usually between nomadic and settled peoples, where they are continguous, there is constant movement from one to the other.[11] Nor should it be overlooked that nomads lay claim to the "territory" of their particular wanderings, even though they do not settle down in it. A human community needs a geographic dimension of its own within which and through which to express

---

distingue pas entre l'aspect ethnico-politique que est en effet propre au peuple particulier d'Israël, et l'aspect proprement religieux que devait selon le plan de Dieu s'étendre en s'élargissant à toute la communauté humaine. [p. 149] The Christian demand for the deterritorialization of faith does not of necessity ignore or deny the natural and justifiable ethnic-political necessities of the Jewish people, The claims of Jewish ethnicity were wrestled with in the earliest period of the Christian movement (see W. D. Davies, "Paul and the People of Israel," especially pp. 31–36). That they were subsequently ignored is part of the tragedy of Christian history. For the sake of completeness, albeit not to exonerate Christianity for its neglect of the problem of ethnicity and territory in Judiasm, it should be noted that some expressions of Judaism itself have been equally concerned to detach themselves from that problem. Thus B. M. Bokser, in a review of *GL*, can write of the rabbis after 70 C.E.:

Torah, as the rabbis saw it, contains the key to the world and to the nature of existence. Of course, some rabbinic circles provided means to remember the Temple. But holiness was now divorced from a single place. The way of Torah enabled each individual to bring holiness into daily life, no longer by means of the Temple. The new set of metaphors reflects a conscious discontinuity, in contrast to the Christian concept which merely continued the old motif of holiness of Temple in a new way. The holiness of a single person, Jesus, replaces that of a single place, in faith, the Christian community represents the true Temple. *In contrast, Torah, in the emerging rabbinic movement, was not just a comfort to Jews without a Temple, but was the basis for a new piety, one quite different from that of Christianity and the Second Temple.* [p. 74. Italics added.]

That deterritorialization was only slowly achieved in Christianity appears from Vair, "The Old Testament Promise of the Land"; see, too, Max Warren, "The Concept and Historic Experience with Land in Major Western Religious Traditions," in the *Proceedings of the Jerusalem Colloquium on Religion, Peoplehood, Nation, and Land*, and the discussion in ibid., pp. 201–8.

11. See Lesley Hazleton, "The Forgotten Israelis."

itself. Judaism's insistence that the occupancy of The Land is not absolute but conditioned by obedience to the Torah, that observance and nonobservance of the commandments have geographic, territorial, and cosmic consequences, points to the truth that ecology is indissoluble from morality, land and law being mutually dependent, and that a people is ultimately responsible for the maintenance of its "place."

The Jewish people's experience of exile as a "chaos" to be overcome, although often creative, reveals the price probably paid by all peoples whose territorial roots are cut.[12] The Jewish engagement with The Land is, therefore, a paradigm of most, if not all peoples' engagement with their lands. 'Abd Al-Tāfahum has expressed the same truth: "We do not rightly understand the Old Testament's sense of place and people unless we know that it mirrors and educates the self-awareness of all lands and dwellers. The nationhood of Israel, the love of Zion, has its counterpart in every continent."[13]

The struggles between Judaism and Christianity in past centuries, when the latter in its mainstream chose disenlandisement (to employ the ugly word used by 'Abd Al Tāfahum), can no longer govern our thinking on the question of The Land. Without the concreteness of the demand to express community in and through the actualities of space—without the soiling of hands with the soil, so to speak—we

12. On exile as "chaos," see J. Z. Smith, *Map Is Not Territory*, p. 119. The views of Sir Isaiah Berlin seem largely to converge with those expressed here (see J. Lieberson and S. Morgenbesser, "The Choices of Isaiah Berlin," a review of *The Idea of Freedom: Essays in Honor of Isaiah Berlin,* ed. Alan Ryan, and Berlin's *Against the Current: Essays on the History of Ideas).* Berlin agrees with Herder that eluding or denying the need to be rooted in a particular group robs men of dignity and self-identity. Different nations or cultures can emerge alongside one another, respecting each other's activities, without engendering conflict. "The values of a group are neither portable nor exchangeable but unique, historical, irreplaceable," write Lieberson and Morgenbesser (p. 11). So Herder, and so Berlin apparently. It is imperative to recognize that the self-expression of a group or people, and even more of a nation, can be twisted into aggressive nationalism, as in Europe and elsewhere in the nineteenth and twentieth centuries; but its denial is as dangerous as its jingoistic affirmation. Such doctrines as that of The Land are clearly and notoriously prone to political and ideological distortion, especially when dressed up in terms of psychology and biology. As Mr. Richard Holway has reminded me, science tends to lend authority to any ideology. Davidic imperial ambitions possibly influenced the doctrine of The Land. But the misuse of a doctrine is no proof either of its truth or falsity; its value can be assessed apart from its misuse. The aim here has been to stimulate reflection on the meaning and value of the doctrine of The Land, not to foreclose discussion of its beneficial potentialities or dangers.

13. 'Abd Al-Tāfahum, "Doctrine."

are in danger of unrealism. The false romanticism, the unrealism, and the individualistic, otherworldly spirituality and false dualism of much in Christian history, although it has other sources in Hellenism and in recent years in a revolt against technological secularism, may not be wholly unconnected with the radical break with The Land as much of Judaism has understood it. It has been held by some that this was one of the factors that ultimately led to the massive protest of early Marxism against false spirituality. The events of our time, in which we have seen the horrendous consequences of deterritorializing peoples in the Far East, the Near East, and Europe, have confirmed that this is to cut their deepest psychological and cultural roots. Many Christian peoples in the West have often been able to ignore these consequences and to escape conceptually into an unrooted universalism. But this is because they have for the most part been able to assume their rootedness and have never known any territorial break comparable with that experienced by Jews, nor been compelled to come to terms even with the possibility of such. The uniqueness of the Jewish doctrine lies not in the emotional experience that gave it birth, however, but in the theological intensity with which it is held.

At this point, the choice is clear. One may assume, in the manner of modern rationalism, that Jewish religion, as is the case with all religions, is the natural outgrowth of a people's efforts to ensure its own survival and find answers to the problems of existence. If so, the theological aspect of the doctrine of The Land can be dismissed.[14] Or one may follow the path suggested by Amos Wilder:

14. The issue has again been renewed in a very important study by Norman K. Gottwald, *The Tribes of Yahweh*. Even had this come to hand earlier, I do not have the competence to assess adequately its massive knowledge and honest wrestling with themes related to that dealt with here. If I understand Gottwald aright, he regards the doctrine of chosenness to be an outgrowth of the sociological context of the early tribes of Israel. These tribes differed radically from their neighbors in various significant ways and strove to preserve or ensure this difference through the development of that doctrine (see pp. 692–93, 702 f., 799 n. 639). This means, it seems to me, that the theology of the doctrine is dissolved into, or absorbed by, sociology. At the risk of impertinence in responding to such an erudite volume in a footnote, I hesitatingly submit two reflections.

First, the doctrine of Israel as the "Chosen People," with which is tied up the doctrine of The Land, certainly only reached definiteness in the postexilic period, however much it may be related to the earlier sociological context described by Gottwald. The theological terms *baḥar* (to choose) and *bâḥûr* (chosen), used in connection with the people of Israel, are creations of the Deuteronomic school and of Deutero-Isaiah respectively—that is, they emerged at a time much later than that dealt with by Gottwald (see T. C.

There is an inseparable link between God's People, Law and Land. Without this "materialism" Judaism could not have made its fundamental contribution to Christianity, nor could it continue to bear its full witness to the world. It is true that the new faith universalized Zion. But the families and kindreds and peoples in Christendom have each their own form of rootedness and love

---

Vriezen, *Die Erwählung Israels nach dem A.T.,* and H. H. Rowley, *The Biblical Doctrine of Election).*

And, secondly, I may put the same kind of simple question to Gottwald that I posed to H. R. Trevor-Roper, who found the clue to the peculiarity of Israel's history in its geographical context (see *GL,* p. 89 n. 27). Until Gottwald's analysis is further examined, can we be sure that the sociological context of the tribes of Israel was unique? We may presume that they shared much of their geographical and, however distinctive, surely also much of their sociological background with other contemporary and contiguous groups. Why, then, should the doctrine of chosenness and of The Land emerge only among them? Gottwald acutely and impressively raises again an old question: does the recognition of the uniqueness of the sociological context of the early tribes of Israel (if such uniqueness be admitted) adequately account for the distinctiveness of their theology? Can we finally dissolve theology into sociology in the study of Jewish history? It is undeniable that the sociological *conditions* the theological. But does it *determine* the latter? Was it not precisely the peculiarity of its religious experience—that is, its experience of a revelation of the Divine—that explains the very radical difference between the response of the tribes of Israel to the surrounding milieu and that of other contemporary and contiguous groups? Backgrounds and influences, sociological, historical, and other, *are* important for the understanding of the doctrine of chosenness and of The Land, as of other doctrines. But Judaism as a phenomenon in human history must be seen in terms of depths as well as of horizontal links. Here the idea of revelation has its rights. In a letter to me in 1976 commenting on the mysterious faith which goes back to Abraham, Dr. J. S. Whale put the matter forcibly [to make his words directly pertinent in response to Gottwald, "born of social circumstances" has been inserted after "ideology"]:

> What if so thoroughgoing and absolute a belief in God and his covenantal purpose, the *Sh'ma'* . . . should mean that here in Abraham ideology [born of social circumstances] really becomes theology? What if the obsessive, subjective "cognition" expressed in the *Sh'ma'* should point to objective reality? . . . What if the Hexateuch should be right and Marcion wrong?

To answer the question thus posed in the negative is to reduce Judaism and Christianity to a tragic illusion, however many ways that illusion may or may not be conceded to have been efficacious and beneficial. Ben Gurion could treat this illusion with levity, jauntily claiming that "God did not create the Jews, the Jews created God." No one could accuse Gottwald of such levity. But does his position finally lead to any other conclusion than that of Ben Gurion?

of land; and God blesses and rules in and through these dimensions—but also limits and judges them all, including Zionism, in terms of his wider purposes. . . .

How far from understanding the human texture of God's working are all these mysticisms and spiritualisms which attract so many today![15]

Wilder's reference to the judgment on all nations leads us to the final stage of our response to the territorial doctrine of Judaism. By some strange alchemy this most earthly doctrine has often, apparently without difficulty, been transformed almost to its opposite. The Land has been spiritualized and transcendentalized—that is, it has been made into a symbol of an ideal order either in this world or in the supernatural "world to come." Jews and Christians have both been engaged in this exercise across the centuries. The evidence for this in Judaism is clear in the Mishnah and earlier. In both Eastern and Western Christianity, such transcendentalizing and spiritualizing has persisted from the first century to the present—for example, in the hope for "a land of pure delight, where saints immortal reign" and for "Jerusalem the Golden." It is natural to see in all this simply a means of depriving the doctrine of The Land of the "crass" materiality which makes it a scandal to the "spiritual," and of circumventing the problem posed by territorial particularity both for Judaism and Christianity. But the process of transcendentalizing and spiritualizing The Land is more than this. It points to the recognition in both religions that, however desirable, the fulfillment of the terrestrial hope for The Land, or for any land, would not suffice to assuage the more than terrestrial aspirations of Israel or of any people. As Lurianism among many other movements shows, Israel and humanity as a whole have been concerned not only with a terrestrial destiny, but—so to put it—with what will be "when earth and man are gone / and suns and universes cease to be," when all terrestrial concerns have been swallowed up in "that day" when the whole temple of man's achievement will be buried in the debris of a universe in ruins. The hope for "The Land," transcendentalized and spiritualized, has enabled many to face "that day," and given assurance that their destiny lies in an eternal order, which "eye hath not seen nor ear heard." Paradoxically, The Land as actual geographic reality has sustained the people of Israel in its historical terrestrial pilgrimage. In the twentieth century this paradox is particularly significant. A new sensitivity, born of our experience in the space age, to our common perilous existence on what Archibald MacLeish calls "the little, lonely, floating planet, that tiny raft in the enormous empty night" which we call earth, has made us more acutely conscious of the questionableness of overemphasizing territorial divisions, however

15. In a private letter dated 3 October 1979.

desirable. Simultaneously, on the contrary, our awareness of spatial immensities has increased the felt need to have "roots," "a place," "a territory." The need to be rooted, which engendered among Jews the doctrine of The Land anchored in the will of the Deity, is now more than ever a living need for every people. At the same time, the transitoriness and precariousness of human existence in the nuclear age compels a search for "The Land" which defies time and space. The doctrine of The Land as cherished by Judaism and reinterpreted both in that faith and in Christianity, points to the twofold human need for terrestrial roots and for the transcendent. The words of Psalm 62:11 can be said of it: "One thing God has spoken: two things have I learnt."

Finally, it must be recognized that, whether convincing or not, any effort to discover meaning in Judaism's understanding of The Land will appear to two kinds of Jews as irrelevant. The rabbis often sought what they called the grounds or reasons for the commandments, which so often appeared irrational, but only within limits. In the last resort, they submitted to the impregnable, infallible rock of the Tanak, which inseparably connected a chosen land with a chosen people. "The essence of Judaism," it has been asserted, "is the affirmation that the Jews are the chosen people; all else is commentary.[16] In its overemphasis on the isolation of one aspect of the Tanak, this is an exaggeration. But to religious Jews it is an exaggeration of a fundamental truth, carrying with it the eternal chosenness of The Land. To such Jews, rooted in their biblical certainties, such inquiry will appear irrelevant, trivial and, indeed, possibly impious.

But our efforts will seem equally irrelevant to Jews who have become detached, if not alienated, from the tradition of Judaism. The vast majority of Jews have been, and are, primarily concerned with survival and positive or negative assimilation in the lands where they find themselves,[17] and The Land is remote from the actualities of their lives. This was driven home very forcibly by Stanley Kunitz, who read parts of this work:

The critical question for me is the transition from historic Judaism to existential Jewishness, a phenomenon separable from religious practice. How to define

16. A. Hertzberg, *The Condition of Jewish Belief*, p. 90. Compare D. Patterson, *The Foundations of Modern Hebrew Literature* (London: Liberal Jewish Synagogue Press, 1961), pp. 7–8, and "Modern Hebrew Literature Goes on Aliyah," *Journal of Jewish Studies* 29 (Spring 1978): 75–84.

17. In this context, by negative assimilation is meant that process whereby Jews allow themselves to be swallowed up by a surrounding culture, so that they cease to be Jews; by positive assimilation, the effort made by Jews to make elements in surrounding cultures serve their own religious needs (see J. J. Petuchowski, *Zion Reconsidered*, pp. 124–29).

it? I am reminded of the twelfth century poet, Yang Wan-li, one of the Four Masters of Southern Sung poetry, who, after experiencing "enlightenment," addressed his disciples in these terms.
Now what is poetry? If you say it is simply a matter of words, I will say, A good poet gets rid of words. If you say it is simply a matter of meaning, I will say, A good poet gets rid of meaning. But you will say, if words and meaning are gotten rid of, where is the poetry? To this I reply, Get rid of words and meaning, and there is still poetry.
So, too, one might say, "Get rid of Land and Torah, and you still have Jews.". . . The nostalgia of exile is entwined with the passion of survivorship, all of it steeped in vestigial tribal feelings. I have always assumed that states of crisis and paradox are part of the birthright.[18]

The history of the doctrine of The Land is so complex that any endorsement of a simple literal understanding of the promise (as understood in Jewish orthodoxy) is critically unacceptable. At the same time the age-long engagement of Judaism with The Land in religious terms indicates that ethnicity and religion—despite the view expressed by Kunitz—are finally inseparable in Judaism. For us, nurtured though we be by the Enlightenment, that age long religious engagement constitutes part of the mystery of Israel in history. The obscurity of antiquity surrounds the origins of the doctrine of The Land with which we have been concerned. But although those origins and their detailed development ultimately elude us, what Jews believe to have happened has become a factor of undeniable historical and theological significance. That belief itself has become a historical datum. Its reality as an undeniable aspect of Judaism cannot be ignored. Across the centuries, Judaism has not usually displayed a rigid, unchangeable attitude towards and claim for The Land, but adaptability and compromise with the exigencies: its most characteristic aspect has been flexibility. A striking fact, previously mentioned, points to this: the term "holy land" seldom occurs in the Tanak, where the holiness of The Land is derivative (so that paradoxically the phrase "The Holy Land" is more native to Christians than to Jews). Later, the rabbis simply refarred to The Land, even while revering it. Judaism has shied away from absolutizing the claims of The Land, subordinating them to the Torah.[19]

18. Letter to the author dated 28 February 1980.
19. See *GL*, p. 29. We have failed to indicate previously that the devotion to The Land in Judaism has been what might be called a "generalized" one. Apart from the unmistakable attachment to Jerusalem (which is the quintessence of The Land, see *GL*, pp. 131–50), Judaism has certainly not been marked by especial devotion to "holy places" to which historical events have lent significance, as Christianity has been. This truism has often been expressed by claiming that Judaism reveres a "holy place"—The Land—and Christianity

It is arguable that the sober "myth" of Jamnia has longer and better served the survival of Jews and Judaism (if, indeed, these phenomena can ultimately be separated) than the more spectacular "myth" of Masada. In this century, no less than in the first, patient pliability and moderated enthusiasm are more likely to be constructive for Israel and the world than intransigence, however heroic.[20]

"holy places," such as Bethlehem, Galilee, Calvary and the site of the Resurrection. This explains why those Jews who settled in The Land did not concentrate on specific places (Jerusalem always being excepted), but were content to be "in The Land." In a letter dated 21 July 1980, Abba Eban writes:

[We] distinguish between a *general* sentiment of attachment to the Land of Israel—and a selective or preferential approach to those specific parts of the land that are most associated with the biblical story. In Zionist ideology, the Land of Israel is a generic term, and the biblical literature is a strong factor in determining the legitimacy of the return. As I point out, however, in my letter, there is no evidence in Zionist practice or rhetoric of any lesser feeling [for] newly settled areas in comparison with those of which the names resound throughout history.

One interesting point to remember is that during the twenty years of Israeli statehood prior to 1967, there is hardly any nostalgic literature about Hebron, Shechem, Bethel, or other places that lay outside Israel's jurisdiction. Since 1967, Hebron is the only place where there has been an ambition to create a Jewish presence in direct association with biblical memories. Here too, however, the desire to renew the attachment owes just as much to the fact of a Jewish settlement up to 1929 as to Hebron's lineage in terms of biblical associations.

20. On the two "myths" of Masada and Jamnia (which are interpretations of actual events, although the rabbinic sources never refer to Masada), see an illuminating study by Baila R. Shargel, "The Evolution of the Masada Myth." There is evidence that the "Masadic myth" is being found wanting by twentieth century Jewry, as it was by the sages in the first century. See Werblowsky p. 114 below for a moving statement.

5

The Territorial Dimension
of Judaism:
A Symposium

I
Kenneth Cragg

It is odd how identical roots can yield contrasted words. Thus *tempus* gives us both "temporal" and "temporary," while the corresponding *chronos* in Greek makes for "chronic" which is far from temporary when applied to a human condition. *Terra,* likewise, supplies both "territory," which can be localized and private, and "terrestrial" which applies to all on the spaceship of the globe. The same "earth" which carries the cargo of humanity can be dug with the individual spade.

The point in beginning this way is to illustrate that there are two crucial issues in and for Jewish existence, today as ever: How to have particularity without tragedy and how to marry a distinctive identity with a human universal. Neither problem is unique to Jewry but Jewish uniqueness gives a radical quality to both. "Territory" and the "terrestrial" dimension may be said to symbolize and also to embody this double situation. To try, if only briefly, to set W. D. Davies' *Territorial Dimension of Judaism* in the wider context of the terrestrial and the human will perhaps be the surest tribute to his careful scholarship and perceptive presentation. This current study has all the discipline and sensitivity evident in his earlier publications, especially among those in this field *The Gospel and the Land.* One's only complaint might be a regret that on several occasions here he allowed himself to lay aside a question with the surely inappropriate plea, ". . . a matter with which we are not competent to deal."

But, holding closely and unfailingly to his immediate brief, Davies documents with admirable balance and citation the nuances and the logic of the sense of The Land within the Jewish soul. The specialist will find here a sound analysis. A general reader is likely to want to pursue two related questions after first registering a general point. The related questions have to do with The Land's involvement with other inhabitants and with the inevitable corollary of power (keeping in mind the significance of the author's invariable usage of capital letters for his theme throughout his text). The general point is the degree to which what is here uniquely Hebraic nevertheless partakes of features elemental to all human habitat and history. Some simple review in this form may best serve to ponder the territorial/terrestrial dimension that Judaism occupies and which (often in tragic terms) occupies Judaism.

Birth/ancestry, land/habitation, and history/memory are manifestly universal human denominators in all awareness of identity. Those components consist of *who* we are *qua* tribe, or people, or seed; *where* we are in landscape and possession; and *whence* we came in time and story. They are also known as the ethnic dimension, the territorial dimension, and the historical dimension. Hebraic identity possesses all these in the awareness of Abraham and all the patriarchs, in the possession of the land of promise, and in the indelible memory of Exodus printed deeply in the entire psychic incorporation of Jewry.[1] It is important to realize that these are common human realities, implicit and explicit in all self-collectives. Jomo Kenyatta wrote in *Facing Mount Kenya:*

According to the tribal legend . . . in the beginning of things . . . the man Gikuyu, the founder of the tribe, was called by the Mogai (the Divider of the Universe), and was given as his share the land with the ravines, the rivers, the forests, the game and all the gifts that the Lord of Nature (Mogai) bestowed on mankind. At the same time Mogai made a big mountain which he called *Kere-Nyaga* (Mount Kenya), as his resting place when on inspection tour and as a sign of his wonders. He then took the man Gikuyu to the top of the mountain of mystery and showed him the beauty of the country that Mogai had given him.[2]

There is, of course, no suggestion that this is equatable with the texture—and certainly not with the relevance—of Yahweh, Abraham, Moses, Zion, and all that is Hebraic. Rather, it is to say that who, where, and whence we are denominate equally and universally all human being and meaning, and constitute indifferently all human difference. The biblical distinctiveness lies in the transcendental, mystical, metaphysical status understood by Hebraic faith to belong with

1. See David Daube: *The Exodus Patterns in the Bible* (London: Faber & Faber, 1963), with its intriguing case for the interplay of Exodus memory and Jewish social and legal forms and usages. The telling of the story incorporates aspects of law, e.g., in respect of slavery and its "redemption" while the former in turn inspires and symbolizes what "liberation" means and sets up a reason for it.

2. Jomo Kenyatta: *Facing Mount Kenya: The Tribal Life of the Gikuyu People,* with an Introduction by B. Malinowski (New York: Vintage Press, n.d.), p. 5.

Hebraic experience of seed, Land, and Exodus. "All our fathers . . . brought out . . . brought in . . . by an outstretched arm. . . ." "Wisdom pitched its tent in Israel." Whether seen by the outsider as a faith in faith, or understood inwardly as a divine *fiat* accountable to none but divine counsels, that rooted assurance of covenanted territory to a covenanted people through a covenanted story is the distinctive mark of the Hebraic, the Judaic, the Israeli readings of themselves.

It is also the perpetual crisis, for it pits distinctiveness against other inhabitants and thus necessitates the dimension of power. There never have been either in geographical or in historical settings of peoplehood any vacant lands or any past escaping times. There is always the actuality of competing occupancy and of disputed or disrupted memories. Davies only refers to these aspects at a tangent, so strictly does he interpret his attention to The Land per se.

What of the other inhabitants, whose names for the land, or parts of it—Canaan, Philistia—are often used in Hebrew story? ("Zion" itself is "the archaic name of the Jebusite acropolis that had *become* the city of David" [p. 82].) In the Joshua episode, their expulsion serves both the effective immigration of the Hebrew tribes and the condign retribution of an idolatrous people. Where an original "native" right is acknowledged it is understood to be overruled by the discretionary power of the God of Israel. The contemporary (or perhaps we should now say "recent") form of this issue within Zionism has been the idea that territory could be delimited by demography in the interests of homogeneity (witness the interesting piece here from Abba Eban pp. 76–77), with the parallel notion of "partitionability" of the land so as to ensure, approximately speaking, "a land without a people for a people without a land." But, except as a comfort to honorably troubled consciences, that hope has never been feasible and was categorically excluded by then Prime Minister Begin's policy of total territoriality. Homogeneity of Jewish population can perhaps be solved gradually in other ways: it certainly no longer pleads any forgoing in its interests of Eretz Yisrael.

By the same token—and, indeed, by several other tokens as well—there abides the problem of power. In the end land is untenable without statehood. This has certainly been the logic of political Zionism. The tradition of Joshua, David, and the Maccabees confirms it. "Return involved control of the land" (p. 81). The stockade of the settler became also the rampart of the defender. Other occupants made it inevitably so, just as the condition of Diaspora (which Zionism so tenaciously disavowed) was by contrast always the risk and the reality of sufferance. Just as the story in the Hexateuch was in no way the exchange of slavery in Egypt for tutelage in Canaan, so it was no part of the thrust of Zionism to have a Palestinian host country rather than a European one.

This inescapable political dimension of The Land still means what it meant in the biblical history, namely a perpetual tension with the "other" human. As that tension obtains, sadly but ineluctably, within a mandate that is transcendental, it acquires a pathos and a mystique that preoccupies the Jewish soul with survival over against the world. In the words of Rabbi Dow Marmur, "the mystical bond" between God and His People, of which The Land is the sacramental focus, constitutes "the neurotic tangle" which makes Judaic existence an antagonizing experience of antagonism.[3] We are all tragically caught in the shame and enormity of anti-Semitism, on the Gentile side, and in the jeopardy and anguish and frustration of Judaic countering, on the Judaic. The State of Israel, tragically, though conceived as a final solution, is proving only another installment of the same pain of being the Judaic particular.[4]

It is for this reason that the ultimate question, which must be asked in and beyond *The Territorial Dimension of Judaism,* takes us to the heart of what it is to "belong with humankind." For us all, in a contemporary history that is urgent for world community, identities must somehow be participatory. To be sure, there are no citizens of the world, if only for the reason that the world is not one city. Our particularities of birth and land and story are inescapable. But their sanctions must be within and not against the human whole. This is why the "territorial" must be also the "terrestrial." There are few tasks more spiritually strenuous than those which have to do with the Judaic part and the human whole.

KENNETH CRAGG is a Bishop in the Church of England and author of, among other works, *This Year in Jerusalem: Israel in Experience.*

II

David Noel Freedman

A fundamental category of scholarly literature is that which contributes to our understanding of things thought to be familiar by treating them from an original and stimulating point of view. W. D. Davies' *Territorial Dimension of Judaism* is a splendid exemplar of this category. Davies is

3. Dow Marmur: *Beyond Survival: Reflections on the Future of Judaism* (London: Darton, Longman & Todd, 1982), p. 93.

4. Reasons of space preclude a fuller treatment of this underlying issue of the Judaic within the human. Some contemporary aspects of it in the achievement, the paradoxes, and the tragedy evident in Zionism and Israel today, as this writer sees them, may be found in his *This Year in Jerusalem: Israel in Experience* (London: Darton, Longman & Todd, 1982).

an outstanding figure in New Testament scholarship, especially with regard to the relationship between early Christianity and contemporary Judaism. He has now embarked on an important study of a related but much neglected area, the place of The Land in biblical and post-biblical thought. He first wrote a major volume in *The Gospel and the Land* and has now supplemented it with a discussion of Jewish thought and doctrine on this topic of The Land. The material with which he deals is mostly familiar, but the insights provided and the approach pursued are of importance primarily because of his stature as a Christian scholar dealing with a subject of special contemporary importance and gravity. The question of the territoriality of Judaism is fraught with dangerous possibilities, and a dispassionate evaluation of this idea from the viewpoint of a Christian exegete and theologian is of great value.

Davies' scholarship is superior. At the same time the scholarship in this work eschews profundity in favor of extensiveness; Davies is attempting to cover a vast territory and must inevitably rely on secondary sources and scholarly opinions. His attempt at a synthesis is valiant and his message important. Perhaps the author or other scholars will pursue the matter further in the future, providing both the breadth and the depth of scholarship that should inform a task of this magnitude. This book, however, is intended to be programmatic, and it easily fulfills its role. The author calls attention to matters that have been neglected for too long in the dialogue between Christianity and Judaism, especially by those outside Judaism. It was neither necessary nor desirable to produce a volume large and thoroughly documented in order to make the main point. Moreover, a serious scholarly treatise on *The Gospel and The Land* lies behind this work; *The Territorial Dimension of Judaism* must be considered in the light of that earlier book.

No work that I can think of competes with this one. It opens up to discussion and debate the issue of The Land in biblical religion, especially as it was interpreted and understood by Judaism. The coming together of Christian scholar with Jewish territoriality is not unique, but Davies brings rare credentials and a remarkably balanced viewpoint.

It is difficult to assess the importance of this book. It raises serious and important questions, providing challenging insights and partial answers. It is well-balanced and readable, short and occasionally incisive. It is a mature statement by a senior, major scholar. At the same time it seems unfinished. At the end the reader is left with more quandaries than solutions, more doubts than certainties, though perhaps that is inevitable. One problem left unexplored is that of the historical dimension of Judaism and Christianity; the nearest thing to a theory of history in this work is a kind of cyclical view whereby the Jews occupy the land, are driven from it, wander about, and then reoccupy the land, like an endlessly replaying record. This portrayal may in fact reflect what happened, but it goes against the grain of biblical understanding and direction—that is, the last understanding of history that the Bible would sustain. Davies' book, then, tacitly assumes a disjuncture between biblical and postbiblical tradition and the course of history.

Unfortunately, Davies' usual freshness and incisiveness of style are not so well exemplified in this book as they might be, and a certain hastiness, perhaps induced by the effort to cover a great deal of material in a very circumscribed space, marks the work. Organization is also a problem; a certain amount of backing and filling, repetition and resumption, obscures the strong and important central theme of the work.

The Territorial Dimension of Judaism makes a significant contribution to the study of this highly charged subject; Davies quite rightly offers a mixed or two-pronged commentary on the question of territoriality in Judaism. The doctrine of The Land persists throughout Jewish history, but its meaning and implications are diverse. Further, he correctly points out that a material, historical interpretation of the doctrine and a spiritual, transcendental interpretation flow into and out of each other so that it is difficult to separate them even in extreme cases. Where does one idea begin and the other end?

Perhaps we expect too much in hoping for resolution. Even the longed-for guidance for the thinking of serious people, puzzled and disturbed by the apparent historical consequences of the doctrine of The Land in the lives of peoples and lands in the Near East today, almost a reenactment of the first Exodus, conquest, and settlement, may be too much to ask. If questions were raised about the ultimate meaning of the doctrine of The Land in those first days of Judaism, they must have died with the questioners; at least they were not preserved in the canon. Do we have better insights today? A more vigorous and determined position on the part of the author would help; if the inevitable position is equivocal or balanced, his statement might at least be more forceful.

Davies has written a very important book. It is straightforward and unsentimental, and it lays bare one of the central problems confronting those of either branch of the family of faith. Perhaps finally only those who live within the life-structure of the Torah can understand what it means to Jews, and hence only those who share in the destiny of the Jewish people can appreciate what the territorial doctrine of Judaism signifies to them.

DAVID NOEL FREEDMAN, general editor of the Anchor Bible Series, is Professor of Hebrew Bible and Director of the Program on Studies in Religion at the University of Michigan.

III

Arthur Hertzberg

W. D. Davies is a learned, exact, brilliant, and profound scholar of what those in the "trade" call intertestamentary studies—that is, of the period in Jewish history in which sects abounded, rabbinic Judaism was fashioned, and Christianity seceded to undertake its mission to the Gentiles. He belongs to a distinguished line of Christian scholars of rabbinic Judaism, which was graced in the last generation by George Foot Moore and Travers Herford, among others.

All of his citations are correct and in place, and they add up to an intelligent and convincing description of the place of the Holy Land in Judaism—and yet, correct though he is on every page, a close reading of the Davies book has convinced me that he is indeed profoundly Christian, for his preconceptions, as unstated premises, descend from the Christian outlook and not from rabbinic Judaism.

He has, not incidentally, succeeded in persuading me, since his book has forced me to be critical both of his preconceptions and of mine, that I remain a Pharisee among Pharisees, *tout entier.*

The fundamental issue between us is the category of the Jewish religion that he mentions on occasion but that he essentially scants— that of people, the community, and the Holy Nation. Judaism is not, as he says several times, especially in his conclusion, a triad of God, The Land, and the Torah, with The Land in question as equally important, and certainly not religiously indispensable. The oft-quoted rabbinic saying (it is a summary of Talmudic attitudes, though as such it does not exist in the early literature) is that "Israel, God, and the Torah are one." Here The Land is not even mentioned, though rabbinic Judaism insists, as Davies quite correctly says repeatedly, that it is the place to which God led The People.

Why does Davies, the learned Christian scholar of rabbinics, construct a triadic description of Judaism of his own to substitute for the one that rabbinic Jews have themselves constructed?

I suspect that the answer to this question—and to my insistence on raising it—lies deep in both our earlier histories. Having been raised as a Christian, Davies can deal easily with the description of Judaism in which the unbreakable essence is God and the Torah, parallel to the unbreakable essence of Christianity, which is Christ and the gospel. The connection to The Land became dispensable early on to Christians and this connection can easily, and even correctly, be described as much more central to Jews, but not fundamental even to them, as they went out into the Diaspora to live on Torah and the universal elements of their religion.

Community and people are much more difficult concepts for Jews and Christians to agree upon, even subconsciously. Here is where the essential break (I argue from my Jewish perspective) between Judaism and Christianity occurred. Rabbinic Judaism insisted that biblical universalism meant, even in its widest outreach, the mission of Israel according to the flesh, of God's Chosen People among the nations of the world. It could never mean the breaking of this category, at least not until the end of time and history. Rabbinic Judaism rejected the idea that time and history ended one Friday afternoon on Golgotha.

Davies knows this, of course, and he regards such emphasis on the Chosen People as "an exaggeration"; he gently chides me on something I have written on this subject in one of the concluding pages of his book. An exaggeration is precisely what it is not—it is the cornerstone and capstone of rabbinic Judaism.

It is self-evident in historic fact that Judaism can survive elsewhere than The Land of Israel; it has done precisely that for at least twenty centuries. From the perspective of rabbinic Judaism, the religious question is: Does Judaism in the Diaspora survive in its full stature? Here the answer is an unequivocal no. The bulk of the 613 positive and negative commandments refer to situations that can occur only in The Land of Israel, even in pre-messianic times, before the Temple is restored and its worship is reinstituted, for there is a whole host of *mitzvot* that apply to agriculture in the Holy Land. The observant Jew in the Diaspora is, from the very beginning, a less obedient one, a truncated version of the fullness of Judaism.

It is this religious insight that is a prime source of modern Zionism. In the nineteenth century, various quite secularist thinkers and politicians pointed out that assimilation and anti-Semitism were both forms of pressure on Jewish existence which were destructive of the community and of what remained of its authenticity and its dignity. The most deeply religious of these figures, A. B. Gordon and Martin Buber, both pointed out that the character of the Jewish people had been fashioned through its contact with the Holy Land and that it could return to its authenticity by reencountering The Land. The persistent outcry of all wings of modern Zionism for an end of powerlessness, which means that Jews should no longer be under the rule of Gentiles, is an expression of an age-old insistence on the full life of an untroubled community, "every man under his own vine and every man under his own fig tree." A partial Judaism can live everywhere, and that part can even be exaggeratedly intensified to make up for the rest that is not possible, but the whole of Judaism can live only in the Holy Land. The doctrine of Land in the Jewish religion is thus in my view a function not of the relationship between God and the Torah but of the encounter of Israel (according to the flesh) and Torah.

Though I agree with Davies that the Jewish religion reechoes even in the most secular versions of Zionism (very often despite themselves), I think that he underestimates that side of Zionism which is profoundly revolutionary. It was no accident that the majority of the Orthodox rejected, and ideologically still reject, Zionism as a modern movement. They do not see the restoration of Jews to The Land as the culmination of Jewish history, for the religious drama is still waiting to be played out. Modern Zionism is itself a deep quarrel about the meaning of Jewish history and only a minority of the religious, the Mizrachi, ever accepted even the notion that human effort towards the restoration of Jews to Zion was a necessary preamble to the redemption, and that that redemption had now begun. The majority of the believers and the majority of the secularists agreed that modern Zionism was a response to nineteenth- and twentieth-century conditions. It was as much a revolt against the religious past—an attempt to consign it to a prior stage of Jewish history—as was assimilation, the archenemy of Zionism.

Zionism is not being reconquered at present by religion, even though the influence of the religious minority is growing in the affairs of the Jewish state. One needs only to walk the streets of Tel Aviv on the Sabbath to be aware that the struggle between the Jewish past and the secular present of its majority is as yet unresolved. What unites both segments of the Jewish people is their sense of belonging to one people, to a community, both within The Land and worldwide.

ARTHUR HERTZBERG is Professor Emeritus in the Department of Religion at Dartmouth College, Hanover, New Hampshire. His most recent book is *Being Jewish in America* (Schocken Books).

IV

Jacob Neusner

Judaism focuses upon a particular place, but from the perspective of nowhere in particular. It is locative in the setting of utopia. The paradox flows from the peculiar circumstance in which the definitive documents of Judaism took shape. The Hexateuch—the five books of Moses plus Joshua—as well as the principal historical and prophetic books of the Scriptures—Judges, Samuel, and Kings—all reached their final closure outside of The Land of Israel and in consequence of the loss of The Land to Israel. From exile all eyes then turn to Jerusalem—no wonder the obsession! The greater part of biblical literature comes to us from writers bearing full knowledge of the loss of The Land—and of its recovery. It is no surprise, then, that The Land should stand as a principal mark of the enduring covenant between God and Israel. The other Torah, the oral one, moreover, reaches its fulfillment in the

Babylonian Talmud, which thus shapes the law of Judaism in complete awareness of a Land once held, then lost, and sorely missed. Accordingly, the yearning for The Land speaks out of the heart of the exiled nation. Judaism as we have known it imagines one place at its center, while framing life for Israel wherever Israel endures, so, as I said, becoming a locative religion emerging from utopia.

If the ambiguous circumstance of the exile's dreaming of home accounts for the utopian-locative paradox of Judaism, the Babylonian Talmud, for its part, knows no doubt that one may practice the holy way of life anywhere, anytime. The issues of the kind of Judaism founded upon the Talmud concern the sanctification of Israel wherever they may be: personal status, commercial transactions, the passing of the seasons. The system finds ample place for the Temple, hence for the holy city and the cult, to be sure. And why not, since, for the sages of the Babylonian Talmud, the return to Zion and the rebuilding of Jerusalem comprise the center of the symbolism of the messianic hope? There was no reason to leave such matters out. They contained no ambiguity about the present circumstances and served full well to join the messianic hope to the rabbinical discipline: Do this, so that will come about. Indeed, rabbinical Judaism is inconceivable without the messianic hope, hence without the full repertoire of Land-centered symbols into which it was cast. However, the Babylonian Talmudic sages nonetheless managed to bypass the critical issue of Land, by omitting from their program of study—hence, the tractates they created—all attention to what in the Mishnah, fully expresses and exposes the Land-centeredness of Judaism.

It is in the law, beginning with Scripture and proceeding to the Mishnah, that Judaism fully exposes its theology. The theology of the Mishnah, upon which the Babylonian Talmud rests, is one-sided: Israel can be Israel only in The Land of Israel. This position is expressed in two of six fundamental divisions of the Mishnah.

In the case of the massive legal system on the subject of cultic cleanness, the Mishnah's sixth and largest division (about 26 percent of the whole in volume), one simply cannot attain cultic cleanness outside of The Land of Israel. All foreign land is by definition unclean with corpse-uncleanness. Accordingly, someone located outside of The Land of Israel is as if he were dead; a corpse is irremediably unclean so far as the system of cultic cleanness is concerned. Death is beyond the frontiers, life is within. The Babylonian Talmud ignores the whole of the Mishnah's repertoire of laws on cultic cleanness, except for the one on woman's menstrual uncleanness, pertinent anywhere Israel might find itself.

In the case of the equally critical legal system on the subject of Israel's obligation to God for its sustenance through The Land, the Mishnah's first division, on agriculture, the message is equally clear. Israel holds The Land of Israel only as tenant; God is the landlord.

Israel must hand over rations designated by God for his servants, the priests, and other parts of the produce of The Land, as a rental fee or sacred tax owed to God for use of God's land (the view of Lev. 27:30). The point at which Israel becomes liable to pay this rent is the moment at which the farmer proposes to take for his own use the crops he has raised. In his study of Mishnah-tractate Masserot, the fundamental legal statement on this matter, Martin Jaffee says, "God's claims against the Land's produce . . . are . . . reflexes of those very claims on the part of Israelite farmers. God's interest in his share of the harvest is first provoked by the desire of the farmer for the ripened fruit of his labor. His claim to that fruit . . . become binding only when the farmer makes ready to claim his own rights to its use." The point is simple: for the Mishnah, to be Israel and clean, so holy, is to live in The Land and to eat, so share in its bounty with God, the owner, in a relationship of mutuality and reciprocity.

How does the Babylonian Talmud deal with these stunning and fundamental assertions of what it means to be Israel? The Mishnah's view, in the cited divisions, is that Israel lives only in the Holy Land. What it means to be Israel is to live life within the same framework of possession and emotion as God. The Babylonian Talmud ignores both divisions entirely. It turns the Mishnah as a whole into something quite different, serviceable everywhere in general, restricted to nowhere in particular.

The upshot is that when Israel in exile formed its fundamental vision of itself, it saw exile and redemption as the poles of its existence; life was lived everywhere within the aching heart, a yearning for some one place. At the same time, whenever the view from The Land became uppermost, the exiles managed to dispose of the claim that Israel could be Israel only in The Land (and State) of Israel by ignoring it. The great sages of Babylonia transmitted the Mishnah without its definitive divisions on agriculture and cleanness, turning it into something serviceable for the Golah.

American Jews of our own day, confronted once again with the claim that normality is to live in The Land and abnormality is to live abroad, authenticity is to be in Tel Aviv, inauthenticity anywhere else, do precisely what they want. They concede it all—amiably even professing feelings of remorse and guilt—and this they do in the English language, not in Hebrew, in statements composed on the other side of the world from Jerusalem. If there is anything normative in the territorial dimension of Judaism, it is in the never-to-be-resolved tensions, to be sure of a chronic, not an acute, nature, imposed upon the existence and imagination of the Jewish nation.

JACOB NEUSNER is Graduate Research Professor of Religious Studies at the University of South Florida, Tampa. He is a prolific scholar; several of his books are published by Fortress Press.

V
Krister Stendahl

W. D. Davies is a master of nuance. He does not have an equal among
New Testament scholars who are serious students of Jewish texts.
Since he now has graciously condensed and enriched his *The Gospel
and the Land: Early Christianity and Jewish Territorial Doctrine,* the full
spectrum is there. It is all there: the expansions and contractions, the
explosions and spiritualizations, the frustrations and realizations, Exodus and Conquest, Exile and Aliyah, Dispersion and Life in The
Land where the Torah is full. Nor is he just writing in the pattern of
"both-and," but the overt and covert interplays of motifs give reality
to the pictures that emerge.

With those pictures from history before us, a major question arises
in my mind. What then is the use(s) of this history—beyond the
indispensable and beautiful satisfaction of knowledge—in this case
richly tuned knowledge?

A student of this history is struck by the creativity of Jewish interpretation through the ages. Historians often tend to read such creativity negatively. Their nineteenth century heritage of establishing
"what actually happened" disposes them to see creative interpretations
as manipulations, making the best of what is, making virtues out of
necessities. The philosopher can say that if God has died, it is by
thousands of manipulative reinterpretations. Christians tend to think
of Jews as "the people of the Old Testament" in an anachronistic
fashion—not as the people seeking *(darash)* faith-filled interpretation
of the Torah, both "written" and "oral." Therefore the first lesson of
this history is that the Jewish people have a distinct gift of creative
and diverse interpretations. That is one sign of its resourcefulness, and
its capacity of survival and renewal.

It is often argued—especially by historians—that those who forget
their history will have to relive it. True enough, but it is equally true
that history never repeats itself fully. The analogies with the present
are never complete, and the variances, big or small, are as important
as the similarities. That is why the capacity of creative interpretation
is precious in a people with a long and revered history. This is so since
God is the creator *now* and not only in a sacred past or sacred book.
Here goes the line between philosophies or ideologies of history—and
a living faith in God.

The pictures presented by W. D. Davies are thus not motifs to
choose from; nor are they to be played against one another in a dialectic
fashion (the title of Davies' last chapter can lead one's thoughts in that
direction: "The Contradiction Resolved?"); nor should the final result
be a relativism where anything and nothing can be normative. Of
course, the pictures that emerge undercut the historical truisms of

tourist guides (those secular fundamentalists). Of course, the loud slogans of propagandists are seriously questioned. Of course, we learn to suspect self-righteous spiritualizations of safely landed· Christians. But the use of this historical panorama of Jewish thinking and feeling about The Land is not to supply the options from which to choose the right and the true ones. It seems to me that for the Jewish people this history rather calls for new acts of creative interpretation in the ongoing history of religious vision.

The State of Israel is a new thing. It is a modern, democratic nation among nations. It is not like Joshua's, David's, or Herod's. Analogies from history have limited density: nineteenth- and twentieth-century nationalism was the midwife of the State of Israel. It is irritating to listen to those who now fault Israel for having bought into the dated idea of nationalism, out of which all national liberation movements have grown. The political science discussion of the flaws and alternatives to nation-states with self-determination is significant. But it is a little much to hear it used against the liberation movement called Zionism, especially when such arguments are buttressed by references to Hermann Cohen's and other Jewish thinkers' glorification of Diaspora life.

In a certain sense Zionism—like all national liberation movements—achieved its goal with the establishment of nationhood and self-determination. The midwife, equipped with the secular skills to deliver, has done her duty. Now the agenda and the challenges are quite different. It is a question of *nurturing* the child born out of the womb of the Jewish people and out of the hope against hope for this child—not from a one hundred-year-old couple like Sarah and Abraham, but out of two thousand years of longing. And more than three thousand years of pondering and interpreting God's will.

Israel is a new thing with new joys and sorrows, duties and gifts. It is a nation among nations in a world of global interdependence. Its nationhood bears the marks of nineteenth-century nationalism, and its constitution the marks of twentieth-century Western democracy. In the world of nations Israel makes the Jewish people visible in new ways.

Furthermore, the establishment of Israel has engendered a Palestinian Arab struggle for national liberation and self-determination. Human Rights—that Enlightenment concept so different from benevolent attitudes toward strangers and sojourners in the biblical and Islamic traditions—is part of the agenda of Israel as of any nation.

In all these and many other respects Israel is a new thing in a new world. There are analogies, experience, and wisdom in the long tradition of the Jewish people. But they are analogies—all with a difference, and none ready for duplicating in the now.

The genius of Jewish tradition—perhaps most strikingly at Jamnia and at the other academies, building on the program of the earlier

Sages of Pharisaism—has been the eye for continuity by changes when the time and the situation made ancient truth uncouth. Such times and such situations were seen as a challenge to the teachers to "act for God" by creative and daringly new interpretation (Mishnah Berakoth 9:5 and its following teachings). This dimension of Jewish history lends special weight to the observation often made that Judaism is not so much a set of doctrines as it is a tradition of interpretation which is open-ended by definition.

What could be more obviously a new situation than a sovereign Israel in The Land after two thousand years, with insight and wisdom gathered in exile and dispersion? What a marvelous challenge to a people of creative interpretation!

Does my perspective differ from that of W. D. Davies? Perhaps it does, but I am not sure. It is as if he believes that the historian and the exegete could unearth a pure "theology" which would supply the answers, perhaps by synthesizing the long and diverse history of Jewish thoughts about The Land. He now and then voices the theologian's and exegete's fears of psychology, sociology, and anthropology. But when all is said and done, his most personal thoughts draw exactly on those "suspect" disciplines—as would I—for those supply tools by which we can best discern what constitutes the situation which now cries out for creative interpretations by Jews, and for us all.

KRISTER STENDAHL is the Andrew W. Mellon Professor Emeritus and Chaplain at Harvard Divinity School and former Bishop of Stockholm.

VI

R. J. Zwi Werblowsky

W. D. Davies' recent little book deserves to be not only carefully read but also thoughtfully pondered. High seriousness, impeccable scholarship, and an enviable lucidity are hallmarks of all his work. Since the appearance of *The Gospel and the Land* (I mention only the larger work and not the shorter articles dealing with the same and related themes) his name has come to be associated with what I consider to be an essentially correct thesis: Over and against the people- and territory-centered notion of holiness and of vocation as exemplified by the Jewish experience and articulated in the Hebrew Bible and later historical data, the New Testament has carried out a de-ethnization and especially de-territorialization of basic religious orientations. It was obvious that sooner or later Davies would have to address himself in greater detail to the specific nature, history, and varying social and spiritual roles played by this "territorial dimension" said to be so essential to, and so central in, Judaism. It is a pity that Davies as much as mentioned Ardrey, whose concept of a biological "territorial imperative" is the surest way to block any understanding of the biblical and postbiblical realities.

But the basic questions remain. How essential and central is "territory" in Judaism—and in precisely what sense? Was it always of the same kind or were there variations in accordance with varying historical circumstances? What exactly is this territorial hang-up (as modern American slang would call it) if examined on the basis of actual behavior (e.g., messianic movements or other movements of returning to the land), of eschatological postponement permitting accommodation with a theoretically short-term but de facto long-term Diaspora (or even "exile") condition, and of religious, and especially liturgical traditions relativizing these accommodations while keeping alive the basic principle of, and the commitment to, the territorial dimension— a commitment which could, potentially, always be reactivated and converted from theory (messianic hope, theological doctrine, nationalist ideology) into practice? To what extent was there a "spiritualization" of these originally very concrete conceptions? These are some of the questions addressed and discussed.

Yet in spite of the book's careful and exemplary scholarship, one cannot help detecting some serious flaws—the writer of these lines is aware that he is laying himself open to the charge of letting his ideological parti pris cloud his judgment instead of having scholarly objectivity illuminate it. Let others, and especially my friend and colleague W. D. Davies, judge.

In the first place it seems rather strange that the author, in spite of his genuine and profound understanding of the liturgical tradition and its significance, somehow fails to appreciate sufficiently its role in keeping the territorial dimension alive and preserving it in its full intensity (often in the teeth of social realities pulling in another direction) to the point where it could be inherited—duly transformed and secularized—by modern Judaism. Was there ever any real spiritualization of this dimension? Surely not, and especially not in Kabbalistic-mystical thought. Unlike Christianity, Judaism had a way of adding spiritual dimensions to earthly realities without "spiritualizing away" anything. Would Davies really consider the ideological and concomitant liturgical reforms of postemancipation Jewry (including their deletion of references to The Land) as "spiritual"? Whatever they were, they were certainly not that! The disjunction Jamnia versus Masada, that poor overworked horse, is a mirage, or rather a deliberate misunderstanding of the existential alternative between the strength to persevere in this territorial bond with long-term faith and hope versus an impatience that cannot brook long-term postponement. This false and misleading disjunction has caused some writers (not Davies!) to use the mischievous and, in fact, vicious expression "Masada Complex." What Masada really means is: "Jamnia was right. We want and must live. But if we must die, we'd rather die the Masada way than the Auschwitz way."

Is modern Zionism really a completely modern, political, secular-nationalist phenomenon? Might it not just be a modern transformation, a translation into modern political idiom of something that has much deeper roots? Was the evolution from the territorial solution of the Jewish problem (as originally envisaged by Pinsker and others) to Zionism the result of politico-socio-historical circumstance only or was it a genuine renaissance—that is, a return to the roots? Theologians nowadays never tire of pointing out the continuities with traditional religious ideas exhibited even by secular utopias. Apparently what is good for the Marxist goose does not apply to the Zionist gander.

At this point we touch what seems to me the essential weakness of Davies' study. The author proves himself a careful and sensitive exegete, but of a type that I would describe as very old school and very Protestant—were I not afraid of being completely misunderstood in my choice of these terms. What I am trying to say is that Davies is so much an "old school" exegete that in his devotion to historical description and interpretation he fails to be a historian, that is, to see the dynamic character of history. Understanding history means to grasp its open-endedness, to realize that to get at the essence of a historical phenomenon (and essence is both a critical principle and a developmental principle) one has to view it as an entity with "an inner, living flexibility, and a productive power . . . a germinative principle . . . not a metaphorical or dogmatic idea but a driving spiritual force which contains within itself purposes and values, and which elaborates these both consistently and accommodatingly." Understanding involves "at one and the same time both critical selection and historical fulfillment for the present and the future." It is therefore a creative act for those who not only see history but live it. That which is objective (in the dialectics between subjectivity and objectivity) is not "something that is just there to be simply picked up, but every time it is newly created, and *it is binding* because of the meshing together of what is possessed historically and the personal, conscientious shaping and transforming activity." These quotations are from an article written by Ernst Troeltsch at the beginning of this century. Most contemporary exegetical work, however scholarly and careful, has not yet caught up with the Troeltsch of eighty years ago.

One final remark. Davies seems occasionally to confuse "messianic" with "theological." It is—at least theoretically, and for those whose style of thinking is religious—quite possible to view the contemporary and very partial realization of the bond between the people and The

Land, in spite of or perhaps precisely because of its secularity, in a theological light while denying it any messianic/eschatological qualities. The resolute de-messianization of Zionism and the State of Israel could be (and probably is) a correct and religiously meaningful theological option in the struggle for an adequate Zionist and Israeli, and for that matter Jewish, self-understanding. The identification of theology with messianism may be a Christian conditioned reflex; it is a Jewish non sequitur (theoretically) as well as aberration (practically).

R. J. ZWI WERBLOWSKY is Martin Buber Professor of Comparative Religion at Hebrew University.

VII

J. S. Whale

Porphyry wrote contemptuously of Origen that he lives as a Christian but played the Greek. The Neoplatonist's sneer would hardly touch a modern Origen, for today our theologians play the Hebrew. None have been more effective in this role than W. D. Davies. He has enlarged our twentieth-century awareness of the Hebraic genius of the New Testament, and has declined to see the distinction between Jewish Torah and Christian gospel as a rigid dualism. His judgments are as careful as his learning is profound. His pro-Semitic sympathies are presented with the critical honesty of the great Alexandrian. Here, then, is an expert's appraisal and defense of the enduring Zionist faith that, as God of Israel, the God of the whole earth has a narrower territorial commitment. What are we to make of such divine parochialism?

The fundamental and ultimate issue which it raises is "the offense of particularity," of which chosen people and promised land (like the Incarnation itself) are notorious illustrations. Many now feel that the defensive war which Hebraic-Christian religion has long been fighting against the scientific and historical attacks of the Enlightenment is already largely lost, and that secularism is here to stay.

That is hardly the impression left by this masterly essay. It does not dispute, of course, the stubborn actuality of facts to which even sacrosanct tradition has to yield: Galileo, the real founder of the modern world, demolished such obscurantism once and for all. Israelite origins, concealed and disclosed by the swirling mists of tendentious legend, are acknowledged to have been tidied up by rabbinism in the five books of Moses. The promise to Abraham is therefore not as verifiable as the signings of the Magna Carta or the Declaration of Independence. Davies also reckons with the awkward fact that after 135 C.E. formal rabbinic theology virtually ignored the issue of The Land until modern times. Yet he argues convincingly that the closing verses of Amos have expressed the very essence of Judaism, and have been its most persistently held tradition, for almost three millennia.

His apologia for religious zeal so immensely creative might be more convincing if it were less reticent. He is not blind, of course, to Judaism's own record of its divinely sanctioned aggressions and savageries in Joshua and 1 Samuel, though he might well claim with Popper that values are not prejudiced by their origins and their pedigrees. He must know that conquest is always cruel, even when perpetrated by God's Elect; and that empire is always huge robbery, whether Roman or British, Muslim or Christian. Patriotism's territorial dimension is not peculiar to Israel; Milton himself could write of "God's Englishmen."

There is reticence too in a learned historical analysis which stops short of modern actualities in the Near East. It makes no mention of sworn evidence to an evil side to Judaism there, which the researches of the Dutch Dominican, Lucas Grollenberg, have made familiar. While Davies is deploring the "horrendous" price paid by a people whose territorial roots are cut, he is strangely forgetful of the ancient inhabitants of Canaan: had Philistines, Hivites, Jebusites, and others no territorial roots? And what of dispossessed Palestinians? Sauce for the goose is sauce for the gander. History abounds in conquests and dispossessions. If the Jewish engagement with The Land were the paradigm it is here alleged to be, the clock of world history itself would have to be put back to the first syllable of recorded time for all nations and peoples: which is absurd. And here the Diaspora is relevant, as Davies is careful to show. It was widespread long before 70 C.E., and multitudes of modern Jews prefer "exile" in the "wilderness" of their dispersion to a "return" to their promised land.

The preeminent and vital fact about Zionism is that its territorial obsession is primarily religious rather than political. Its Land is sacramental, symbolizing and conveying what is constitutive of and essential to this chosen people. Its belief in God is no mere theism, an academic theory, but existential and dynamic faith. Wellhausen, that prince of textual critics, himself observed that prayer is the only adequate confession of faith. Every synagogue means just that.

Zionism, like all true religion, is Anselm's famous Ontological Argument brought down to the brass tacks of concrete interpretation. This argument, the greatest of the classic "proofs" of the existence of God, asserts that the most perfect being conceivable by us must exist, since a perfection limited to an object of thought would obviously be less than a perfection including being. The very idea of God presupposes the fact of God standing behind it. If this were not so we could never rely on the power of the human mind to get at any truth at all. Belief in God is thus axiomatic for all rational enquiry.

Yes. But this substantially sound argument is ultimately dictated by faith: it is not proof. Anselm is still "betting his life" that *id quo nihil magis cogitary potest* really exists, really *is*. Thus the vital issue here is how this Absolute of our highest thought is to be interpreted. As personal? As Zeus or Yahweh? As God and Father of the Lord Jesus Christ? Here the classic religious answers differ. Many people (including many Jews) think that Land—a piece of real estate—can have no more than a contingent and temporal significance. It is not an eternal reality in the heart of God. Ben-Gurion's levity in saying "God did not create the Jews; the Jews created God" neatly popularized Kant's criticism of Anselm that the thought of $100 does not involve its existence in the pocket.

The last word here has to come from the self-authenticating truth and power of religious faith. It acquires its seminal and dynamic reality by being lived. Humanity's enduring religious insights have the stubborn actuality of facts since they are facts. Thomas Hardy once wrote the word "small" as a verb ("his shape smalled in the distance"); but, thinking of the probable objections of literary purists, he turned to Oxford's hugely detailed New English Dictionary for reassurance, and found his use of the word confirmed—by a quotation from an early novel by Thomas Hardy! The genius of the creator of *Tess* was its own authority. "I believe in order that I may understand" wrote the great Anselm: Abraham, whether an eponymous hero or not, must have said much the same thing.

J. S. WHALE is a theologian and historian who has taught at universities throughout Great Britain and the United States, including Oxford and Princeton, where he was senior fellow of the Council of Humanities. He is the author of *The Protestant Tradition* and *Christian Reunion: Historic Divisions Reconsidered*.

6

Further Reflections:
Response to a Symposium

W. D. DAVIES

Is most writing autobiographical? Certainly this study is the fruit of years of trying to do justice to Jewish existence and to wrestle with its mystery as I have encountered its amazingly rich but often tragic actuality. In this wrestling many have shared: David Daube, Louis Finkelstein, and Marc Tannenbaum in this country, Raphael Loews in the United Kingdom, and Shemaryahu Talmon, and Günter Stemberger in Austria. Four others I cannot forget—the late Abraham Heschel, James Parkes, Marcel Simon, and Ephraim Urbach of like spirit all who shared the same concerns and furthered them. My deepest appreciation goes to the editor of *Midstream*[1] for permission to reprint the Symposium on pp. 99–117 herein, and particularly to the contributors to it for their rich, careful, and penetrating responses to this little study—Kenneth Cragg, David N. Freedman, Arthur Hertzberg, Jacob Neusner, Krister Stendahl, R. J. Zwi Werblowsky and J. S. Whale. None of these named, however, is responsible for the judgments here expressed.

As in the Symposium, so generally there has been little criticism of the factual presentation offered here of the Jewish tradition bearing on The Land, although I am fully aware that the *halakic* (legal) evidence has only been briefly referred to; that remains to be presented elsewhere (see especially Neusner herein pp. 107 ff., and in many of his works). Apart from this gap, which only Rabbinical specialists can adequately fill, certain important matters have been pointed to as either inadequately emphasized or as missing. Such criticisms are not surprising; one could not handle all aspects of the theme in such a small volume. My chief aim in this, as in the former volume, *The Gospel and the Land,* was to inform and stimulate discussion. I shall here offer reflections largely evoked by the very constructive criticisms and comments offered mainly in the Symposium.

THE LAND AND THE HOLOCAUST

A Jewish colleague, Professor Joseph Jacob Blum, Duke University, expressed amazement and a polite resentment at my failure to relate

1. *Midstream* 29 (1983) 32–43.

the doctrine of The Land to the Holocaust. I myself was amazed to discover that I had even omitted to include the term "Holocaust" in the index. A detective story by G. K. Chesterton leaped to mind. Detectives from Scotland Yard had been called in as a last resort to solve what seemed a straightforward case of murder, but to no purpose. They had examined every possible clue without success, but omitted to consider a familiar figure who turned out to have been the murderer—the friendly postman who, as everyone knew, regularly went to the house of the victim to deliver mail. What had stared them in the face they had failed to see, and they had assumed the obvious. So it is with this little book. I must plead guilty to having assumed the obvious—the fact and significance of the Holocaust. We have been so numbed by the banality of evil[2]—its horrors have so weighed upon us and have been so placarded before us in films, on television, and in books that they have rightly become part of the very furniture of our twentieth-century minds. Thus I have always understood and justified the very creation of the State of Israel in terms of the Holocaust. Lest there be any misunderstanding on this score, let it be stated again that the Holocaust sealed long centuries of Jewish suffering and ipso facto established the conviction that the return to The Land and the creation of the State of Israel in The Land were a necessity. *The Proclamation of The Independence of Israel* contains the following words: "The holocaust that in our time destroyed millions of Jews in Europe, again proved beyond doubt that compelling need to solve the problem of Jewish homelessness and dependence by the renewal of the Jewish State in the Land of Israel. . . ."[3] There are other sanctions for the State of Israel. Hertzberg summarizes them as follows:

The right of the Jewish State to exist . . . was rooted in the unique tie of Jews to the land of their ancestors, on a need of the Jews for a homeland of their own in a dangerous century, on the growing assent of many nations, beginning with the Balfour Declaration and the League of Nations mandatory that Jewish needs and Jewish history had validity in their own right; and on the dedicated willingness of Jews to share mutual control of the territory with a Palestinian Arab state."[4]

2. See W. H. Poteat, *The Banality of Evil: The Darkness at the Centre,* The Loy H. Witherspoon Lecture (Charlotte, N.C.: University of North Carolina, 1988), referring to Hannah Arendt, *Eichmann in Jerusalem: A Report on the Banality of Evil (New York: Penguin, 1977).* See David K. Shipler, *Arab and Jew: Wounded Spirits in a Promised Land* (New York, Times Books 1986), 148, for example.

3. See Zev Vilnay, *Israel Guide,* 12th edition, 1968, pp. 46–48.

4. *The New York Review of Books,* (vol. 38, number 4, no. 5, November 7, 1990, p. 53).

The Holocaust is the most certainly inescapable sanction. I fully concur with Cragg's statement: "The Nazi Holocaust in Europe is the irrefutable, indubitable sanction for the utter legitimacy of the State of Israel."[5] Such different figures as Abraham Heschel, Arthur Hertzberg, Jacob Neusner, Gershom Scholem, and Elie Wiesel reflect the mind of most, if not all, Jews when they link the need for the State of Israel with the Holocaust; That horrendous baptism of fire powerfully propelled the urge of much twentieth-century Jewry to return to The Land. It convinced most Jews, especially those who had been undecided and ambiguous, that dependence, powerlessness, and passivity would not avail for Jews, and it reinforced among Zionists the aggressive militancy demanded by the creation of the State of Israel as, it would seem, of every state. In this paradoxical way, the Holocaust, the supreme expression of the outcome of Jewish powerlessness before the Nazi genocide, became the justification of, and a main instigation for the creation of a powerful state. Reaction to the Holocaust helped, very significantly, to erode the long tradition of "quietism" which had marked Jewish life in Palestine and in the Diaspora since the middle of the second century. In the minds of many, Jews and Gentiles alike, this quietism, although accused of fostering mere "passivity," had lent to Judaism much of its nobility and moral sensitivity. Again in the minds of many Jews and Gentiles, the Holocaust understandably but tragically—by way of reaction to it—evoked among certain elements of Jewry a centuries-long reemergence mutatis mutandis of a spirit not altogether unlike that of the Zealots of the first century.[6] This impact of the Holocaust, however, is not to be overemphasized by the ascription to Jews of what has wrongly been called a Masada complex.[7]

But, cogent as is the criticism that we have not dealt with the significance of the Holocaust, it has to be differentiated from the essential concern of this study. Certainly in the twentieth century the Holocaust must be part of the overarching context of the doctrine of The Land. But that context, although it *informs*, does not *determine* the content of that doctrine. It is arguable that the doctrine of The Land was primordial in the Jewish consciousness:[8] it has persisted through

5. See his remarkable work, *This Year in Jerusalem* (London, 1982), p. 130 (Cragg's reference to p. 93 is erroneous).
6. See David K. Shipler, *Arab and Jew.*
7. See Werblowsky, p. 114, above.
8. The origins of "Israel," as a people, are obscure. Whether they be traced to Abraham in the patriarchal period or to the Exodus, the promise of and hope for The Land are prominent in the sources. The promise is certainly so in the story of Abraham, and Levenson has recently emphasized that the central motif even in the story of the Exodus is not the deliverance from slavery in

centuries of often terrible historical vicissitudes. Undoubtedly for many Jews the Holocaust lent a desperate urgency to the doctrine, but it did not create it de novo. Probably, if not certainly, what the Holocaust did was to make the connection between the doctrine of The Land and the necessity of a State in The Land unavoidably explicit. Before the Holocaust that connection had not for many been unmistakably and unambiguously clear.

JEWS AND PALESTINIANS

A second criticism, we shall see, is not unrelated to the first. The culmination of the persecution of Jews which we call the Holocaust occurred outside Palestine in Europe. Not Europe, however, but Palestine, a land and people who were not responsible for the Holocaust, had to incur and pay the price for its dire consequences in the tragic dislocation and suffering involved for Jews (not only from Europe, but also in the Middle East itself) and in the lives of Palestinian Arabs. The incursion of Jews into Palestine from Europe and elsewhere and the creation of the State of Israel were accompanied by the displacement of previous Arab inhabitants of that land. Cragg points out that, except to plead incompetence to deal with it, I had not recognized the consequences that displacement involved for Palestinians. Referring to words of Rabbi Dow Marmur, he urged that "the mystical bond" between God and his people, of which The Land is the sacramental focus, constitutes a "neurotic tangle" which makes Judaic existence an "antagonizing experience of antagonism."[9] The evidence that the active pursuit and implementation of the doctrine of The Land have brought forth immense human suffering and tension which has led to new revolt in Palestine and elsewhere needs no recital. It is impossible here to trace that mutually antagonizing experience. Only rough figures can be adduced, but the incursion of two million (these figures have been increased this year, 1991, by the arrival of thousands from Russia and Falashas from Ethiopia to settle) Jews into Palestine and the State of Israel resulted in the emigration of eight thousand Arabs; what was actually involved in all this we can only leave to the imagination.

For many reasons the enmity between Palestinian Arabs and Israelis has not abated through the years. Cragg and Whale insist that the

---

Egypt so much emphasized in contemporary liberation theology. That deliverance was not for *all* those oppressed in Egypt but only for oppressed Israelites to whom The Land had been promised. The center of the Exodus story lies rather in the repatriation of the people of Israel in the Promised Land (see Jon D. Levenson, "Liberation Theology and the Exodus," in *Reflections* [Yale Divinity School], Spring 1991, pp. 2–12.

9. See Dow Marmur, *Beyond Survival: Reflections on the Future of Judaism* (London, 1982), p. 93, p. 102 above.

distinctive doctrine of The Land in Judaism has carried, as a corollary, a failure to deal with the claims of those who inhabited Palestine before and who now live with the Israelis in the State of Israel. That is, Judaism has so emphasized the covenanted territory of a covenanted chosen people that it has inevitably created tension between Jews and the Palestinians, who had claim to the same land. What is indubitable is that the nature and purpose of Zionism willy-nilly carry within themselves the potentiality for conflict with the Palestinians. The Jews, who created the State of Israel, did so to escape the humiliation of being at the mercy of the Gentile world. The host countries of Jews in the Diaspora sometimes had welcomed but more often had only tolerated them, mainly because they were useful or profitable: there were "good" Jews, that is, those who were economically and otherwise profitable for the host countries, and "bad" Jews, that is, those who were not such but undesirable. When they created the State in Palestine, Jews had no intention to be simply guests of the Palestinian Arabs, who were to be their hosts: that would have been only to reproduce the conditions of the Diaspora. Abba Eban's letter, cited on p. 98 above, makes clear that many early Zionists were not unaware of the menace of and of the need to defuse the conflict with Arabs. He orally pointed out later to me that, for example, Ben-Gurion's constant pre-occupation with the Negev, confirmed by his decision to live there in retirement, was governed by his desire to avoid the settlement of Jews in areas considerably populated by Arabs and to encourage settlements which were not likely to be in areas of potential conflict. However, among many Jews there was a tendency to think simplistically of Palestine as a land without a people into which a people without a land could enter without undue difficulty: there was no Arab State in Palestine before 1948, only people under a mandatory power. The outcome was inevitable—the creation of a situation in Palestine oddly similar to that in the Diaspora: Jews simply exchanged the animosity they had known outside Palestine for animosity inside Palestine. What-ever the numbers and condition of the Arabs who were in Palestine before the creation of the State of Israel, there is little doubt that their confrontation with Israel engendered among Palestinians a communal consciousness and the will to survive as a recognized nation. This was to be expected. The kind of thinking and experience which had led Jews to demand a state of their own in a land of their own has also, naturally, led Palestinians to make the same demand for themselves. Who better than Jews could understand why this should be so?

Two necessities, then, came to coincide in the same land: The necessity for Jews to have a state of their own and the necessity for Palestinians to have a similar privilege. The discussions over partition, binationalism and the territorial and demographic distribution of Jews and Arabs would require volumes to describe. Nor can the immense complexity of the cultural and geographic variety in the Jewish immigration into Palestine be overlooked. The leaders of Zionism, like the very different "Lovers of the Land" who had previously settled in Palestine, were largely Europeans, and the children of the Enlightenment (Ashkenazi and others). At the time of the birth of the state, these combined with Jews, from the Yemen and elsewhere in the Middle East and North Africa, who were of a vastly different cultural and social background, sometimes medieval and certainly preindustrial. It was this tangled combination of European and Middle Eastern Jews which together confronted the Arab inhabitants of Palestine. Nationalist, cultural and religious differences and interests, both within Jewry and without, ensured conflict. The military, political, and social history of this conflict between Jews and Arabs in Palestine has often been written. The actual course of events has been hard to come by, because the accounts of them vary according to the point of view, but the history of Israeli-Arab relations in Palestine provokes two questions:

1. Are we to conclude from that history that the doctrine of The Land, logically pursued to its conclusion in the creation of the State of Israel, necessarily produces an intransigence which makes deadly conflict between Jews and Palestinians inevitable? Does the doctrine of The Land demand that a peaceful and mutually acceptable coexistence of Jews and Palestinians in one land will never be possible?

At this point we must recognize that to isolate the doctrine of The Land and so to concentrate on it that all other aspects of Judaism are not allowed to impinge upon it to supply controls and correctives is to invite a positive answer to this question, that is, that there can never be a peaceful coexistence. However, the possession of The Land, important as it is, is not the central or the sole concern of Judaism. There is no single doctrine which expresses the essence of Judaism. Two other aspects of that faith, at least, serve to "hedge in" the doctrine of The Land and to deliver it from its exclusive intransigence—the claims of the Torah (which includes the Prophets and the Law) and the claims of the People, both claims grounded in the divine. In these reflections we cannot supply the evidence for this statement, but it is cogent. One of our greatest needs is for an awareness of the way in which the Torah demands that The Land should be possessed and how the claims of the inhabitants of The Land other than Jews should be honored. Hertzberg holds that, not the triad "God, The Land and the Torah," but the triad "Israel, God and the Torah" best expresses the nature of Rabbinic Judaism; not the doctrine of The Land, but that of the Chosen People is its cornerstone and its capstone (see p. 105). Hertzberg's claim, at the least, serves as a very important corrective to any ascription of preeminent, absolute status to The Land in Judaism; one would be bold to dispute or wholly dismiss his understanding of that faith. According to Broyde and Rachman, the overwhelming majority of halakic scholars, including those in Israel and the Diaspora, agree that the sanctity of life is a higher value than the inviolability of land ownership.[10] This implies, as Hertzberg holds, that the people come first. The Torah thus provides a resource to restrain the absolutism that many have been tempted to give to the claims of The Land on the loyalty of Jews—its possession, maintenance, and retention.

2. This leads to the second question raised by the history of Israeli-Arab relations in Palestine. Given the actual situation that has developed in Israel, how is it to be met? The two necessities we referred to have led to tragic and prolonged suffering and continue to do so.[11] To allow the principle that human life is of higher value than territory has a direct bearing on that situation. J. D. Bleich states unequivocally that "it is halachically legitimate to barter 'Land for peace' if doing so will preserve the lives of the inhabitants of Israel . . . I believe this view is shared by the majority of authoritative halachic decisions."[12] Further, Broyde and Rachman write, "The weight of rabbinic authority is that Jews are under no religious obligation to retain all, or any part of the land of Israel if such retention will involve loss of

10. See Michael Broyde and Emmanuel Rachman, *Midstream* 36/2 (1990), p. 11 on "Halacha and the State of Israel."

11. The physical effects in poverty and deprivation and the military expenses involved in the Israeli-Palestinian conflict cannot be exaggerated. They are more immediately apparent than the profound psychological effects among both Israelis and Palestinians. Like other communal enemies facing each other, in hostility, hate, and fear, the two groups have developed similar characteristics. Terrorism has marked the Israeli and the Palestinian sides, the educational systems on both sides have been manipulated for political ends, religious beliefs on both sides have been intermingled with nationalism, a Palestinian Diaspora has developed to parallel the Jewish Diaspora, a hope for a return among Palestinians has also appeared. Mutual hatred, often deliberately nurtured, bears the same face on both sides. The multiple expressions of all these phenomena and their human dimensions are well brought out by David K. Shipler, op. cit., passim.

12. Cited by Broyde and Rachman, op. cit., p. 12. J. D. Bleich has dealt with the issue of "Land for Peace" necessarily agitating Israel in two volumes, *Contemporary Halakhic Problems* (vols ii and iii), (New York: KTAV Publishing House, 1983, 1989). See vol. iii, pp. 293–305 on 'Of Land, Peace and Divine Command,' and vol. ii, pp. 169–221 on 'The Sanctity of the Liberated Territories' and 'Judaea and Samaria: Settlement and Return.' Bleich makes one thing clear (see vol. iii, pp. 15 and 17): the principle 'Land for Peace' involves not only respect for the lives of Jews in the land (as one scholar to whom I submitted these pages before publication claims) but for the lives of Gentiles also.

life."[13] Within the fullness of the Jewish religious traditions—the prophetic and the halakic—the doctrine of The Land is, then, hedged against inflexible absolutism.

The position of the main stream of Judaism as such seems clear. In view of what we have written, contrary to much popular and even sophisticated opinion, it is not the main religious elements in Israel that constitute the chief obstacle to Israeli-Palestinian coexistence and peace. That the halakah has been misused and misinterpreted by religious extremists (such as the Gush Emunim, among the followers of the late Rabbi Kahane, and among the late Rabbi Cook and his followers) so that Judaism has been blamed for fostering inflexibility, intolerance, and even terrorism, does not alter this fact. Rather, it is arguable that, along with the apathy and indifference of many of the religious Jews, it is mainly the secularist, nationalist leaders of the Jewish State, like Ben-Gurion, Begin, Sharon, and others, who have elevated the claims of The Land above all else.[14] There are significant,

13. Op. cit., p. 11, n.4.

14. This assessment of the role of religious belief is not to be taken to imply insignificance. The Bible and the Koran are the foundation documents of Jews and Arabs respectively. In varying degrees those two documents inescapably color and impinge upon the minds of Israelis and Palestinians, secular as well as religious, who are informed by them. It is true that the religious tradition does not *directly* govern the thinking of most Israelis and Arabs about The Land; it is primarily the needs of military security that do so: a figure like General Sharon on the Jewish side illustrates this. Probably only about 10–11 percent of Israelis are observant Jews and of these only about 3 percent can be regarded as highly committed to the active pursuit of the repossession of The Land: most Israelis are secularists unmoved by the *biblical* arguments for the possession of The Land and for its retention within all its present boundaries. However, just as there is an Islamic fundamentalism, so there is among the small minority referred to a Jewish fundamentalism. For that minority The Land has become an essential, central concern. And it is the fundamentalist enthusiasm of these that has fed the intolerance and extremism with which religious Israelis are all often unjustly tarred. In particular, the very influential "mystical" figure, Rabbi Abraham Yitshak Kook, the first Ashkenazi Chief Rabbi of Palestine, although he had a universalist as well as a particularistic emphasis—Israel was to serve the world—provided a link between the religious tradition and Zionism by his insistence on the essential relation between the sacred and the secular. His disciples, including his son, Rabbi Zvi Yehuda Kook, found in the control of the West Bank by Israel after 1967 a sign that the messianic redemption was already breaking in and progressing. The creation of the state and its expansion in the settlement of the West Bank, the Judea and Samaria of the biblical tradition, after 1967 came to be regarded as the fulfillment of the destiny of the Chosen People. In this way religion and nationalism in certain circles coalesced into a dangerous, inflamatory mixture.

if often overlooked, religious and other forces at work in Israel, in such groups as *OZ ve SHALOM* (Religious Zionists for Strength and Peace), who struggle against such a position.

What then are we to conclude? The two necessities which have met head on in Israel have generated a third—the necessity for compromise.[15] This is an inescapable conclusion. If continued tragedy is to be avoided, both Israelis and Palestinians are called upon to recognize the imperative of compromise. The nature of the compromise required, however, is not immediately clear, and to enlarge upon the nature of the arrangements to be made to meet the demands of this absolutely necessary compromise is beyond the scope and competence of this study. Certain avenues of approach considered can be mentioned. First, the earlier vision of a binational state in which Jews and Arabs were to live together on equal terms *will* assert itself. The claims of such a binational state, possibly taking a federalist form, were taken very seriously by early Western European Zionist leaders in Israel. They had been influenced by the liberal principles of statehood that were widely accepted in the West and recently were championed by Pierre Trudeau, for example, for Canada. Those principles are expressed in words from Lord Acton, quoted by Trudeau:

A great democracy must either sacrifice self-government to unity or preserve it by federalism. The coexistence of several nations under the same State is a

15. Hertzberg uses the term "compromise" without hesitation or explanation (see p. 129 above), and we follow him. Some Jewish scholars object, as do a colleague, Kelman Bland, Duke University, and Neusner (*Who, Where, and What Is Israel?: Zionist Perspectives on Israeli and American Judaism* [Larham, N.Y. and London: University Press of America, 1989]). Bland insists on the outright, unconditional recognition of the State of Israel by the Palestinians before there can be any agreement. A glance at the *Oxford English Dictionary* (vol. 1, p. 497; Oxford, 1971), where the term "compromise" is given two columns, justifies its use. To refer to the need for a compromise is to refer to a necessarily bargaining situation which begins—as my colleague Professor Arthur Larsen, the International Lawyer at Duke University, informs me— *without "compromise,"* but implies that a "compromise" is eventually possible. To take up a "bargaining position" willy-nilly implies the mutual recognition of the parties involved. When, therefore, we desire a compromise we mean that we urge an agreement to a rearrangement of the existing situation, the settling of differences and conflicting claims. The term "compromise" is not a strictly legal term; it is not a recognized part of legal terminology. It would be tragic if a semantic difficulty should be allowed to stand in the way of a settlement or rearrangement. It might be wise to avoid the use of the term "compromise" altogether, because by its use we do not imply any abandonment of principle (as its use sometimes indicates). As we use it, the term is not prejorative.

test, as well as the best security, of its freedom. It is also one of the chief instruments of civilization. . . . The combination of different nations in one State is as necessary a condition of civilized life as the combination of men in society. Where political and national boundaries coincide, society ceases to advance, and nations relapse into a condition corresponding to that of men who renounce intercourse with their fellow men. . . . A State which is incompetent to satisfy different races condemns itself; a State which labors to neutralize, to absorb, or to expel them is destitute of the chief basis of self-government. . . .[16]

In the twentieth century these words of Lord Acton's seem a counsel of perfection: they are not likely to be heeded by Israel, because the shadow of the Holocaust overcasts its sky, as well as the events of the wars of 1948, 1967 and 1973 and now 1990–91. It is claimed to be possible, if not probable, that in a binational or federalist state Jews would almost certainly in a short time be seriously outnumbered by Palestinians; they would be liable to become subordinates to or to become again "guests" of Palestinian "hosts." The fear of this at present is too real in the Israeli mind for it to be accepted. Can the ghost of the Holocaust and the fear of Arab attack ever be exorcised from the mind of Israel? And, on the other side, can Palestinians so grasp the utterly profound, traumatic, impact of the horror of the Holocaust on the mind of Jewry so as to begin to understand the attitudes it has helped to engender and to recognize the necessity of the existence of the State of Israel?

Second, then, given the "Utopian" character of the hope for a binational federalist state, under the present circumstances, and the irrepressible claim of Palestinians for a state of their own, the position represented and expressed realistically and forcibly by Hertzberg (among others) must register very powerfully. Hertzberg writes:

The one clear result of many decades of conflict between Israelis and Palestinians is that neither is willing to disappear in order to accommodate the desires of the other side. Israel will have no peace unless the demand of the Palestinians for a state of their own on the soil of part of Palestine is accepted. The Palestinians will have no peace unless they accept finally and irrevocably that Israel has a clear right to national existence as a state. The lives and hopes of millions of people have been distorted, ruined or destroyed by this conflict. All who are involved in this destructive conflict must move beyond debating with one another about the past and, indeed, help make a start on a decent compromise to save the future.[17]

16. Pierre Trudeau, *News Perspective Quarterly,* (The Center for the Study of Democratic Institutions) Los Angeles, vol. 7, no. 3, Summer 1990, p. 61.

17. Hertzberg, *New York Review of Books,* vol. 38, no. 5, March 7, 1991, p. 53.

Third, we now merely indicate the way in which Israelis and Palestinians have confronted each other in The Land in recent years. They have both been governed by fear, distrust and suspicion, and entrenched attitudes, hardened and inflexible, although there are on both sides elements of concern to change this. The State of Israel has handled its relationships with the Palestinians in terms of the occupation of territories taken over by military means and continuing to require military control—the West Bank, the Gaza Strip, the Golan Heights. This occupation can, in the Israeli view, develop and be modified in time to permit and foster Palestinian autonomy: it can be flexible as time and circumstance allow. This approach, thus crudely summarized, presents an immense obstacle to Palestinians, because it denies to them a right Israelis have claimed for themselves. This denial has had profound psychological consequences among Palestinians in their painful awareness that Israel deems it infeasible to risk granting them their own State; the Palestinians are only, in fact, to be "guests" in the Israeli home despite all protestations that they are to be treated equally. On the other hand, the way in which Israel has occupied the territories has left Israel not only with a wounded spirit because of the suffering it has inflicted on the Palestinians and with a "gnawing self-criticism," but also open to the charge that it has repudiated the authority of the very body, the United Nations, successor to the League of Nations, to which it has appealed to reinforce the recognition of its own existence as a state by the nations of the world.[18] At the same time Palestinians have also been adamant against clearly and unambiguously recognizing the right of Israel to exist despite the international confirmation of that right by the United Nations. The result has been violence: violence on both sides begets violence and will do so until the vicious cycle be broken. Sissela Bok has again shown how in violent conflict each side becomes blind to the virtues of the other and enlarges the vices: "Vansittartism" did not die with the end of the First World War: the pot still calls the kettle black. This is the transforming power of violence. This is what makes compromise an utter necessity. The prime movers in that compromise must be the Israelis and the Palestinians themselves, that is, those who have to live with it and make it workable. Whatever the exact form the compromise will take or have to take (conditions are constantly changing), the precondition of its success will be the willed determination on both sides to make it succeed. This involves the recognition both by Israelis and Palestinians of the desperate need of each for their own land and the equally desperate need of each for a reconciliation in which each honors the other's right to a state. Perhaps, if they could look into

18. Shipler op. cit., p. 91.

each other's eyes and see in them the same human tragedy, they would be moved to compromise.[19]

In short, what is needed is an immense leap in empathetic and sympathetic imagination on both sides. Such language may not be regarded as valid currency in the halls of *Realpolitik,* but, when *Realpolitik* has so far so dismally and tragically failed to achieve the necessary compromise, is it not imperative to try another way? A compromise in the spirit of costly mutual understanding and forgiveness would ultimately prove to be not a loss or deprivation for either Israelis or Palestinians, but their mutual enrichment and, indeed, possibly the ground of their very survival. It is highly temerarious for a biblical student to pass judgment on the political practicalities to be

19. Sissela Bok, *Strategy for Peace,* (New York: Pantheon Books, 1989), 10–16. A Jewish journalist, Ari Shavit, writing on Israeli prison camps for captured members of the Intifada, has put in a nutshell what many Jews inside and outside Israel have come to fear, that is, the effect of the present situation on (to use a shorthand) "the soul of Israel." He points to the tragic irony that it is not clear who are the confined and who are the confiners, and concludes that "It is not at this house, a matter of territories in exchange for peace. It is a matter of territories in exchange for our humanity" (see *The New York Review of Books,* Vol. xxxviii, Number 13, July 18th 1991, p. 6). It is sentiments such as these that seem to inform the disillusion or disenchantment which one detects in the work of Vital and among Jewish thinkers who often implicitly express the thought nostalgically, that to travel hopefully was better than to have arrived in the Land. See also Harry Berger, Jr., in *Representations* 25 (Winter 1989), pp. 119–37, on "The Lie of the Land: The Text beyond Canaan." This bears on the issue raised by Vital. Drawing on Walter Brueggemann's work *The Land* and his article on "Trajectories in the Old Testament Literature and the Sociology of Ancient Israel," *JBL* 98 (1979), pp. 161–85, Berger comes to what must seem to many a very staggering conclusion. For him "The Old Testament has its genesis shortly after the zenith of the unified monarchy that embodies the political triumph of the 'great nation.' It continues to grow and change during the period of the divided monarchy, during the Babylonian exile and captivity, and after the return and rebuilding. Its message to all those who possess the promised land, or who long for it, is clear: *to possess the land is to lose the promise"* (p. 136). Only in the text itself, for Berger, does the Tanak find "the seed of the one community, that can gather around the holy of holies at its center, the circumference of which is nowhere and that can bear it and birth it through time, the hermeneutical community, the community of *textual* desire" (ibid., emphasis mine). By implication, does not Vital find himself to be driven to the same conclusion? But is the text the only viable center for Judaism? Must the quest for The Land be regarded as a wild-goose chase? Here the need to keep The Land and The People and The Text in perspective again asserts itself lest the essential "triangle" of Judaism fall apart.

implemented in achieving that indispensable compromise to which we have referred. But reflection and concern, the sources in the Jewish and Christian traditions, and the demand of the times do point—so it seems to us—to the direction of the policy to be followed, a direction indicated by Hertzberg so clearly. Abba Eban and others have pointed out the many possibilities open to such a policy and the models it might follow in Europe and elsewhere.

To urge consideration of a Palestinian State is to touch one of the most sensitive nerves of many Israelis, especially Zionists; it is to attack "the dream they had lived for—the achievement of the State of Israel."[20] Israeli Jews and Palestinians can contemplate coexistence in the same space on a *personal* level: Israelis often like or respond positively to Arabs and Arab culture; there is some intermarriage. But to allow the Palestinians' dream of a state for themselves changes the personal to a communal, political relationship, and at this point Israelis naturally become defensive; their own dream seems placed in jeopardy. Shipley recalls the immutable law of physics: "Two bodies cannot occupy the same space at the same time."[21] But peoples are not merely "bodies." Cannot two peoples with sensitivity and adjustment learn to coexist while cherishing their own dreams? This is what the situation demands in Israel and Palestine. As in to other relationships, compatibility in the national and international spheres is not a given but usually a costly achievement. The extreme difficulty among many Jews of even recognizing the existence of a Palestinian people as such is illustrated in Joel Carmichael.[22] He describes the "invention of a new people, Palestinians," as "perhaps the most brilliant feat of psychological warfare in history." If Carmichael is right, the Western world has certainly been guilty of "extreme gullibility": it has been duped by "the political stratum" of the Palestinians, most of whom are Arabs, and by the major news media of the West; it has accepted "a fairy tale as a reality."[23] According to Carmichael, "the portentousness of the bogus scholarship claiming the national viability of the Palestinian Arabs can hardly be exaggerated" (ibid.). Carmichael overlooks that events are creative and have an afterlife. The conflicts between Israeli Jews and Arabs in Palestine have brought into being a new phenomenon not imposed by any artificial invention but growing out of the actual situation created by those conflicts. The *Intifada* cannot in the judgment of most observers be explained away simply as the manipulation of outsiders, of Arab or other external influences. It does not seem justifiable to

20. Shipler, op. cit., p. 76.

21. Ibid., 77.

22. Joel Carmichael, "The Palestinian People: A Lethal Fiction," *Midstream* 37/2 (February–March, 1991), pp. 6–8.

23. Carmichael, op. cit., p. 8.

deny a national consciousness to Palestinian Arabs. Carmichael stands in a tradition of "denial" that goes back to the beginnings of the Zionist movement, although not universal within it: we comprehend his sensitivity but cannot share his view.

THE LAND AND THE DIASPORA

While the doctrine of the chosen Land and the chosen people, as we saw, have had "inevitable" consequences inside Palestine in the relationships between Jews (Israelis) and Palestinians, they long had had equally "inevitable" consequences for Jews in their relationships with Gentiles outside Palestine in the Diaspora before the emergence of the State of Israel. And they have had such especially since then. To examine the causes of the anti-Semitism which ultimately necessitated the creation of the State of Israel is not possible here. Let it simply be recognized that the doctrine of the "chosen people" in all its expressions has involved Jews in various forms and degrees of separation and isolation from the societies within which they found themselves in the Diaspora. As we indicated above, pp. 61–67, the role of Diaspora Jews in Jewish history cannot be exaggerated. Paradoxically, the State of Israel, which was created to enable Jews to escape from their suffering in the Diaspora, has only been able to continue in existence by means of the support—financial, military, and cultural—of Diaspora Jews: the State of Israel largely depends on the very phenomenon that the Zionists, who created it, held in contempt and sought to annul. The desired life in The Land has turned out to be possible only with the aid of the despised life outside it. Perhaps we did not sufficiently emphasize this paradoxical situation.

However, two considerations are pertinent. The doctrines of the chosenness of the People and of The Land *have* often historically called forth antagonism against Jews among Gentiles. They have outraged the sense of justice of some, as Whale's comments illustrate (he is even led to invoke his "discredited" ontological argument against the doctrine of The Land [see pp. 115–17]). But it is arguable that this is because the doctrine of chosenness has often been corrupted by Jews and misinterpreted by Gentiles. Vriezen (see above, p. 94) long ago established that that doctrine was governed not by status conferred, as it was so often misunderstood to imply, but by service demanded: the chosen *(bahur, eklektos)* is the servant *('ebed, doulos)*. If The People and The Land are conceived of as being chosen for the sake of others, that is, to serve humankind, as the notion of chosenness emerges in the Tanak and Rabbinic sources, should such a doctrine offend? Tragically, as in Christianity so in Judaism, a doctrine, despite its intent, can be easily perverted. This has happened both among Jews and Gentiles. The doctrine of chosenness has been popularly regarded as conferring favor or privilege and, therefore, as implying partiality in the divine purpose. Just as, until very recently in the United States, the notion that "separate" could be reconciled and equated with "equal" was once acceptable, but is so no longer ("separated" being now claimed to denote "unequal"), so it is with the doctrine of chosenness. Mutatis mutandis most Gentiles find it unacceptable because, in their view, it is unjustly discriminatory. The intent of the doctrine has been lost sight of.[24]

Since the creation of the State of Israel another element has come into play. Before the rise of Zionism, devotion to The Land had a "mystical" or religiously intense quality which did not concern itself with *Realpolitik*. "The Lovers of Zion" were content to live on The Land indifferent as to who controlled it politically. But Zionism involved politics—the need to assert a national will which demanded the use of power. Zionists had to resolve the traditional Jewish ambiguity about statehood, and they could do so only through the assumption of political, including military, responsibilities. They sought the "conversion" of a religious (and, from their point of view, ineffective or even futile) concern with The Land to a political nationalism. This, in turn, has involved not only the transformation, or rather the supersession, of the mentality of the earlier "Lovers of Zion," but an immense intensification and extension of the need for help from the Jews of the Diaspora to enable the State of Israel to persist. The Land as a religious center did not call for the same degree of massive aid from Diaspora Jews as did and does The Land as the locus of the State of Israel. That state has had to be engaged in unavoidable political, necessarily compromising, activity, military and other, especially in what could be interpreted as the repressive containment of the Palestinians who have revolted in the Intifada and in the wars outside The Land in Lebanon and elsewhere. As in the Maccabean period the military activity of Jews gave rise to criticism of them and instigated animosity against them, so has that of the modern State of Israel. What concerns us particularly is the effect that this has had upon the relationship between The Land and the Diaspora. This question we did not face in our study. It has now become so acute that some consider that the State of Israel has often so alienated many Jews of the Diaspora by its conduct that it has very seriously strained the relationship between them. Two scholars, Professors David Vital and Jacob Neusner, have dealt directly with this issue, with different results: we take them as representative of two positions.

According to Vital the relationship between The Land and the Diaspora has now been strained to breaking point. Is he justified in

24. See on "Chosenness," Dow Marmur, *Beyond Survival* (London, 1982), pp. 173–179, esp. p. 177.

thus describing the situation in his recent penetrating and challenging book, *The Future of the Jews: A People at the Crossroads?*[25] This is why we previously suggested that, apart from its purely human, agonizing dimensions, the Holocaust is crucially important as having so sealed the conviction of the utter necessity of a militarily powerful Jewish state, that it has, for most Jews and many Gentiles, finally and fully justified its creation. (In this sense, the Holocaust has a role in Jewish history comparable to that played by Constantine in Christian history.) But, according to Vital, the result has been acutely paradoxical and is likely in the future to be disastrously so. The creation of the State of Israel, because of its necessary involvement in the compromises of politics, has helped to ensure that the notion of "Israel" as the center of a living unity of all Jews everywhere, within The Land and outside it, is dying and will continue to die. For most Jews, Vital holds, The Land has become less central than it was in their tradition and also less necessary: their interests, that is, those of Diaspora Jews, differ from those of Israelis. We suggested above (pp. 82–84) that The Land, if not of the *esse* of Judaism, was of its *bene esse*. This view has been endorsed in the excellent work of Eisen on the *Galut.*[26] In short, in the past *The Land* provided a focus or center for the unity of the Jewish people everywhere. But according to Vital, *the State* in The Land, by its necessary activity, has put strains on that unity and eroded it. For reasons we cannot here pursue, the erosion of that unity—again if Vital's position be accepted—had begun in the Enlightenment, but, in his view, an almost fatal blow was given to it when, as he puts it, there was injected into the life of Jewry "the hard, clearly defined body of a sovereign state. . . ."[27] called upon to play its part among other states. According to Vital:

The rise of an independent state has both revolutionized and destabilized the Jewish world . . . the *interests,* and therefore the underlying tendencies and viewpoints, of American and other Jewries, cannot fail to differ crucially from those of Israeli Jewry. And that is one key reason, quite conceivably the chief reason, why willy-nilly the Jewish world—beaten by assimilation on the one hand and by destruction and threats of further punishment on the other—is now coming apart. Where there was once a single, if certainly a scattered and far from monolithic people—indeed, a nation—there is now a sort of archipelago of discrete islands composed of rather shaky communities of all qualities, shapes, and sizes, in which the Island of Israel, as it were, is fated increasingly to be in a class by itself.

25. David Vital, *The Future of the Jews: A People at the Crossroads,* (Cambridge, Mass.: Harvard University Press, 1990).

26. Arnold M. Eisen, *Galut: Modern Jewish Reflection on Homelessness and Homecoming* (Bloomington, Ind.: Indiana University Press, 1980).

27. Vital, *Future of the Jews,* p. 144.

In sum, the unity of Jewry, however fragile, however problematic, essentially a function of the old sense, and, yes, the old reality of nationhood, lies shattered today, almost beyond repair.[28]

We simply reiterate here that behind the revolutionizing and destabilizing of the Jewish world to which Vital refers lies the Holocaust, which finally propelled the creation of The State.

From Vital's point of view, then, the Zionist movement, which so concentrated on The Land, and those elements of Judaism that also so concentrated, have had a strange, paradoxical dénouement. The pursuit of The Land has involved the disintegration—nigh fatal in Vital's eyes—of the unity of the Jewish people:[29] its victory in the emergence of the State of Israel was a Pyrrhic one.

Neusner, on the other hand, is not so pessimistic. In numerous essays conveniently gathered in *Who, Where and What Is Israel? Zionist Perspectives on Israeli and American Judaism*,[30] he presents a more dialectic and more ambiguous point of view than does Vital. There can be no doubt of Neusner's commitment to the State of Israel and his celebration of its creation and achievement. He writes: "Seen in the perspective of the long history of the Jewish People from 70, the creation of the State of Israel in 1948 dominates the scene, the definitive fact that redefines everything that happened from 70 to 1948 and that has taken place since that time."[31] But for Neusner this does not involve an alienation of the Diaspora. Dealing only with America, he takes that country to be the Promised Land for Jews and holds that "America, the freest and most open society Jews have ever known, is not only

28. Op. cit., p. 147.
29. There is here a conundrum in Vital's work. He distinguishes between Judaism and Jews as a nation (op. cit., p. 145). But can these phenomena be distinguished? He asks "whether their [the Jews'] ancient faith should be seen primarily as the instrument of their national preservation, or contrariwise, whether it is their peoplehood that should be seen as the means whereby their religion was defended and preserved, and not without success, against successive, near fatal onslaughts by pagan, Christian, and Muslim rivals" (op. cit., p. 140). One might agree that there can be Jews without Judaism, but can there be Judaism without Jews? Would not the end of Jews imply the end of Judaism? This question is not a theoretical one. In our work on *The History of Judaism* for Cambridge University Press, Dr. Louis Finkelstein and I found it impossible to distinguish "the history of Judaism" from "the history of the Jews." Is Vital's distinction between Judaism and Jews a distinction without a difference? This is simply to assert the commonplace that religion and ethnicity are inextricable in the Jewish tradition.
30. Jacob Neusner, *Who, Where, and What Is Israel?*
31. Op. cit., p. 153.

good for the Jews but better, for the Jews, than the State of Israel. . . ."[32] The life in the American Diaspora does not present for him
the picture of a disintegrating splintering community that Vital sees,
but of a free, creative, cohesive one, secure in its foreseeable future.[33]
Neusner's admiration for Israel and for America can also coexist with
drastic criticism of both.[34] His loyalty to The Land does not negate
for him admiration for the life of the Diaspora, at least as he has known
it in America.

Both Vital and Neusner indirectly highlight the significance of the
doctrine of The Land. Vital's book, as far as we know, has not been
widely discussed, but we hesitate to endorse it. This much can be
asserted: The modern is not the only period when the Diaspora has
gone its own way without disrupting what Vital calls "the myth" of
the unity of Jewry. The Diaspora in Egypt, for example, before the
Common Era, even developed its own temple and yet remained "in
communion with" the Palestinian community. The Jewish presence
in Palestine across the centuries, on the other hand, has often been so
decimated that it apparently sometimes became a trickle: it could not
solely have supplied a focus for Jewish unity. In order to survive, that
unity must have had another focus or other foci than only The Land
itself. Such considerations suggest that Neusner's critical optimism
about the Diaspora, particularly in America, may appeal to history
for support. In our time also, will not the Jewish people survive any
dissatisfaction with and rejection of the activity of the State of Israel
as it has survived perhaps even greater challenges to its unity in the
past?[35] But it is wise to recall the proverb ascribed to the Chinese,
"Prediction is always precarious, especially about the future."

32. Op. cit., p. 113.
33. Op. cit., p. 113, 114.
34. Op. cit., pp. 113ff.
35. Has Vital overlooked two factors: (1) the *shared* memories of Israelis
and (2) the intercommunication of Jewry everywhere through the ubiquitous
Synagogue—two agencies of an enduring, tenacious continuity? And is Vital
in danger of what Shipler calls "nostalgia, a romance of the past," which
contains an element of falsehood? As Shipler puts it, "For Israeli Jews, too
close to their formative past to face it squarely, the years in which the state
was built exists suspended from reality as expressions of the dream [of the
promised land]. Those who now decry anti-Arab bigotry, religious zealotry,
Jewish terrorism, and the affinity for violence [in the State of Israel—those
factors which Vital sees as causing disaffection from present-day Israel among
Jews of the Diaspora] often fall into the passionate misconception that these
are wholly new ingredients in the Jewish state, that the humane moralism of
the initial venture was once pristine and has been lost, that something precious
has been stolen from the lofty enterprise" (op. cit., p. 32). Shipler provides

THE LAND IN PERSPECTIVE

This last question leads to another, that raised by Hertzberg. What exactly is the *comparative* role or importance of The Land in Judaism? As we noted previously, he rejects the description of Judaism as "a fortunate blend of a people, a land and their God" (which I had, in fact, derived from Arthur Marmorstein, a leading Jewish scholar in the United Kingdom at the beginning of this century) as giving too much weight to The Land. Instead he prefers, in his own words, (p. 105 above), "the oft-quoted rabbinic saying (it is a summary of Talmudic attitudes, though as such it does not exist in the early literature) . . . that 'Israel, God and the Torah are one.' "[36] For Hertzberg "what unites both segments of the Jewish people [he is specifically referring to religious and secularist Jews in The Land] is their sense of belonging to one people, to a community both within The Land and worldwide" (p. 107 above). Hertzberg, in short, raises the fundamental question, What is the unifying heart of Judaism or its animating power? He finds the cornerstone and capstone of Rabbinic Judaism to be "the chosen people." Not The Land but The People is central.[37] As does his brilliant statement of it elsewhere, Hertzberg's succinct statement of his case

---

evidence (op. cit., pp. 31–57). Correspondence with Israeli scholars in recent years confirms this. Has this "nostalgia," which Vital himself seems to reflect (op. cit., pp. vii–ix), led him to overemphasize the negative impact of the developments in the State of Israel on the Diaspora Jews or at least to lend them a negative significance not essentially different from that of an earlier time before 1948, when already there was disenchantment?

36. So also Dow Marmur, op. cit., p. 57. For a reservation about overemphasis on the People, see p. 58.

37. Michael Loewe and Shemaryahu Talmon have particularly emphasized the necessity of holding the three pillars in perspective, both orally and through correspondence, especially one letter from Michael Loewe dated May 15, 1989. See also his insightful article, "Judaism's 'Eternal Triangle,' " *Religious Studies* 23 (1937), 309–23. I once asked President Louis Finkelstein what he regarded as the "essence" of Judaism. His reply was the following (letter dated June 12, 1990):

It is very difficult for me to formulate in a single sentence what might be called the essence of Judaism if that means that some things are more important than others. The Torah is what holds us together. We love to observe its laws and that can only be done by community. The Torah also commands that all of us, if we can do so, live in Israel and observe the commandments, which can only be fulfilled there. But I do not think that there is an essence of Judaism in the sense that some things are more important than others. The Divine Commandments are all equally important.

See also Cragg above, p. 100–101, also.

points to a simple fact which implicitly breaks through the comments of all the contributors to the symposium and which my earliest teachers of theology taught me. It is this: to deal adequately with any one particular doctrine in any theology so as to see it in true perspective, one has to relate it to *all* other aspects of that theology as a totality. To isolate a doctrine and concentrate exclusively upon it is ipso facto to magnify and distort it. So is it with the doctrine of The Land. Hertzberg is fully justified: to deal rightly with that doctrine, without overemphasis on its role and significance, it is imperative to relate it to the totality of Judaism. We may still ask whether Hertzberg's own elevation of the chosen people to a position of such preeminence is not itself an overemphasis. He raises the whole question of the nature of Judaism which Vital describes as a "great complex (not to say tangle) of history, high culture, belief and social and ritual practice and all this with a national component." (op. cit., p. 1). To answer the question raised demands, of course, far more than could be even only suggested here.[38]

THE DOCTRINE OF THE LAND
AND CULTURAL PRESSURES

The comments of Stendahl and Werblowsky, finally, bring to the fore one other aspect of the doctrine of The Land, that is, the way in which, like all theological doctrines, it was and is conditioned or motivated by the social and cultural milieux within which it was initially enunciated and subsequently developed. The sociological has long invaded theological scholarship and we have fully recognized this.[39]

Stendahl is justified in connecting the emphasis on The Land in recent Judaism with the rise of Zionism, which he, like many others, understands in terms of the nationalist movements of nineteenth-century Europe. "The State of Israel," he writes, "is a new thing. It is a modern democratic nation among nations." He rejects criticisms

38. Op. cit., p. 1. Dow Marmur, op. cit., p. 57, writes: "The faith of Israel rests on three pillars: trust in God; belief in the authenticity and validity of His will as revealed in the Torah; and the conviction that the Jewish people has been given the task to make His will, and thereby His presence, known to the world and manifest in its own actions and lifestyle. Judaism becomes dangerously lop-sided and disturbed when it rests on only one or two of these pillars."

39. We need only recall Finkelstein's "class struggle" interpretation of the Pharisees or recent treatments of papal infallibility in Roman Catholic theology by way of example for the interpretation of the sociological and theological, and a recent work, drawing on Max Weber, by I. M. Zeitlin, *Jesus and the Judaism of His Time* (Cambridge, England: Polity Press, 1988).

of Israel for having, as he puts it, "bought into the dated [sic] idea of nationalism." At first sight Stendahl and Werblowsky might seem to differ in this matter. The latter asks, "Is modern Zionism really a completely 'modern' political, secular-nationalist phenomenon? Might it not just be a modern 'transformation,' a translation into modern political idiom of something that has much deeper roots. . . ?" (p. 114). For Werblowsky, in short, Zionism is a reinterpretation of the tradition about The Land, not a *new* phenomenon. Contrast Stendahl's view. We may question them both. Of Werblowsky we ask, Why, if Zionism is not in some sense disturbingly new, has it found it so difficult to find acceptance among so many of the most established traditionalist elements in Judaism and why is it still rejected by so many of these? Since Judaism is at home with the constant reinterpretation of its tradition, we may ask whether a mere reinterpretation (if Zionism be only such) is likely to have been so tenaciously repulsed and rejected within Judaism itself. And of Stendahl we ask why, while he rightly and clearly emphasizes the role of the continuous reinterpretation of the tradition in Judaism, he can so easily dismiss the connection of Zionism (whose affinities with and indebtedness to nineteenth-century nationalism he finds obvious) with an ancient tradition recognized among Jews and regard it as a new phenomenon? However, there is truth in what both Werblowsky and Stendahl assert. Territorialism failed to motivate the Jewish mind. Zionism is ultimately hardly conceivable without the long tradition of a hope for the promised land upon which it could and did unconsciously and consciously draw when territorialism proved abortive. This is why the Jews who created the State of Israel chose the evocative name of Zion in the title of their movement: all this confirms Werblowsky's position. But, at the same time, there was present in Zionism the firm desire (compare Hertzberg pp. 106–07: "this religious insight is a prime source of modern Zionism.") to be radically distanced from the traditional religious attitudes; this emerges in the deliberate avoidance of the Divine Name and the use of the circumlocution "The Rock" for it in the very Constitution of the State, in the choice of the Star of David, which is not a traditional Jewish religious symbol, as the emblem of the State, in the staggering, paradoxical use of the term "Holocaust" for Jewish suffering, and in other ways. Conversation with Jewish scholars in modern Jerusalem and elsewhere still makes one immediately aware of the conscious, sometimes virulent, distancing from the religious tradition among some of them at least. All this points to Zionism not necessarily as a new phenomenon, but as a new step or stage in a long continuing tradition to this extent. Stendahl is endorsed. But while he rightly recognizes the break in the tradition which the Zionist creation of the State of Israel involved, he fails to appreciate that there are continuities in Judaism which inform and thereby survive the breaks in it. Zionism is a break *in* the tradition, but not *with* it. We have preferred to embrace both the positions illustrated in the comments of Werblowsky and Stendahl and to hold them in tension, as—if we understand him aright—does Neusner. This preference we still affirm. Werblowsky, Stendahl, and, in a different way, Freedman raise the question of the interpretation of the tradition about The Land—the appropriate attitudes and methods to be applied to it. Stendahl tentatively suggests that in this study we were governed by a very simplistic aim—"to unearth a pure 'theology' which could supply the answers, perhaps by synthesizing the long and diverse history of Jewish thoughts about The Land." He himself, by contrast, prefers to regard Jewish tradition as constantly in the process of reinterpretation and, therefore, as open-ended. Freedman's comments are pertinent here also.

The aim of this study, however, was not to discover or uncover any "pure theology of The Land," but more simply to find out what exactly the tradition states about The Land and, in doing this, to bear in mind the questions posed to us in the twentieth century by the data and by their results in the life of The Land in our time. This procedure presupposes that the Jewish tradition, particularly the Hebrew Scriptures, have something to say to us today. But it first demands the effort to hear what the tradition, particularly in the Hebrew Scriptures, spoke to its own time. Historical reconstruction must precede interpretation or rather must proceed along with interpretation. Merely to state the tradition as a phenomenon of the past, as a pure theology, is not enough, but the history of the tradition is nonetheless essential to its true interpretation; the horizon of the tradition and our own horizon must be focused. Therefore I have sought to point out the substance of the tradition, to understand the problems which at various stages it addressed, to listen in to them, as it were, and to bear in mind at the same time the problems confronting our day. Necessarily this study is very limited, for example, in its comparative neglect of the liturgy, as Werblowsky points out. The liturgy is a major source about and for the sentiment for The Land. A glance at my larger work might allay some of this criticism. In the little space of the present study our aim was not to be exhaustive (this would take a lifetime), but rather to serve as an agent provocateur to stimulate further discussion.[40]

---

40. It is a pleasure to note that since *The Gospel and The Land* (1974) was published, other important studies have appeared, especially: Walter Brueggemann, *The Land* (Philadelphia: Fortress Press, 1980); Arnold M. Eisen, *Galut: Modern Jewish Reflection*; and Doron Mendels, *The Land of Israel as a Political Concept in Hasmonaean Literature: Recourse to History in 2nd Century* B.C. *Claims to the Holy Land* (Tübingen: J. C. B. Mohr [Paul Siebeck], 1987) (Mendels' volume also has rich bibliographical guidance). These scholars have

These reflections cover a vast area, as did this little study. I am acutely aware of their inadequacy to begin to deal with the questions to which they advert, and how temerarious the attempt to do so. But their outcome is not without force; this can be briefly summarized. To ignore the territorial (The Land) and the national (the People) is as disastrous as to absolutize them; they are both to be honored, but the territorial is to be hedged in by the terrestrial—to use Cragg's words— and the national by the universal. The doctrine of The Land has its due, proper, and indeed "essential" place, but is it too much to hope that it can be seen in the light of the larger hope, familiar to Judaism and to Christianity, which in the last century was expressed in terms of "the Parliament of Man and the Federation of the World"? Is all of this a utopian illusion? Is it not rather a truism—a plain, self-evident truth to be pondered by both Israelis and Palestinians as by all peoples?

---

carried the discussion of The Land further, not to mention researches in sociology and political science. In this connection I have been grateful for correspondence with Jonathan Boyarin, New School for Social Research, New York, and especially to Professor Gunter Stemberger for his published work in *Kairos* 25 (1983), pp. 176–99 on *Die Bedeütung des Landes Israel in der Rabbinischen Tradition* and also *Juden und Christen im Heiligen Land* (Munich: Verlag C. H. Beck, 1987). See also, Ruth Kark, editor, *The Land that Became Israel,* (New Haven, Conn.: Yale University Press, 1990). This work deals almost entirely with highly useful historical and geographic themes, but only has one very helpful chapter on "Perceptions and Images of the Holy Land" by Jehoshua Ben-Ariek, pp. 37–56. We need a comparable volume by Jewish scholars from the theological point of view. There are illuminating reviews of *The Gospel and the Land* especially by Pierre Benoit, Shemaryahu Talmon and David Flusser in *Christian News from Israel* 25 (November 3 [19], 1975), pp. 132–39. It needs to be noted that since he published the work referred to on pages 93–94 n. 4, Gottwald has further elaborated the link between society and theology in ancient Israel. See "The Theological Task after *The Tribes of Israel,*" in *The Bible and Liberation: Political and Social Hermeneutics* (Maryknoll: Orbis Books, 1983), pp. 190–200; "Social Matrix and Canonical Shape," in *Theology Today* 42 (1983), pp. 307–21; and "Religious Conversion and the Societal Origins of Ancient Israel," in *Perspectives in Religious Studies* 15 (1988), pp. 49–65.

Glossary

Apocalyptic: [from the Greek verb *apocaluptein*, "to reveal"] The doctrines about the end of all things (although the term also included other doctrines) and the extensive literature in which these doctrines are set forth. It flourished in the Hellenistic and Roman periods.

Apocrypha: The body of Jewish religious literature written between the second century B.C.E. and the second century C.E., not included in the Hebrew Bible, but incorporated in the Roman Catholic Old Testament. Other writings dealing with apocalyptic materials, generally referred to as the Pseudepigrapha, emerged in the same period. These Pseudepigrapha were thrust aside by the growth of rabbinical literature and were all but lost to the Jewish tradition, their preservation being largely due to the Christian Church. See *APOT* and now the recent edition by J. H. Charlesworth.

Diaspora: Literally, "dispersion." The Greek word used to refer to Jewish communities outside Palestine, both before and after the fall of Jerusalem in 70 C.E., composed both of voluntary and involuntary emigrants from Eretz Israel. There is much debate in modern Jewry as to whether the term still has overtones of "exile" (see n. 1 to chap. 3) or is simply to be taken as denoting the geographically widespread Jewish communities outside The Land.

Gemara: Literally, "completion," (i.e., of the Mishnah). The usual designation for the comment and discussion around the Mishnah. There are a Palestinian *gemara* and a Babylonian *gemara* to the Mishnah, but to many tractates no *gemara* is extant.

Haggadah: Literally, "narration." Generally the term denotes nonlegal elements in the Jewish sources and tradition—homilectics and morals, history and legend, scientific facts and philosophical reflections, biblical and rabbinical narratives. Specifically it describes the liturgical manual for the domestic service for Passover Eve.

Halakah: Literally, "the way to walk" (from the verb *hâlak*, "to walk"). The technical term for the whole body of rabbinic law and for particular provisions which by majority vote are accepted as legally binding. It covers trial, civil, ceremonial, and criminal law.

Hasidim: Literally, "pious ones." A group, usually taken to be the precursors of the Pharisees, which arose in the second century B.C.E., and at first participated in the Maccabaean revolt. The term is used to denote groups of pietists throughout the course of Jewish history and especially very pious Eastern European Jews of the eighteenth century, whose descendants can be found in colonies in the United States.

Jamnia: A city near Joppa where the rabbis gathered under the leadership of Johanan ben Zakkai after the Jewish Wars. According to modern scholars, the reorganization of post-70 C.E. Judaism and the collection and writing down of the halachic and haggadic oral traditions began there, but historical details are disputed.

Lurianism: The school of mysticism founded by the Qabbalist Isaac Luria (1534–72) in Safed, Israel. It had a profound influence on the whole Jewish world, forming the basis for much of late hasidic thought.

Mekilta: One of the oldest of the Tannaitic Midrashim, giving an exposition of a large part of the book of Exodus, and dealing with almost all the laws of that book and with some of its most important narrative portions.

Midrash, pl. Midrashim: Literally, "investigation," "enquiry" (from the root *dârash,* "to inquire," "to investigate"). Midrash denotes writings that interpret Scripture in order to extract its full implications and meanings and also to impart contemporary relevance to biblical events. These writings are of two kinds: halakic midrashim, dealing with Mosaic Law, and haggadic midrashim, expounding nonlegal parts of Scripture. The Midrash Haggadah flourished greatly after the Mishnaic period.

Mishnah, The: [from the verb meaning "to repeat," "to learn," "to study," hence "learning," "study"] The systematized collection of laws (halakoth) finally codified by Judah the Prince around 220 C.E. More than simply a "code," the Mishnah is a textbook giving the essence of the Oral Law as it was known to the sages of that time, and remains the authoritative source for Jewish law. It consists of six orders (Shishah Sedarim), each divided into tractates, chapters, and paragraphs:
1. Zeraim ("Seeds"), eleven tractates, mainly on agricultural laws
2. Moed ("Appointed Times"), twelve tractates on the laws of festivals and feasts

3. Nashim ("Women"), seven tractates, chiefly on marriage, divorce, and vows
4. Nezikin ("Damages"), ten tractates on civil and criminal law
5. Kodashim ("Holy Things"), eleven tractates pertaining primarily to Temple services
6. Toharot ("Purity"), twelve tractates on the laws of ritual purity and impurity

The language of the Mishnah is in new (i.e., rabbinic) Hebrew as distinct from the classical language of the Bible.

Philo: Alexandrian Jewish philosopher (ca. 25 B.C.E.–40 C.E.) who combined contemporary Hellenistic philosophy and piety with belief in Revelation and Scripture.

Rashi: The name given to Solomon ben Isaac (1040-1105 C.E.), a leading commentator on the Bible and the Babylonian Talmud, who was born in Troyes, France. His widely acclaimed and influential commentary was published with the first edition of the Talmud, and except for modern editions of a few tractates, no edition of the *BT* has appeared without it.

Sabbatai Svi: Born in Smyrna in 1626, he claimed to be the Messiah, initiated an antinomian messianic movement which spread throughout Jewry with amazing rapidity. In 1666 he apostasized to Islam.

Talmud: Literally, "teaching," "study," "learning." The word is most commonly used as a comprehensive term for the Mishnah and Gemara taken together as a single unit. It is specifically applied to two compilations: the Palestinian Talmud, often wrongly referred to as the Jerusalem Talmud (Talmud Jerushalmi), and the Babylonian Talmud (Talmud Babli). These are the record of discussions over a period of about eight centuries by Jewish sages working continually in the academies of Palestine and Babylonia. To the sages up to the formation of the Mishnah (128 in all), the term *tannaim* is applied; and to the students, teachers, and reciters who followed, the term *amoraim*. The Palestinian Talmud was finally redacted at Tiberias around 400 C.E., and the Babylonian Talmud, which is regarded as the authoritative work, around 500 C.E.

Tanak: Formed from the initial letters of *Torah, Nebi'im, Kethubim* (i.e., Pentateuch, Prophets, Writings), this is the usual word among Jews for the Jewish Bible (which is also the Protestant, but not the Roman Catholic, Old Testament).

Tosephta: A collection of laws parallel to the Mishnah.

Selected Bibliography

Allegro, J. "4 Q Florilegium." *Journal of Biblical Literature* 75 (1956): 176–77; 77 (1958): 350–54.

Al-Tāfahum, 'Abd. "Doctrine." In *Religion and the Middle East*, vol. 2, edited by A. J. Arberry, pp. 365–412. Cambridge: Cambridge University Press, 1969.

Ardrey, R. *The Territorial Imperative*. New York: Atheneum, 1966.

Arendt, H. *Eichmann in Jerusalem: A Report on the Banality of Evil*. New York: Penguin, 1977.

———. *The Jew as Pariah: Jewish Identity and Politics in the Modern Age*. Edited by R. H. Feldman. New York: Schocken, 1978.

Avigad, Nahman and Yadin, Yigael. *The Genesis Apocryphon*. Jerusalem: Magnes Press of the Hebrew University, 1956.

Babylonian Talmud, The. 35 vols. London: Soncino, 1935–52.

Barthélemy, D., O.P., and Milik, J. T., et al. *Qumran Cave I: Discoveries in the Judaean Desert*, I. Oxford: Clarendon Press, 1955.

Ben-Ariek, J. "Perceptions and Images of the Holy Land" in Ruth Kark, ed. *The Land that Became Israel*. New Haven, Conn.: Yale University Press, 1990.

Bennett, W. H. *The Post-Exilic Prophets*. Edinburgh: T. & T. Clark, 1907.

Benoit, Pierre. "Judaïsme et Christianisme." *Revue Biblique* 84 (January 1977): 147–50.

Berger, H., Jr. "The Lie of the Land: The Text Beyond Canaan." *Representations* 25 (1989): 119–37.

Bickerman, E. J. *Four Strange Books of the Bible*. New York: Schocken, 1967.

———. *From Ezra to the Last of the Maccabees*. New York: Schocken, 1962.

Bleich, J. D. *Contemporary Halakhic Problems*. New York: KTAV, 1983, 1989.

Bonsirven, J. *Le Judaïsme Palestinien*. Paris: Beauchesne, 1934–35.

Bok, S. *Strategy for Peace*. New York: Pantheon Books, 1989.

Bokser, B. M. Review of *The Gospel and the Land* by W. D. Davies. *Conservative Judaism* 30 (1975): 71–74.

Bowman, J. W. *Which Jesus?* Philadelphia: Fortress, 1970.

Brody, H., ed. *Selected Poems of Jehudah Halevi*. Translated by N. Salaman. Philadelphia: Jewish Publications of America, 1924.

Brown, P. *The World of Late Antiquity.* London: Thames & Hudson, 1971.

Broyde, M. and Rachman, E. "Halacha and the State of Israel." *Midstream* 36/2 (1990).

Brueggemann, W. *The Land.* Philadelphia: Fortress, 1977.

_____. "Trajectories in the Old Testament Literature and the Sociology of Ancient Israel." *JBL* 98 (1979): 161–85.

Buber, M[artin]. *Israel und Palestina.* Zurich, 1950. Translated by S. Godman as *Israel and Palestine.* London: East and West Library, 1952.

Buber, Martin, ed. *Jüdische Künstler.* Berlin: Jüdischer Verlag, 1903.

Caquot, A. "Le Rouleau du Temple de Qoumran." *Etudes Théologique* 4 (1978): 443–500.

Carmichael, J. "The Palestinian People: A Lethal Fiction." *Midstream* 37/2 (1991): 6–8.

Charles, R. H., ed. *The Apocrypha and Pseudepigrapha of the Old Testament.* 2 vols. Oxford: Clarendon Press, 1913.

Childs, B. S. *Introduction to the Old Testament as Scripture.* Philadelphia: Fortress, 1979.

Chouraqui, André. *The People and the Faith of the Bible.* Translated by W. V. Gugli. Amherst, Mass.: University of Massachusetts Press, 1975.

Clements, R. E. *Abraham and David.* London: S. C. M. Press, 1967.

Cohen, Hermann. *Die Religion der Vernunft aus den Quellen des Judentums.* Frankfurt: Melzer, 1959.

Condition of Jewish Belief, The. A Symposium Compiled by the Editors of *Commentary* Magazine. New York: Macmillan, 1966.

Cullmann, O. *Christ and Time.* Philadelphia: Westminster, 1950.

Danby, H. *The Mishnah.* Oxford: Oxford University Press, 1933.

Davies, W. D. *The Gospel and the Land: Early Christianity and Jewish Territorial Doctrine.* Berkeley and Los Angeles: University of California Press, 1974.

_____. "Israel, Mormans, and The Land." in *Reflections on Mormonism,* edited by T. G. Madsen, pp. 79–97. Provo, Utah: Brigham Young University, 1978.

_____. "Paul and the People of Israel." *New Testament Studies* 24 (October 1977): 4–39.

_____. "Reflections on the Spirit in the Mekilta: A Suggestion." In *Proceedings of the Sixth World Congress of Jewish Studies,* pp. 159–73. Jerusalem: Hebrew University, 1977.

de Gaulle, Charles. *Memoirs of Hope.* Translated by T. Kilmartin. New York: Simon and Schuster, 1971.

de Vaux, R. "Jerusalem and the Prophets." In *Interpreting the Prophetic Tradition,* edited by H. M. Orlinsky, pp. 275–300. Cincinnati: Hebrew Union College Press, 1969.

Dillistone, F. W. *Traditional Symbols and the Contemporary World*. London: Epworth, 1973.

Dreyfus, T. "The Commentary of Franz Rosenzweig to the Poems of Jehudah Halevi. " *Tarbiz* 47 (March–October 1978): 91 ff.

Eckert, W. P., Levinson, N. P. and Söhr, M., eds. *Jüdische Volk, gelobtes Land*. Munich: Kaiser, 1970.

Eisen, A. M. *Galut: Modern Jewish Reflection on Homelessness and Homecoming*. Bloomington, Ind.: Indiana University Press, 1980.

Finkelstein, L. "Israel as a Spiritual Force." In *Israel: Its Role in Civilization*, edited by M. Davis. New York: Harper, 1956.

———. *New Light from the Prophets*. London: Vallentine, Mitchell, 1969.

———. "Rabbinic Theology and Ethics." In *The Cambridge History of Judaism*, edited by W. D. Davies and L. Finkelstein. Cambridge: Cambridge University Press, 1984.

Finkelstein, L., and Davies, W. D. *The History of Judaism*. Cambridge, England: Cambridge University Press, 1984, 1989.

Freedman, D. N. "Divine Commitment and Human Obligation: The Covenant Theme." *Interpretation* 18 (October 1964): 3–15.

———. Review of *The Gospel and The Land* by W. D. Davies. *Journal of Biblical Literature* 95 (1976): 503–6.

———. Reviews of *The Gospel and The Land* by W. D. Davies. *Christian News from Israel* 25 (1975): 132–39.

Gottwald, N. "Religious Conversion and the Societal Origins of Ancient Israel," in *Perspectives in Religious Studies* 15 (1988): 49–65.

———. "Social Matrix and Canonical Shape," in *Theology Today* 42 (1983): 307–21.

———. "The Theological Task after *The Tribes of Israel*," in *The Bible and Liberation: Political and Social Hermeneutics*. Maryknoll: Orbis Books, 1983, 190–200.

———. *The Tribes of Yahweh: A Sociology of the Religion of Liberated Israel, 1250–1050* B.C.E. Maryknoll, N.Y.: Orbis, 1979.

Goudover, J. van. "Tora und Galut." in *Jüdische Volk, gelobtes Land*, edited by W. P. Eckert, N. P. Levinson, and M. Söhr, pp. 197–202. Munich: Kaiser, 1970.

Halkin, A. S. *Zion in Jewish Literature*. New York: Schocken, 1961.

Halpern, B. *The Idea of the Jewish State*. 2nd ed. Cambridge, Mass.: Harvard University Press, 1969.

Hazleton, L. "The Forgotten Israelis." *New York Review of Books* 27 (29 March 1980): 43–5.

Hertzberg, A. *The Condition of Jewish Belief. A Symposium Compiled by the Editors of "Commentary" Magazine*. New York, 1960.

———. *The French Enlightenment and the Jews*. New York: Columbia University Press, 1968.

———. *The Zionist Idea*. New York: Atheneum, 1968.

Heschel, A. *Israel: An Echo of Eternity.* New York: Farrar, Straus and Giroux, 1969.

Huesman, J. "Archaeology and Early Israel: The Scene Today." *Catholic Bible Quarterly* 37 (1975): 1–16.

Hüttenmeister, F., and Reeg, G. *Die antiken Synagogen in Israel. Beihefte zum Tübingen Atlas des Vorderen Orients,* vol. 12. Wiesbaden: Ludwig Reichert, 1977.

Jacob, E. *Israël dans la perspective biblique.* Strasbourg: Editions Oberlin, 1968.

———. "Les Trois Racines d'une théologie de la 'Terre' dans *l'A.T.*" *Revue d'Histoire et de Philosophie Religieuses* 4 (1975): 476–8.

James, M. R., ed. *Liber Antiquitatum Biblicarum.* New York: Macmillan, 1917.

Josephus, Flavius. *Josephus.* Introduction and English translation by H. St. J. Thackery. 8 vols. Loeb Classical Library. New York: G. P. Putnam's Sons, 1926–65.

Kadashin, M. "Aspects of the Rabbinic Concept of Israel." *Hebrew Union College Annual* 19 (1945–46): 57–96.

Kark, R., ed. *The Land that Became Israel.* New Haven, Conn.: Yale University Press, 1990.

Katz, J. "The Forerunners of Zionism." *Jerusalem Quarterly* 7 (1978): 10–21.

Kochan, Lionel. *The Jew and His History.* London: Macmillan, 1977.

Kohler, K. "The Testament of Job: An Essene Midrash on the Book of Job, Re-edited and Translated with Introductory and Exegetical Notes." in *Semitic Studies in Memory of Rev. Dr. Alexander Kohut,* edited by G. A. Kohut, pp. 264–95. Berlin: Calvary, 1897.

Lacocque, A. "Une Terre qui découle de lait et de miel." *Vav: Revue de Dialogue* 2 (1966): 28–36.

Leibowitz, Yehayahu. "State and Religion." *The Jerusalem Quarterly,* No. 14 (Winter 1980), pp. 59–67.

Levenson, J. D. "Liberation Theology and the Exodus," *Reflections* (1991): 2–12.

Lieberman, S. "Response." *Proceedings of the Rabbinical Assembly Of America* 12 (1949): 272–89.

Lieberson, Jonathan, and Morgenbesser, Sidney. "The Choices of Isaiah Berlin."*New York Review of Books* 17 (20 March 1980): 30 ff.

Loewe, M. "Judaism's 'Eternal Triangle' " *Religious Studies* 23 (1937): 309–23.

Maier, J. *Die Tempelrolle vom Toten Meer.* Munich: Reinhardt, 1978.

Maimon, Rabbi Moses ben [Maimonides]. *The Guide of the Perplexed.* Translated by S. Pines. Chicago: Chicago University Press, 1963.

Marmur, D. *Beyond Survival: Reflections on the Future of Judaism.* London: Dartom, Longman and Todd, 1982.

Marquardt, F. W. *Die Juden und ihr Land.* Hamburg: Siebenstern-Taschenbuch, 1975.

Mekilta de Rabbi Ishmael. Edited by J. Lauterbach. 3 vols. Philadelphia: Jewish Publication Society of America, 1933–35.

Mendels, D. *The Land of Israel as a Political Concept in Hasmonaean Literature: Recourse to History in 2nd Century* B.C. *Claims to the Holy Land.* Tübingen: J.C.B. Mohr (Paul Siebeck), 1987.

Meyers, Eric M. *Jewish Ossuaries: Reburial and Rebirth.* Rome: Biblical Institute, 1971

Midrash Rabbah. Edited and translated by H. Freedman and M. Simon. 9 vols. London: Soncino, 1939.

Milgrom, J. "The Temple Scroll." *Biblical Archaeologist* 41 (1978): 105–20.

Montague, Ashley. "The New Litany of Innate Depravity, or Original Sin Revisited." In *Man and Agression,* edited by F. Ashley Montague, pp. 3–16. New York: Oxford University Press, 1968.

Moore, G. F. *Judaism.* 3 vols. New York: Schocken, 1971.

Nave, Prina. "Zentrum und Peripherie im Geschichte und Gegenwart." *In Jüdische Volk, gelobtes Land,* edited by W. P. Eckert, N. P. Levinson, and M. Söhr, pp. 82–97. Munich: Kaiser, 1970.

Neher, André. "David Gans (1541–1613), disciple du Maharal de Prague et assistant de Tycho Brahé et de Jean Kepler," *Revue d'Histoire et de Philosophie Religieuses* 52 (1972): 407–14.

_____. *L'Existence Juive.* Paris: Editions du Seuil, 1962.

_____. *Moses and the Vocation of the Jewish People.* New York: Harper & Row, 1959.

_____. *L'Etat d'Israël: Actes du Collogue Judéo—Chrétien—Le Peuple de Dieu, Fevrier 1970,* in *Rencontre-Vav* (Paris, 1972), pp. 74–90.

Neusner, Jacob. "Map Without Territory: Mishnah's System of Sacrifice and Sanctuary." *History of Religions* 19 (November 1979): 103–27.

_____. *Who, Where, and What Is Israel? Zionist Perspectives on Israeli and American Judaism.* Larham, N.Y. and London: University Press of America, 1989.

New English Bible, The. Cambridge and Oxford: Oxford University Press, 1970.

Otto, R. *The Kingdom of God and the Son of Man.* New rev. ed. London: Lutterworth, 1943.

Patterson, D. *The Foundations of Modern Hebrew Literature.* London: Liberal Jewish Synagogue Press, 1961.

_____. "Modern Hebrew Literature Goes on Aliyah," *Journal of Jewish Studies* 29 (Spring 1978): 75–84.

Petuchowski, J. J. "Diaspora Judaism—An Abnormality?" *Judaism* 9 (1960): 17–28.

_____. *Zion Reconsidered.* New York: Twayne, 1966.

Philo Judaeus. *Philo Judaeus*. Edited and translated by F. H. Colson and G. H. Whitaker. Loeb Classical Library. New York: G. P. Putnam's Sons, 1929–62.

Poteat, W. H. *The Banality of Evil: The Darkness at the Centre*. Charlotte, N.C.: University of North Carolina, 1988.

Price, R. E. "A Lexiographical Study of *glh, šbh and šwb* in Reference to Exile in the Tanach." Dissertation, Duke University, 1977.

Raitt, T. M. *A Theology of Exile, Judgment and Deliverance in Jeremiah and Ezekiel*. Philadelphia: Fortress, 1977.

Rendtorff, R. *Israel und seine Land*. Munich: Kaiser, 1978.

———. "Die religiosen und geistigen Wurzeln des Zionismus." *Aus Politik und Zeit Geschichte* 49 (4 December 1976): 3–49.

Revised Standard Version of the Bible, The. 2nd ed. New York: Nelson, 1971.

Rotenstreich, Nathan. "Réflexions sur la pensée nationale juive moderne."*Jerusalem Quarterly* 7 (1978): 3–9.

Rowley, H. H. *The Biblical Doctrine of Election*. London: Lutterworth, 1950.

Rubenstein, R. *After Auschwitz. Radical Theology and Contemporary Judaism*. Indianapolis: Bobbs-Merrill, 1966.

Samuel, M. *The World of Scholem Aleichem*. 1945. Reprint, New York: Knopf, 1965.

Sanders, J. A. "Adaptable for Life: The Nature and Function of Canon." In *Magnalia Dei: Festschrift for G. Ernest Wright*, edited by F. M. Cross et al., pp. 531-60. Garden City, N.Y.: Doubleday, 1976.

———. "Text and Canon." *Journal of Biblical Literature* 98 (1979): 5–29.

———. *Torah and Canon*. Philadelphia: Fortress. 1972.

Schaff, Philip. *Creeds of Christendom*. 3 vols. New York: Harper & Row, 1919.

Schmidt, K. L. "Diaspora." In *Theologisches Wörterbuch zum Neuen Testament*, edited by G. Kittel, vol. 2, pp. 98–105. Stuttgart: Kohlhammer, 1935.

Schoffeleers, J. M. *Guardians of the Land: Essays on the Central African Territorial Cults*. Gwelo: Mambo Press, 1979.

Scholem, Gershom. *Jews and Judaism in Crisis*. Edited by W. J. Dannhauser. New York: Schocken, 1976.

Scott, R. B. Y. *The Relevance of the Prophets*. New York: Macmillan, 1968.

Shargel, B. R. "The Evolution of the Masada Myth." *Judaism 28* (Spring 1979): 357–81.

Shashar, Michael. "The State of Israel and the Land of Israel." *The Jerusalem Quarterly*, No. 17 (Fall 1980), pp. 56–65.

Shipler, D. K. *Arab and Jew: Wounded Spirits in a Promised Land*. New York: Times Books, 1986.

Skinner, J. *Prophecy and Religion.* Cambridge: Cambridge University Press, 1922.

Smith, J. Z. *Map Is Not Territory.* Leiden: E. J. Brill, 1978.

Stemberger, G. *Die Bedeutung des Landes Israel in der Rabbinischen Tradition.*

———. *Juden und Christen im Heiligen Land.* Munich: Verlag C. H. Beck, 1987.

———. *Kairos* 25 (1983): 176–99.

Tal, U. "Historical and Metahistorical Self-Views." In *Religious Zionism.* Tel Aviv: University of Tel Aviv Press, 1984.

———. "The Land and the State of Israel in Israeli Religious Life." In *Proceedings of the Rabbinical Assembly,* 76th Annual Convention, 38:1–40. Grossinger, N.Y.: Rabbinical Assembly, 1977.

———. "The Nationalism of Gush Emunin in Historical Perspective. *Forum on the Jewish People, Zionism, and Israel,* no. 36 (Fall/Winter 1979).

Le Talmud de Jerusalem. Translated by M. Schwab. 12 vols. Paris: Librairie Orientale et Americaine, 1932–33.

Thompson, T. L. *The Historicity of the Patriarchal Narratives: The Quest for the Historical Abraham.* New York: W. De Gruyter, 1974.

Trudeau, P. *News Perspective Quarterly* 7/3 (1990): 61.

Urbach, E. E. "Center and Periphery in Jewish Historical Consciousness: Contemporary Implications." In *World Jewry and the State of Israel,* edited by M. Davis, pp. 217–35. New York: Arno, 1977.

Vair, R. J. "The Old Testament Promise of the Land as Reinterpreted in First- and Second-Century Christianity." Dissertation, Graduate Theological Union, Berkeley, 1979.

Van Seters, J. *Abraham in History and Tradition.* New Haven, Conn.: Yale University Press, 1975.

Vaux, R. de. "Jerusalem and the Prophets." In *Interpreting the Prophetic Tradition,* edited by H. M. Ortinsky, pp. 275–300. Cincinnati: Hebrew Union College Press, 1969.

Vermes, G. *The Dead Sea Scrolls in English.* 2nd ed. London: Penguin, 1975.

Vital, D. *The Future of the Jews: A People at the Crossroads.* Cambridge, Mass.: Harvard University Press, 1990.

———. *The Origins of Zionism.* Oxford: Oxford University Press, 1975.

Von Rad, G. *The Problem of the Hexateuch and Other Essays.* Translated by E. W. T. Dicken. New York: McGraw-Hill, 1966.

Vriezen, T. C. *Die Erwählung Israels nach dem A. T.* Zürich: Zwingli, 1953.

Warren, M. "The Concept and Historic Experience with Land in the Major Western Religious Traditions." In *Proceedings of the Jerusalem Colloquium on Religion, Peoplehood, Nation and Land,* edited by M. H. Tanenbaum and R. J. Zwi Werblowsky, pp. 187–200. Truman

Research Institute Publication No. 7. Jerusalem: Hebrew University, 1972.

Werblowsky, R. J. Zwi. "Israël et Eretz Israël," *Les Temps Modernes* 253 (1967) 371–93.

Zeitein, I. M. *Jesus and the Judaism of His Time*. Cambridge, England: Polity, 1988.

Index of Authors

Subject Index